T0235371

# Lecture Notes in Computer Science 9342

*Commenced Publication in 1973*
Founding and Former Series Editors:
Gerhard Goos, Juris Hartmanis, and Jan van Leeuwen

## Editorial Board

More information about this series at http://www.springer.com/series/7408

Christian Terboven · Bronis R. de Supinski
Pablo Reble · Barbara M. Chapman
Matthias S. Müller (Eds.)

# OpenMP:
# Heterogenous Execution
# and Data Movements

11th International Workshop on OpenMP, IWOMP 2015
Aachen, Germany, October 1–2, 2015
Proceedings

 Springer

*Editors*

Christian Terboven
RWTH Aachen University
Aachen
Germany

Bronis R. de Supinski
Lawrence Livermore National Laboratory
Livermore, CA
USA

Pablo Reble
RWTH Aachen University
Aachen
Germany

Barbara M. Chapman
University of Houston
Houston
USA

Matthias S. Müller
RWTH Aachen University
Aachen
Germany

ISSN 0302-9743           ISSN 1611-3349   (electronic)
Lecture Notes in Computer Science
ISBN 978-3-319-24594-2        ISBN 978-3-319-24595-9   (eBook)
DOI 10.1007/978-3-319-24595-9

Library of Congress Control Number: 2015950929

LNCS Sublibrary: SL2 – Programming and Software Engineering

Springer Cham Heidelberg New York Dordrecht London
© Springer International Publishing Switzerland 2015

Printed on acid-free paper

Springer International Publishing AG Switzerland is part of Springer Science+Business Media
(www.springer.com)

# Preface

OpenMP is a widely accepted, standard application programming interface (API) for high-level shared-memory parallel programming in Fortran, C, and C++. Since its introduction in 1997, OpenMP has gained support from most high-performance compiler and hardware vendors. Under the direction of the OpenMP Architecture Review Board (ARB), the OpenMP specification has evolved up to the release of version 4.0. This version includes several new features like accelerator support for heterogeneous hardware environments, an enhanced tasking model, user-defined reductions, and thread affinity to support binding for performance improvements on non-uniform memory architectures. As indicated in its recently released comment draft, version 4.1 will refine the support for accelerators and expand the constructs to express irregular parallelism and data dependencies.

The evolution of the standard would be impossible without active research in OpenMP compilers, runtime systems, tools, and environments. OpenMP is important both as a programming model for single multicore processors and as part of a hybrid programming model for massively parallel, distributed memory systems built from multicore or manycore processors. Since most of the growth in parallelism in exascale systems is expected to arise within a node, these systems will increase the significance of OpenMP, which offers important features to exploit that capability.

The community of OpenMP researchers and developers in academia and industry is united under cOMPunity (www.compunity.org). This organization has held workshops on OpenMP around the world since 1999: the European Workshop on OpenMP (EWOMP), the North American Workshop on OpenMP Applications and Tools (WOMPAT), and the Asian Workshop on OpenMP Experiences and Implementation (WOMPEI) attracted annual audiences from academia and industry. The International Workshop on OpenMP (IWOMP) consolidated these three workshop series into a single annual international event that rotates across Asia, Europe, and the Americas. The first IWOMP workshop was organized under the auspices of cOMPunity. Since that workshop, the IWOMP Steering Committee has organized these events and guided development of the series. The first IWOMP meeting was held in 2005, in Eugene, Oregon, USA. Since then, meetings have been held each year, in Reims, France, Beijing, China, West Lafayette, USA, Dresden, Germany, Tsukuba, Japan, Chicago, USA, Rome, Italy, Canberra, Australia, and Salvador, Brazil. Each workshop has drawn participants from research and industry throughout the world. IWOMP 2015 continued the series with technical papers, tutorials, and OpenMP status reports. The IWOMP meetings have been successful in large part due to the generous support from numerous sponsors.

The cOMPunity website (www.compunity.org) provides access to the talks given at the meetings and to the photos of the activities. The IWOMP website (www.iwomp.org) provides information on the latest event. This book contains the proceedings of IWOMP 2015.

The workshop program included 19 technical papers, two keynote talks, and advanced tutorials on OpenMP. All technical papers were peer reviewed by at least three different members of the Program Committee.

October 2015

Christian Terboven
Bronis R. de Supinski
Pablo Reble

# Organization

## Program Committee Co-chairs

| | |
|---|---|
| Christian Terboven | RWTH Aachen University, Germany |
| Bronis R. de Supinski | LLNL, USA |

## Tutorials Chair

| | |
|---|---|
| Michael Klemm | Intel, Germany |

## Publication Chair

| | |
|---|---|
| Pablo Reble | RWTH Aachen University, Germany |

## Local Chair

| | |
|---|---|
| Matthias S. Müller | RWTH Aachen University, Germany |

## Local Organization

| | |
|---|---|
| Agnes Ramalho-Mendes | RWTH Aachen University, Germany |
| Marco Carboni | RWTH Aachen University, Germany |

## Program Committee

| | |
|---|---|
| Eduard Ayguadé | BSC and Universitat Politecnica de Catalunya, Spain |
| Mark Bull | EPCC, University of Edinburgh, UK |
| Jacqueline Chame | ISI, USC, USA |
| Nawal Copty | Oracle Corporation, USA |
| Luiz DeRose | Cray Inc., USA |
| Alejandro Duran | Intel, Spain |
| Nasser Giacaman | University of Auckland, New Zealand |
| Chunhua Liao | LLNL, USA |
| Kent Milfeld | TACC, USA |
| Bernd Mohr | Jülich Supercomputing Center, Germany |
| Philippe Navaux | UFRGS, Brazil |
| Stephen Olivier | Sandia National Laboratories, USA |
| Jairo Panetta | ITA, Brazil |
| Vinod Rebello | UFF, Brazil |
| Alistair Rendell | Australian National University, Australia |
| Mitsuhisa Sato | University of Tsukuba, Japan |

| | |
|---|---|
| Seetharami Seelam | IBM Research, USA |
| Dirk Schmidl | RWTH Aachen University, Germany |
| Thomas R.W. Scogland | LLNL, USA |
| Eric Stotzer | Texas Instruments, USA |
| Priya Unnikrishnan | IBM Toronto Laboratory, Canada |
| Ruud van der Pas | Oracle Corporation, USA |

## IWOMP Steering Committee

### Steering Committee Chair

| | |
|---|---|
| Matthias S. Müller | RWTH Aachen University, Germany |

### Steering Committee

| | |
|---|---|
| Dieter an Mey | RWTH Aachen University, Germany |
| Eduard Ayguadé | BSC and Universitat Politecnica de Catalunya, Spain |
| Mark Bull | EPCC, University of Edinburgh, UK |
| Barbara Chapman | University of Houston, USA |
| Bronis R. de Supinski | LLNL, USA |
| Rudolf Eigenmann | Purdue University, USA |
| Guang R. Gao | University of Delaware, USA |
| William Gropp | University of Illinois, USA |
| Kalyan Kumaran | Argonne National Laboratory, USA |
| Federico Massaioli | CASPUR, Italy |
| Larry Meadows | Intel, USA |
| Arnaud Renard | University of Reims, France |
| Mitsuhisa Sato | University of Tsukuba, Japan |
| Sanjiv Shah | Intel, USA |
| Ruud van der Pas | Oracle, USA |
| Matthijs van Waveren | CompilaFlows, France |
| Michael Wong | OpenMP CEO, IBM, Canada |
| Weimin Zheng | Tsinghua University, China |

# Contents

**Extensions**

**Compiler and Runtime**

**Energy**

# Applications

# PAGANtec: OpenMP Parallel Error Correction for Next-Generation Sequencing Data

Markus Joppich[1,2,3]([envelope]), Dirk Schmidl[1], Anthony M. Bolger[2], Torsten Kuhlen[1], and Björn Usadel[2]

[1] JARA – High-Performance Computing, IT Center, RWTH Aachen University, Aachen, Germany
{schmidl,kuhlen}@itc.rwth-aachen.de
[2] Institute for Botany and Molecular Genetics, RWTH Aachen University, Aachen, Germany
{bolger,usadel}@bio1.rwth-aachen.de
[3] Institute for Informatics, Ludwig-Maximilians-Universität Munich, Munich, Germany
joppich@bio.ifi.lmu.de

**Abstract.** Next-generation sequencing techniques reduced the cost of sequencing a genome rapidly, but came with a relatively high error rate. Therefore, error correction of this data is a necessary task before assembly can take place. Since the input data is huge and error correction is compute intensive, parallelizing this work on a modern shared-memory system can help to keep the runtime feasible. In this work we present PAGANtec, a tool for error correction of next-generation sequencing data, based on the novel PAGAN graph structure. PAGANtec was parallelized with OpenMP and a performance analysis and tuning was done. The analysis led to the awareness, that OpenMP tasks are a more suitable paradigm for this work than traditional work-sharing.

## 1 Introduction

The field of biological research has changed with the availability of (short-read) next-generation sequencing (NGS). In contrast to former techniques, NGS reduces the costs of sequencing a genome from $100 million to $10,000 [9]. However, the length of the sequenced fragments is cut from roughly 1000 bp down to several hundreds or less. Putting the produced small fragments together is called *assembly*, *genome assembly* when the genome is being reconstructed, or *transcriptome assembly* if the transcriptome is targeted. It is referred to as *de novo* assembly if performed without referencing previously resolved sequences [13].

There exist mainly two approaches to solve the assembly problem: the overlap-layout-consensus approach (finding a Hamiltonian path) and the $k$-mer based, de-Bruijn graph-like approach (finding one of many Eulerian paths). Both are computationally expensive approaches which have been tackled by the high performance computing (HPC) community [4,7,16].

© Springer International Publishing Switzerland 2015
C. Terboven et al. (Eds.): IWOMP 2015, LNCS 9342, pp. 3–17, 2015.
DOI: 10.1007/978-3-319-24595-9_1

The assembly task becomes even more complex if the input reads contain erroneous information, since errors blow-up the assembly graph structure significantly. NGS techniques typically produce higher error rates than older sequencing techniques. Therefore, error removal is a critical step in making the assembly problem more tractable. Common approaches include trimming of reads to remove parts of the biological preparation or bad-quality bases from a read [3], at the cost of information loss. Still certain errors can not be removed from the reads by trimming. Thus, the need for special error reduction and correction techniques is imposed and tackled [10,11,20].

The PAGAN framework [2] uses a novel graph structure to preserve the actual read information of the sequence. These additional information are crucial for a higher accuracy and precision during assembly and error correction compared to former techniques. In this work, we present the implementation of an error correction tool for *de novo* transcriptome assemblies, PAGANtec. Since these error correcting algorithms are compute intensive and work on huge graph structures, performance is an important goal for the development. We parallelized the algorithms with OpenMP *tasks* and undertook them a performance investigation leading to an optimized version of the parallelization. Besides improving assemblies, PAGANtec delivers insight into how bioinformatics can profit from HPC, and how OpenMP can be applied in this area.

## 2    Related Work

First the most commonly applied graph structure for assembly will be introduced, together with error correction methods. Upon this, possible error scenarios in NGS reads and their effects on the graph are mentioned. Finally general parallelization strategies will be discussed.

### 2.1    *k*-mer Graph and Error Correction

The input of any assembly are the reads retrieved from the biological sequencing experiment. Usually these are in the range of 75 bp up to 300 bp for Illumina platforms. A read is a word/sequence $\Sigma^l$ over the alphabet $\Sigma = \{A, T, C, G\}$, where $A, T, C, G$ denote the four nucleotides deoxyribonucleic acid (DNA) is made of. Its length $l$ is expressed in base-pairs (bp).

Here we focus on techniques based on the $k$-mer-graph. Therefore, reads are first decomposed into the set of all unique $k$-mers (subsequences of length k), which is also called the $k$-mer-spectrum. For creating the $k$-mer-graph, the unique $k$-mers represent the graph's nodes, and edges are drawn if two $k$-mers follow each other in any read sequence.

If a read contains errors, this can manifest in any of the following three characteristics [13]: a spur or *tip*, marking an alternative ending of a path through the graph, a *bubble*, essentially marking an alternative path (and thus sequence), or a *tangle*, making it impossible to understand which path to go within the graph.

While the last is mainly endured due to repeated sections within the graph, the former two must be handled by error correction approaches, as these make the graph structure unnecessarily complicated. Here it must be understood, that a single base error in a read can make up to $k$ new $k$-mers, which must be stored and traversed for assembly!

Error correction algorithms try to correct reads such that fewer tips or bubbles form, making the assembly finally more tractable. In general there are three classes of error correction algorithms, which are reviewed in [19]. Here the focus is on $k$-mer-spectrum based approaches.

Once the $k$-mer-spectrum has been created for all reads, reads are categorized into *solid* and *insolid* reads, if all $k$-mers in a read occur at least a few times, or not, respectively. *Insolid* reads are tried to be converted into solid reads by substituting insolid $k$-mers by solid ones with a minimum number of edit operations. Quake [10] and Reptile [20] are two examples for programs using this approach, which also incorporate the quality scores of the reads. SEECER [11] uses a $k$-mer-spectrum based approach, and incorporates hidden Markov Models. These tools however fail, if reads do not occur at the same frequency for any postion, like in a transcriptomic context.

Early programs like CUDA-EC [17] prove that using the $k$-mer-spectrum is parallelizable on the graphical processing unit (GPU), but misleadingly assume that always the complete data fits into the device's memory. More recent approaches like DecGPU [12] employ a hybrid CUDA- and message-passing interface (MPI)-based approach allowing the distribution of the workload.

## 2.2   Parallelization Options

The massive amounts of data produced by NGS techniques, especially for assembly, pose several problems. These have to be processed in a finite amount of time, requiring the need for parallelization and HPC-techniques, while keeping the amounts of data processable by current computers. Since the amount of input data can go into the hundreds of GB, this is challenging.

There exist several paradigms to achieve concurrency. Only few assemblers rely on MPI implementations, because the distribution of the read information is hard to realize. Besides ABySS for example [18], more recently, the Meraculous assembler based on MPI single-sided communication [7], and Trinity (MPI) [4] have been presented.

Many assemblers and error correctors use threading to distribute their work among the cores of a computer [9]. Here, the shared address space does not force users to distribute the read data.

Using GPUs for general purpose tasks can be found in an increasing amount of programs. New hardware generations, as the Tesla K80 [14], offer up to 24 GB of RAM on a card with 4992 CUDA cores. However, this platform is only suitable if the task fits the architecture and into the memory of these accelerators [17].

High-memory multi-core machines are widely available in the community, being commonly used for assembly purposes. Furthermore, with OpenMP an incremental parallelization is easily possible, it is a widely accepted industry standard [5] and available in most linux distributions. PAGANtec's correction filters would need to process each node, making a later incremental parallelization a conclusive step. Thus, OpenMP has been chosen for parallelization in this work.

## 3    PAGANtec Architecture

PAGAN transcriptome error correction (PAGANtec) corrects NGS-reads for transcriptome assemblies. Within a single read, the majority of errors occurs at the ends of reads [11], but errors within reads exist, too. Thus, error locations can be divided into several categories: an error is either located at the beginning of a read, within the read, or at the end of a read. It is important to note that the first and last case can be handled as one. Thus one must only distinguish between errors at the outer ends of a read and in-line errors. The filters, correcting special types of errors, specifically apply for these cases (Fig. 1).

Errors in the last bases of a sequence create short *tips* at the end of $s$-mers. The second class consists of errors which are not on the leading or trailing tails of a read, thus are within the reads. These errors are called in-line errors, and cause deviations in the graph structure.

### 3.1    Graph Structure

The Probabilistic Algorithm for Genome Assembly for Next-generation Data (PAGAN) graph consists of $s$-mers (nodes) (Fig. 2), implicitly linking each other (edges) by adding the route tail sequence to the sequence of the $s$-mer. The similarity property is maintained, if for each link from $s$-mer$a$ using route $r$ to $s$-mer$b$ there exists a connection from $b$ to $a$ with the complemented route tail sequence $\bar{r}$. An $s$-mer may contain several route entries, each representing a read going through this $s$-mer. Route entries can be collapsed into routes.

A central element for PAGANtec is the flow concept. A flow is a collection of reads which traverse the graph in a common manner. The number of contained reads gives the width of a flow. Here, flows are created around $s$-mers to find the skeleton/main routes within the graph.

### 3.2    Correction Strategies

In general, an error can be identified as only a few reads supporting this path or flow through the graph. Seldom used edges in the graph are a result of erroneous reads and PAGANtec finds such edges to correct errors. The most practical idea for applying corrections is to first take the read out of the graph, and re-insert its corrected form. Since the corrections can involve several nodes, this would require extensive locking to avoid data-races when the algorithm is parallelized.

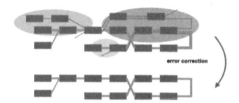

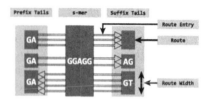

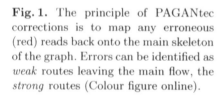

**Fig. 1.** The principle of PAGANtec corrections is to map any erroneous (red) reads back onto the main skeleton of the graph. Errors can be identified as *weak* routes leaving the main flow, the *strong* routes (Colour figure online).

**Fig. 2.** PAGAN terminology explained for one *s*-mer. Each *s*-mer contains routes, which again contain route-width-many route entries which going from prefix- to suffix-side or vice-versa.

As a consequence, saving the changes in memory and applying them to the reads, after all *s*-mers have been processed, has been identified as the most versatile option. In certain cases, when only a few *s*-mers are effected by an error, a direct, on-line correction can be performed (Fig. 1, green background).

When an error occurs within a read (e.g. bubble structure), there are two possible scenarios (Fig. 1). The error can occur at the outer edges of a read, then a long tip structure, spanning multiple *s*-mers, is formed (blue background) or it is placed in the interior of a read, such that the error-prone read folds back onto the main flow, forming a bubble structure (red background). In both cases the correction is buffered and applied at a later stage to the graph. This concept is employed by the *inline error* filter.

All correction filters have a similar structure, requiring the complete graph structure as well as *s*-mers for correction (Algorithm 1). The outer *for*-loop, in which all *s*-mers are processed, seems to be an ideal candidate for OpenMP parallelization.

---

**Algorithm 1.** Loop structure in PAGANtec correction filters

---

**Require:** graph is a valid PAGAN graph, smers contains the *s*-mers to be processed
**Ensure:** Each *s*-mer has been processed
1: **function** APPLYFILTER(graph, smers)
2:    **for** smer ∈ smers **do**
3:        **for** route ∈ smer **do**
4:            **for** route entry ∈ route **do**
5:                CORRECTROUTEENTRY(graph, route entry)
6:            **end for**
7:        **end for**
8:    **end for**
9: **end function**

---

### 3.3   Correcting Errors

The *FilterTips* algorithm is used to correct errors which occur at the ends of a read (Fig. 1, green background). We correct these errors first for two reasons: the corrections made here are directly available in the graph and thus may support any following correction, e.g. by creating stronger flows. Secondly, when the ends are already corrected, it is more likely that bubble structures can form and therefore valid corrections are easier to find.

The principle of this algorithm is described in Fig. 3. Weak routes are identified in a first step, before it is checked whether this weak route is at the start or end of a read. If so, the attempt to find a correction is initiated.

(a) *GGAGG-s*-mer with the top route being weak due to an error. Thus the top route implicitly links to the *AGGAT-s*-mer and the lower route to *AGGGT*.

(b) By correcting the top route's suffix-tail to *GT*, no reference about this route is in *AGGGT*.

(c) A new link must be established in *AGGGT*. This may lead to the creation of two identical route entries (left) which are combined in the next graph loading phase.

**Fig. 3.** Correction process of the top route in the presented *s*-mer. The tail *AT* makes the top route a weak route.

Therefore, possible candidates for correction must be found. A set of possible candidates is retrieved by calculating the flow through the *s*-mer. Then all retrieved flows are compared to the actual read sequence. The best matching flow is used for correction.

A naive way to apply a correction in this filter is to simply replace the tail sequence of the erroneous tail with the correct version (Fig. 3(b)). This however has to be done with care in order to not violate the similarity property. Recalling that reads can start or end either explicitly or implicitly (referred *s*-mer does not exist), two cases have to be considered. First, the *s*-mer referred to by following the corrected tail does not exist. Then no action is required, and the read is corrected after changing the tail. Second, the *s*-mer referred to by following the corrected tail exists (Fig. 3(b)). Then an explicit ending has to be added to the next $s$-mer (Fig. 3(c)). The current $s$-mer GGAGG has to be linked to the next one, AGGGT.

In contrast to tip filtering, *long tip* filtering is only applied to tails which are longer than any of the *strong* tails. Even if an error is in the part covered by shorter tails, these tails can not be used for correction, as these might not be from the same context.

Modifications made by the *long tip* filter are not saved directly in the graph. If these were saved in the graph as explained for tip filtering, in some cases more than two $s$-mers must be changed to maintain the similarity property. As this would require a lot of locking during linking, dramatically increasing the overhead, such corrections are stored in a separate hash-map and are applied when writing the reads to disk again.

The final stage of the error correction process is the *inline error filter*. This filter is responsible to find and correct any error within a read which forms either a tip or a bubble. Any remaining errors from the example case are thus a target of this filter (Fig. 1, blue/red background).

Even if an error is located inside a read, tips at both ends of variable length can be created. This especially happens if the remaining sequence is too short to form a bubble, or in case multiple errors prevent the building of a bubble (Fig. 1, blue background). Again, first weak routes are found and possible corrections, flows, for these are then calculated. If a suitable correction, in the context of both the up- and downstream sequence, is found, a patch for this correction is stored and applied to the read, when writing the reads to disks (as previously). This is done because online manipulations of the graph are not possible.

## 4    Parallelization

In order to interpret NGS-data, the processing requires a lot of memory and time. Thus parallelization is an important aspect in the PAGANtec framework.

Here, an interconnected graph structure needs to be processed. A topologically oriented parallelization would be beneficial to exploit the ccNUMA architecture and distributed memory in general. However, the existence of enough connected regions in the graph is not guaranteed and finding those components would require a massive amount of computational effort beforehand. Therefore a NUMA-aware data-distribution can not be applied here. Not having any large matrices to process, like in numerics, the parallelization has to start at high-level constructs. The presented PAGANtec framework uses two different approaches for parallelization, both based on the $s$-mer-arrays processed by the filters.

For tip filtering, the outer *for*-loop, which applies the correction filter to each $s$-mer is optimal for this purpose. Using the #pragma omp parallel for construct, the filter's workload can be distributed among all available threads (Algorithm 2). With one exception, the link creation, the calculations performed in this filter are $s$-mer specific and thus there is no interference with other $s$-mers, preventing data races or race conditions. If the next $s$-mer exists, a link to this $s$-mer must be established (Fig. 3(c)) requiring an exclusive lock for this $s$-mer to be obtained.

**Algorithm 2.** FOR work-sharing construct implementation

1: **function** APPLYFILTER(graph, smers)
2:      `# pragma omp parallel for schedule(dynamic)`
3:      **for** smer ∈ smers **do**
4:          **for** route ∈ smer **do**
5:              **for** route entry ∈ route **do**
6:                  CORRECTROUTEENTRY(graph, route entry)
7:              **end for**
8:          **end for**
9:      **end for**
10: **end function**

Attempting a correction while potentially another thread is changing routes within this $s$-mer is dangerous, possibly causing a loss of data integrity, and thus must be prohibited. If the next $s$-mer does not exist, no link must be established and any changes may be made directly without requiring a lock. If the next $s$-mer exists, it must be ensured that only one thread at a time changes an $s$-mer (Algorithm 3). It has been observed, that this locking is a possible bottleneck and even might lead to a deadlock, if two nodes try to fix tips in each other. Therefore, only if the lock is obtained, the new tail can be copied over and a link can be formed, because there is no risk of a data race. If the lock is not obtained, two cases are distinguished. If another thread locked the next $s$-mer for error correction, a dead-lock could occur, and thus no changes are attempted to be applied. The correction operation is aborted. If the lock is not obtained and another thread has the next $s$-mer locked for link creation, it is waited until the lock can be acquired. Similarly, if a lock is acquired for correction, it is checked that no other thread is currently holding a lock. However, there is no queuing system for operations.

**Algorithm 3.** Link Creation in FilterTips

1: **function** ATTEMPTLINKCREATION(graph, route)
2:
3:      nextSmer ← GETNEXTSMER(current $s$-mer, graph, route)
4:      **if** nextSmer ∈ graph **then**
5:          ▷ If locked by another thread for correction, skip. If locked for linking, wait.
6:          **if** GETSMERLOCK(nextSmer) **then**
7:              CREATELINK(graph, route, nextSmer)
8:          **end if**
9:      **else**
10:                                        ▷ Next $s$-mer does not exist
11:          CREATELINK(graph, route, nextSmer)
12:      **end if**
13: **end function**

For the long tips and inline filter, the analysis of the contained routes is independent of other $s$-mers. Storing the corrections in a hash-map, however, has to be thread-safe. Thus, while inserting a correction corresponding to the $s$-mers hash, the vector containing the correction has to be locked for this purpose.

### 4.1   Performance Analysis

Here we focus on the performance analysis after stating that no memory leaks have been found in PAGANtec using Valgrind and Intel Inspector XE 2013. To track performance issues, Intel VTune Amplifier XE 2013 [8] has been used. Among the features of this tool are hotspots and concurrency analysis as well as readouts from hardware performance counters.

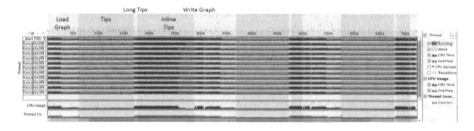

**Fig. 4.** Performance analysis of the task-optimised version of PAGANtec (cluster-tuning [15]). The different stages of the 3 correction runs can be identified. While loading the graph and performing tip filtering, a high overhead rate is seen (red ticks) (Colour figure online).

Analysing the output of the performance analysis (Fig. 4), the three iterations of the error correction can be clearly seen. Each iteration first loads the graph into memory, followed by the filters for tips, with a high spin and overhead rate, the long tips and inline errors. Finally the corrected reads are written to disk.

Regarding the high spin and overhead rate, it has been analysed that this results mainly from the frequency of $s$-mers being locked and unlocked during route creation (load graph) and correction (tips). The exclusive access to an $s$-mer can not be circumvented. The long tip filter does not show significant problems and thus is not discussed here.

Most interestingly, the inline filter, using `pragma omp parallel for` parallelisation, shows a major load imbalance, forcing many threads to wait for only one thread to finish. It can be concluded that this behaviour is neither due to dead-locks or other unwanted side-effects, but is a true load balancing problem. Changing the scheduling strategy from *static* to *dynamic* tries to distribute chunks with uneven workload better among all threads. Still, chunks with over-proportionally large amounts of work being processed very late pose a threat for load balancing and build up a major load imbalance (Fig. 5). In fact, even on a small 25 %-portion of the full dataset, the `schedule(static)` version takes 4.6

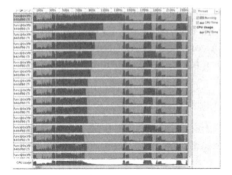

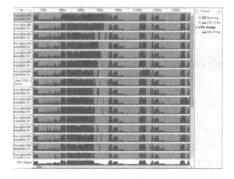

**Fig. 5.** CPU usage per thread for the 0.25-*dus18* sample (*for* parallelized, *dynamic* schedule) with 24 threads on cluster-tuning [15]. Load imbalances can be noticed.

**Fig. 6.** CPU usage of the 0.25-*dus18* sample (task parallelized) with 24 threads on cluster-tuning [15]. In comparison to Fig. 5, less severe load imbalances are seen.

times as long as the `schedule(dynamic)` version. Also the guided scheduling performs worse than dynamic.

Considering that multi-core machines usually have many, but relatively weak, cores, load imbalances pose big problems on such architectures. Thus, the `#pragma omp parallel for` construct turns out to be insufficient for parallelization, because it does not allow fine-grained enough parallelism when needed. Even though a single *s*-mer can be handled by a single thread (e.g. `schedule (dynamic,1)`), this would be applied to *s*-mers with many route entries (potentially high workload) and only few route entries (potentially low workload). Even though the *dynamic* scheduling is well improved over *static* scheduling, still load imbalances can be observed - possibly occurring due to *s*-mers taking considerably longer than others and being worked on only at the end.

The inner loops should not be directly used for parallelism as these show a high variance in workload, often too small to justify the parallelization overhead. OpenMP also offers the `#pragma omp task` construct for more flexibility by defining the workloads explicitly. The code for applying the filter to the *s*-mers has been changed such that *s*-mer-chunks of equal size are created (Algorithm 4 without inner task creation). Analysing the load imbalance further, it could be determined that few *s*-mers take significantly longer to process due to flow creation. To avoid this, the task creation has been amended to create a new task, whenever the current selection of *s*-mers exceeds a fixed number of routes. This could finally reduce the load imbalance, however could not resolve it.

The standard technique for resolving load imbalances is to first process the most expensive tasks, and the smaller tasks at the end. This is not applicable here for two reasons: first, it is unknown beforehand how much work each chunk actually will contain. The width of all routes is an indicator, but even *s*-mers

---

**Algorithm 4.** TASK work-sharing construct implementation

---

```
1: function APPLYFILTER(graph, smers)
2:     #pragma omp parallel
3:     #pragma omp single
4:               ▷ For each chunk of |smervec| s-mers with less than 2000 route entries
5:     for each smervec ⊆ smers ∧ |routeentries(smervec)| ≤ 2000 do
6:         #pragma omp task untied firstprivate(smervec)          ▷ Outer task
7:         for route ∈ smer do
8:             for each entries ⊆ route ∧ |routeentries(entries)| ≤ 400 do
9:                 #pragma omp task untied firstprivate(entries)    ▷ Inner task
10:                {
11:                CORRECTROUTEENTRIES(graph, entries)
12:                }
13:            end for
14:        end for
15:    end for
16: end function
```

---

with many routes could contain only strong routes, not needing any correction. Secondly, this approach would require a sorting of the tasks. Creating first all tasks, then sorting these by workload is not feasible due to memory limitations. Thus, being able to control task scheduling while creating tasks could be beneficial for problems like the presented one. The experimental research compiler Mercurium with OmpSs offers priorities for tasks already [1,6], which would be highly welcome for the here presented purposes in OpenMP, too. While *gcc* and *icc* successfully compile PAGANtec, we have not yet succeeded to compile using Mercurium. Thus we could not evaluate this hypothesis.

With OpenMP 4.0 *depend* clauses have been introduced. These allow a controlled flow of the program, e.g. all tasks requiring $x$ as input wait until all *existing* tasks outputting $x$ have finished. Since only already existing tasks are considered, this does not help in prioritizing tasks - here we want to dynamically put one task before all the rest. In fact, most OpenMP implementations use a first-in-first-out (FIFO)-like mechanism for choosing the next task to work on, such that any large task already begins before any small, following tasks.

Because the inline filter does not change the graph immediately, but collects changes, the parallelism can be propagated to different levels. In addition to the for-loop over $s$-mers, the loop over route entries can be used as another parallelism level (Algorithm 4). In general, the width of a single route is too low to either apply a *parallel for* or a *task* on it directly. Certain $s$-mers have routes containing several hundred route entries. Usually many of these are weak routes and thus are processed by the correction filter. Following this, a high route entry count is an indication for a high workload. Therefore, using the *task* construct, a task is created for every $l = 500$ route entries (empirically determined). By doing so, the load imbalance could be further reduced (Figs. 4 and 6), but still not completely resolved.

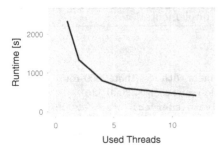

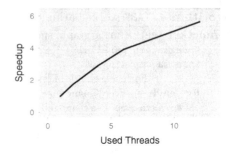

**Fig. 7.** Runtime (`task` parallelized) of the 0.25-dus18 dataset on the 12 core Intel Xeon CPU.

**Fig. 8.** Measured speedup (`task` parallelized) of the 0.25-dus18 dataset on the 12 core Intel Xeon CPU showing a dent after 6 threads.

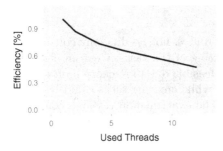

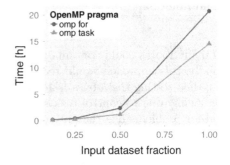

**Fig. 9.** Measured efficiency (`task` parallelized) of the 0.25-dus18 dataset on the 12 core Intel Xeon CPU. Efficiency only reaches about 50 % on 12 threads.

**Fig. 10.** Comparison of the wall clock times (32 threads on a BCS node [15]) on different fractions of the dus18 dataset. For large inputs, the optimised task-version version shows improved performance.

A performance gain between 1 and 2 could be achieved for the low-level *task*-based parallelism (Fig. 10) over the simple *for*-based version - at runtimes of 14 h or more a dramatic change. It can be noticed that with increasing size of the input dataset, the improved parallelism version profits more from the optimization. This is caused by the aforementioned long processing time for certain $s$-mers due to the complex graph structure.

The speedup $s_n = \frac{T_n}{T_1}$ and efficiency $e_n = \frac{s_n}{n}$ are calculated based on the overall runtime (Figs. 7, 8 and 9) on a system with an Intel Xeon X5690 12 core CPU. While the speedup of the total program is linear with the used number of threads, it is still significantly below the ideal speedup. The efficiency only reaches about 50 %. This may have several reasons. The graph loading is parallel, but still has a significant impact on the overall performance: even when run on all threads, the average CPU usage is less than maximally possible (Fig. 4) - similar to tip filtering, a high locking rate produces this problem. On the other hand, accessing the graph structure is not memory-friendly.

First it can be seen that the function responsible for finding the $s$-mer data-structure is responsible for 30 % of offcore responses, and also being the function with the highest count for this event. This suggests that both writing into this data-structure during graph creation as well as retrieval is a possible area of improvement, as threads from several cores need to access data from other cores. Additionally the flow finding function is of interest. From performance analysis it is known that this function is responsible for about 60 % of the total runtime. Also more than 20 % of retired memory instructions are recorded here. This is no surprise since here all $s$-mers associated to the current flow must be retrieved - in case of contained errors, possibly multiple times. Furthermore approximately 40 % of all retired instructions are memory instructions. Possible further optimizations thus should target memory operations for graph accesses. A cycles per instruction (CPI) rate of 1.168 reported by Intel Amplifier underlines that the hardware could be exploited better.

Focusing on the workload per (outer) task (Algorithm 4), first it can be stated that most tasks process several hundred $s$-mers (Fig. 11). Still 871 out of 13, 267 total tasks process less or equal to 5 $s$-mers. Of these, 694 tasks only process a single $s$-mer but do not create any inner tasks. Of all outer tasks, 45 also create inner tasks. 42 of these tasks only process a single $s$-mer (red triangle, Fig. 12). It can also be seen that for most tasks the execution is significantly below $1s$ (median 0.0222 s), with a maximum execution time of 347 s. For those tasks creating inner tasks, the total runtime is in the 100–300 s range. Without the creation of these tasks, the runtime would be longer, thus explaining the

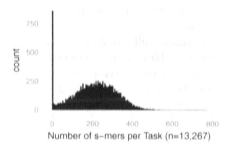

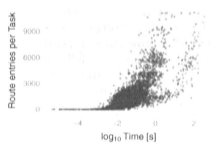

**Fig. 11.** Histogram of created tasks in inner for-loop per outer task (**task** parallelized) in the 0.25-dus18 dataset on the 12 core Intel Xeon CPU.

**Fig. 12.** Runtime versus number of route entries contained in outer task (**task** parallelized) in the 0.25-dus18 dataset on the 12 core Intel Xeon CPU (circle: 0 inner tasks, triangle: $\geq$ inner tasks) (Color figure online)

improvement in load balancing over the outer-task-only version. This shows, that the route entry count is a good indicator for chunk creation and further fine-grained work distribution (inner tasks).

## 5    Conclusion

We have presented PAGANtec, a read error correction for de novo transcriptome assembly. Using OpenMP a speedup of 6 at 12 threads has been achieved. We could show that OpenMP provides a good platform for an incremental parallelization strategy, especially making use of the OpenMP task construct.

As limitation of the `pragma`-based OpenMP, here especially customization problems could be identified. A big class of problems in bioinformatic applications involves graph-like data structures with an uneven load balance. It has been determined that *for*-based parallelism does not permit for general coarse-grained parallelism and fine-grained parallelism when needed. This is possible using OpenMP *task*-based parallelism. However, the default, FIFO-based, scheduling technique for OpenMP tasks does not provide the flexibility needed for scheduling. Expected to be expensive tasks should be prioritizable on construction, such that large pieces are computed first, reducing the risk of load imbalances a lot. The newly available *depend* clause is too limited for these purposes. A performance increase of up to factor 2 by choosing a manual *task*-parallelism underlines the importance of better customization possibilities. A customized scheduling may finally resolve the described load imbalance.

Also, extensive random accesses and locking patterns, common in graph-based problems as presented here, reduce the effect of the parallelization. Here, especially the tip filtering requires locks to prevent simultaneous transactions on a single $s$-mer. OpenMP inbuilt locking mechanisms, eventually also making use of transactional memory, available as a pragma-based directives, would be beneficial for this kind of program. Other memory related problems must be tackled, but do not originate from using OpenMP.

OpenMP proves to be versatile enough to be successfully applied to bioinformatic problems and especially the task-construct enables the usage of OpenMP also on non-standard HPC data-structures, such as indirectly linked graphs. Nonetheless, making use of good work-sharing heuristics as well as standard OpenMP techniques and fine-grained parallelism, which requires more architectural work than pragma-based techniques intend to generate, a speedup of 6 on 12 cores could be achieved for PAGANtec.

## References

1. Badia, R.M., Martorell, X.: Tutorial OmpSs: single node programming. In: Parallel Programming Workshop (2013)
2. Bolger, A.M.: PAGAN Framework. Private Communication (2014)
3. Bolger, A.M., Lohse, M., Usadel, B.: Trimmomatic: a flexible trimmer for illumina sequence data. Bioinformatics **30**, 1–7 (2014)

4. Carrier, P., Long, B., Walsh, R., Dawson, J., Sosa, C.P., Haas, B., Tickle, T., William, T.: The impact of high-performance computing best practice applied to next-generation sequencing workflows. Technical report, April 2015. http://biorxiv.org/content/early/2015/04/07/017665.abstract
5. Dagum, L., Menon, R.: OpenMP: an industry standard API for shared-memory programming. IEEE Comput. Sci. Eng. **5**(1), 46–55 (1998)
6. Duran, A., Ayguade, E., Badia, R.M., Labarta, J., Martinell, L., Martorell, X., Planas, J.: OmpSs: a proposal for programming heterogenous multi-core architectures. Parallel Process. Lett. **21**(02), 173–193 (2011)
7. Georganas, E., Buluç, A., Chapman, J., Oliker, L., Rokhsar, D., Yelick, K.: Parallel De Bruijn Graph Construction and Traversal for De Novo Genome Assembly, pp. 437–448, November 2014
8. Intel: Intel VTune Amplifier XE 2013 (2013). https://software.intel.com/en-us/intel-vtune-amplifier-xe
9. Kaya, K., Hatem, A., Özer, H.G., Huang, K., Çatalyürek, U.V.: High-performance computing in high-throughput sequencing. In: Elloumi, M., Zomaya, A.Y. (eds.) Biological Knowledge Discovery Handbook: Preprocessing, Mining, and Post-processing of Biological Data, Chap. 43, pp. 981–1002. Wiley, Hoboken (2013)
10. Kelley, D.R., Schatz, M.C., Salzberg, S.L.: Quake: quality-aware detection and correction of sequencing errors. Genome Biol. **11**(11), R116 (2010)
11. Le, H.S., Schulz, M.H., McCauley, B.M., Hinman, V.F., Bar-Joseph, Z.: Probabilistic error correction for RNA sequencing. Nucleic Acids Res. **41**(10), e109 (2013)
12. Liu, Y., Schmidt, B., Maskell, D.L.: DecGPU: distributed error correction on massively parallel graphics processing units using CUDA and MPI. BMC Bioinf. **12**, 85 (2011)
13. Miller, J.R., Koren, S., Sutton, G.: Assembly algorithms for next-generation sequencing data. Genomics **95**(6), 315–327 (2010)
14. NVIDIA: Tesla K40 and K80 GPU Accelerators for Servers, December 2014. http://www.nvidia.com/object/tesla-servers.html
15. RWTH Aachen: RWTH Compute Cluster, May 2015. https://doc.itc.rwth-aachen.de/display/CC/Hardware+of+the+RWTH+Compute+Cluster
16. Sachdeva, V., Kim, C., Jordan, K., Winn, M.: Parallelization of the trinity pipeline for De Novo transcriptome assembly. In: 2014 IEEE International Parallel and Distributed Processing Symposium Workshops, pp. 566–575. IEEE, May 2014
17. Schmidt, B., Müller-Wittig, W.: Accelerating error correction in high-throughput short-read DNA sequencing data with CUDA. In: 2009 IEEE International Symposium on Parallel and Distributed Processing, pp. 1–8. IEEE, May 2009
18. Simpson, J.T., Wong, K., Jackman, S.D., Schein, J.E., Jones, S.J.M., Birol, I.: ABySS: a parallel assembler for short read sequence data. Genome Res. **19**(6), 1117–1123 (2009)
19. Yang, X., Chockalingam, S.P., Aluru, S.: A survey of error-correction methods for next-generation sequencing. Briefings Bioinf. **14**(1), 56–66 (2013)
20. Yang, X., Dorman, K.S., Aluru, S.: Reptile: representative tiling for short read error correction. Bioinformatics **26**(20), 2526–2533 (2010). (Oxford, England)

# Composing Low-Overhead Scheduling Strategies for Improving Performance of Scientific Applications

Vivek Kale[(⊠)] and William D. Gropp

University of Illinois at Urbana-Champaign, Urbana, IL 61822, USA
vivek@illinois.edu

**Abstract.** Many different sources of overheads impact the efficiency of a scheduling strategy applied to a parallel loop within a scientific application. In prior work, we handled these overheads using multiple loop scheduling strategies, with each scheduling strategy focusing on mitigating a subset of the overheads. However, mitigating the impact of one source of overhead can lead to an increase in the impact of another source of overhead, and vice versa. In this work, we show that in order to improve efficiency of loop scheduling strategies, one must adapt the loop scheduling strategies so as to handle all overheads simultaneously. To show this, we describe a composition of our existing loop scheduling strategies, and experiment with the composed scheduling strategy on standard benchmarks and application codes. Applying the composed scheduling strategy to three MPI+OpenMP scientific codes run on a cluster of SMPs improves performance an average of 31 % over standard OpenMP static scheduling.

## 1 Introduction

Performance of scientific application code can be impacted by how efficiently iterations of a parallel loop are scheduled to cores. Many different sources of performance loss impact the efficiency of a scheduling strategy applied to a parallel loop, as we will show in Sect. 2. In prior work, we developed multiple loop scheduling strategies, with each scheduling strategy focusing on mitigating a subset of the overheads. However, mitigating the impact of one source of performance loss can lead to an increase in the impact of another source of performance loss, and vice versa. In this work, we show that in order to schedule loops efficiently, we need to compose loop scheduling strategies so as to handle multiple sources of performance loss simultaneously.

Our contribution, in addition to a specific composite scheduling strategy, is a guide to combining scheduling strategies to handle multiple sources of the overhead together, to handle the circumstances and challenges posed by an application and architecture. Such a scheduling strategy can be beneficial to improve performance of scientific applications on clusters of multi-cores, and can be beneficial in the context of next-generation, e.g., exascale, clusters of SMPs.

© Springer International Publishing Switzerland 2015
C. Terboven et al. (Eds.): IWOMP 2015, LNCS 9342, pp. 18–29, 2015.
DOI: 10.1007/978-3-319-24595-9_2

In the sections that follow, we discuss implementation of a scheduling strategy composition containing many different scheduling techniques implemented up to this point. We show results for different scientific application codes, i.e., two CORAL benchmarks and one particle simulation application code, using different types of scheduling strategies. Finally, we conclude the paper through a discussion of scheduling techniques and the scheduling strategy composition in the context of running applications on next-generation architectures.

## 2   Scheduling Strategies

Consider a common structure of scientific applications: outer iterations, e.g., timesteps, which enclose inner iterations that typically loop over data arrays. For these codes, load balancing of the computational work across cores of a node is necessary for obtaining high performance. Load balancing can be attained through the use of OpenMP loop scheduling strategies. However, there are multiple sources of performance loss in parallel scientific applications, and different schedulers affect these sources differently.

Figures 1 and 2 show the sources of performance loss through a breakdown of execution times for widely used loop scheduling strategies applied to two different application codes: a Barnes-Hut code (left) with non-uniform iteration times, i.e., load imbalance across iterations, and a NAS LU code (right) with uniform iteration times. NAS LU can still benefit from dynamic load balancing within a node because such load balancing can deal with imbalances caused by noise, which are *amplified* in synchronous MPI codes [7]. The performance data are for a node of a cluster of Intel Xeon 16-core processors. The execution time breakdown is shown as a stacked bar graph in Fig. 1. Thread idle time is labeled as 'idle' and cost of synchronization is labeled as 'dq'. We measure the time each thread waits at the barrier, and use the average over threads as the cost of thread idle time. We estimate the cost of synchronization by using hpcToolkit to obtain the time spent in the `omp_lock()` function. The computation time, labeled 'comp', is calculated by dividing the sequential execution time by the number of threads. The remaining execution time is attributed to data movement and labeled as 'dm'. Note that this breakdown may not be exact, but it gives us an adequate estimate to understand the impact of overheads to the efficiency of the scheduling strategies. For obtaining the cache misses, we used PAPI counters PAPI_L2_TCM and PAPI_L3_TCM for the L2 and L3 cache misses, respectively. We measured cache misses for each OpenMP parallel loop for thread 0. In Fig. 2, the L3 cache misses are shown.

Using static scheduling for these codes makes data movement small and eliminates synchronization overhead, but does not mitigate load imbalance. For Barnes-Hut, the thread idle time is 21 % of the total execution time. For NAS LU, idle time shown is small, but not negligible, at 2.8 %. Using dynamic scheduling improves load balance almost completely, but dynamic scheduling still causes data movement and synchronization overhead. Also, the synchronization overhead is still noticeable at 5.9 % when dynamic scheduling is applied to the two codes.

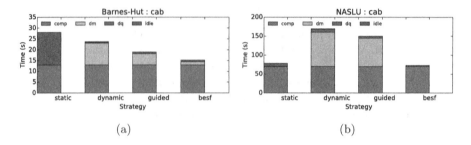

**Fig. 1.** Breakdown of execution time for NAS LU and n-body code.

Finally, guided scheduling can reduce synchronization overhead. However, guided scheduling still incurs data movement across cores, as is seen by the large number of cache misses for Barnes-Hut and NAS LU in Fig. 2.

We have identified three challenges to obtaining good performance using dynamic load balancing within a node: (1) cost of load imbalance due to load imbalances from the application or system noise, (2) data movement overhead, and (3) synchronization overheads from runtimes. None of the scheduling strategies examined was able to handle all sources of performance loss. This challenge provides motivation for developing a new set of scheduling strategies.

To handle all 3 challenges, one could intelligently blend static and dynamic scheduling strategies, where the first $k$ loop iterations are scheduled statically across threads, and the remaining $n-k$ loop iterations are scheduled dynamically across threads [4]. The parameter $k$ is experimentally tuned. We define $\frac{n-k}{n}$ as the dynamic fraction $f_d$. Correspondingly, the static fraction $f_s = 1 - f_d$. We refer to this scheduling strategy as hybrid static/dynamic scheduling. Figure 3a shows loop iterations scheduled statically across 4 cores during one invocation of a threaded computation region. Figure 3b shows the corresponding diagram for the hybrid static/dynamic scheduling strategy.

The $4^{th}$ bars from the left in Fig. 1a and b show the execution time for NAS LU and Barnes-Hut when the hybrid static/dynamic scheduling strategy, labeled *besf*, is used. The hybrid static/dynamic scheduling strategy is the best

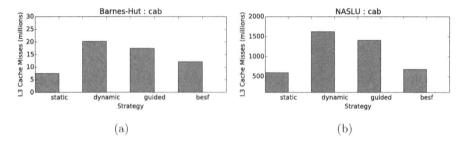

**Fig. 2.** L3 cache misses for different OpenMP scheduling strategies.

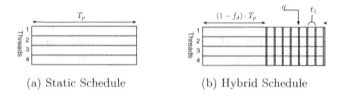

(a) Static Schedule          (b) Hybrid Schedule

**Fig. 3.** Diagram of threaded computation region with different schedules applied to it.

performing of the four scheduling strategies shown. The reason is that data movement overhead is reduced significantly compared to the dynamic scheduling scheme, but the scheduling scheme does enough dynamic scheduling to handle the cost of load imbalance. Using hybrid static/dynamic scheduling for NAS LU does not improve performance significantly over OpenMP static scheduling, but it does not degrade performance either. The hybrid static/dynamic scheduling strategy reduces thread idle time for NAS LU, rather than increasing it. Although NAS LU seems efficient with static scheduling, consider the situation when it is running on a machine with significant OS noise, i.e., the interference created by OS daemons. In this situation, amplification of noise across MPI processes can cause large performance degradation, and dynamic scheduling of loop iterations can potentially mitigate this impact of noise [7].

As we will see in the next section, different circumstances, including architectural/OS and application charactersistics, require different scheduling techniques to modify the above basic hybrid static/dynamic scheduling strategy. We next show what those techniques are and how to compose the techniques into a single effective scheduler.

## 3   Techniques for Composing Scheduling Strategies

In the context of the problem listed in the previous section, we design a scheduling strategy that can handle the many different sources of performance loss and the inefficiencies of the scheduling strategies. We first give a description of each of the elemental scheduling strategies, which are based on existing scheduling strategies from prior work; the existing scheduling strategies are adapted from the perspective of composing the scheduling strategies together. We then show a composition of the scheduling strategies described.

### 3.1   uSched

This scheduling strategy is designed to mitigate the impact of transient events such as OS noise as well as application-induced imbalances. *uSched* first measures its parameters such as iteration time and noise duration [7]. It then uses a model-guided determination of the dynamic fraction (considering both application imbalance and imbalance due to noise) to determine a reasonable baseline value of the static fraction $f_s$, as described in [7]. After this, we conduct an exhaustive search in a small neighborhood around $f_s$. We try different static fractions in the range $[f_s - 0.05, f_s + 0.05]$. This increment can be adjusted by the application programmer and requires knowledge of iteration granularity. The resulting static fraction is $f_{s_{tuned}}$, which is the static fraction used for *uSched*. This is the static fraction used for all nodes.

### 3.2   slackSched

This scheduling strategy is an optimization over *uSched*, as described in prior work [7]. It uses a distinct static fraction for each node based on MPI slack. MPI slack is the deadline that each process has to finish its work, before this process extends the applications critical path thereby increasing the cost of application execution. Because of the way collective calls are implemented in MPI, the slack is different on different processors. We use the call-path method [7,12] for predicting the slack for each collective call. In the context of the scheduling strategy composition that we want to do, the scheduling strategy is put together and works as follows:

1. On each process, start with the static fraction $f_s$ obtained in *uSched*.
    (a) On each process, retrieve that process's invocation of the last MPI collective, where the invocation of the last MPI collective is retrieved through the callsite slack-prediction method, as shown in prior work [7].
    (b) Given the identifier of the last the MPI collective call invoked, estimate that collective call's slack value from the history of slack values stored by the slack-conscious runtime. The slack estimate is based on the slack value recorded in the previous MPI collective invocation, as is done in prior work [7].
2. On each process, adjust its dynamic fraction based on the slack value. This adjustment is done using a performance model and theoretical analysis described in prior work [7].

### 3.3   vSched

This scheduling strategy is based on prior work [8]. The motivation of this scheduling strategy is to improve the spatial locality in the dynamically scheduled iterations. In the above schedulers, the dynamically allocated iterations are grouped at the end of the iteration space. Here, we stagger them, so as to keep the iterations executed by a thread contiguous as much as possible. Let $p$ denote the number of cores on one multi-core node. Let $t$ denote the thread with thread ID $t$. Let $n$ be the number of loop iterations of an OpenMP loop. The static iterations assigned to each thread are from $\lfloor \frac{n \cdot t}{p} \rfloor$ to $\lfloor \frac{n \cdot (t+f_s)}{p} \rfloor$, while dynamic iterations associated with thread $t$ are from $\lfloor \frac{n \cdot (t+f_s)}{p} \rfloor + 1$ to $\lfloor \frac{n \cdot (t+1)}{p} \rfloor - 1$. In the context of the scheduling strategy composition that we want to do, we implement this scheduling strategy by starting with the hybrid static/dynamic scheduling strategy, and then apply the staggering of iterations to this hybrid static/dynamic scheduling strategy.

### 3.4   ComboSched

The comboSched scheduling strategy is vSched, i.e., locality-optimized scheduling, with slackSched, i.e., slack-conscious scheduling, added into it. In other words, one optimization over uSched, slackSched, is composed with another optimization over uSched, vSched, to form the comboSched scheduling strategy. The comboSched scheduling strategy is put together and works as follows:

1. Stagger the iterations, as specified in vSched.
2. Start with the static fraction obtained from the uSched scheduling strategy.
3. Specify the queue to steal from in the vSched scheduling strategy.
4. On each process, adjust its dynamic fraction based on the slack value, as described in slackSched.

In summary, we described a series of scheduling strategies, and showed the design of a scheduling strategy composition using the features of these scheduling strategies. We next show code transformation needed to use the scheduling strategy composition and assess performance of the application of these scheduling strategies and the scheduling strategy composition to three application codes.

## 4   Code Transformation

Below, we show the changes to a simple MPI+OpenMP code needed to use our scheduling strategy. Figure 4 shows an application program containing a basic OpenMP loop. Figure 5 shows the same application code containing the OpenMP loop transformed to use our composed scheduler. The macro functions used for invoking our library's loop scheduling strategies are defined at lines 5–7 of Fig. 5, and the parameter value 'strat' of the macro function indicates the scheduling strategy to be used from our library. The sds parameter value in the macro functions' invocations at lines 24 and 27 specifies the staggered static/dynamic scheduling strategy of our library, i.e., the *vSched* strategy described in Sect. 3. The implementation changes needed for the composition are done within our macro-invoked scheduler. The record struct variable is used to store information about previous invocations of the threaded computation region in lines 25 and 26, and necessary for the slack-conscious scheduling strategy, i.e., the *slackSched* strategy described in Sect. 3. Our scheduling strategy could equivalently be implemented in an OpenMP runtime and offered as an OpenMP loop schedule.

## 5   Results

With the above composition of schedulers, the question we ask is: does our composition of the schedulers and adjustment of the scheduler parameters help provide further performance improvement than each of the schedulers in isolation?

To answer the above, we experimented with three different MPI+OpenMP application codes. The first application code is Rebound [11], an MPI+OpenMP

```
1   #include "mpi.h"
2   #include <omp.h>
3   int main(int argc, char* argv[])
4   {
5     // ...
6     MPI_Init(&argc,&argv);
7     MPI_Comm_size(MPI_COMM_WORLD,&numprocs);
8     MPI_Comm_rank(MPI_COMM_WORLD,&rank);
9     // ...
10    while(timestep < 1000){
11  #pragma omp parallel for
12    for(int i=0; i<n; i++)
13      c[i] += a[i]*b[i];
14      MPI_Allreduce(&sum,&global_sum,1,MPI_DOUBLE,MPI_SUM,MPI_COMM_WORLD);
15      timestep++;
16    }
17    MPI_Finalize();
18  }
```

**Fig. 4.** Code with OpenMP loop.

```
1   #include "mpi.h"
2   #include <omp.h>
3   #include "vSched.h"
4   // ...
5   // In the macros below, strat specifies the sched strategy.
6   #define FORALL_BEGIN(strat, s, e, start, end, tid, numThds) loop_start_ ## strat (s, e, &start,
        &end, tid, numThds); do {
7   #define FORALL_END(strat, start, end, tid) } while(loop_next_ ## strat (&start, &end, tid));
8   int main(int argc, char* argv[]){
9     // ...
10    int tid, numThrds, start, end = 0;
11    double fd, fs;
12    static LoopTimeRecord *record = NULL;
13    MPI_Init(&argc,&argv);
14    MPI_Comm_size(MPI_COMM_WORLD,&numprocs);
15    MPI_Comm_rank(MPI_COMM_WORLD,&rank);
16    vSched_init(numThrds);
17    // ...
18    while(timestep < 1000) {
19        fd = predict_dynamic_fraction(&record); fs = 1.0 - fd;
20  #pragma omp parallel
21        {
22          tid = omp_get_thread_num();
23          numThrds = omp_get_num_threads();
24          FORALL_BEGIN(sds,tid,numThrds,0,n,start,end,fs)
25      for(int i=start;i<end;i++)
26        c[i] += a[i]*b[i];
27          FORALL_END(sds,tid,start,end)
28        }
29        end_timing(&record, n);
30        MPI_Allreduce(&sum,&global_sum,1,MPI_DOUBLE,MPI_SUM,MPI_COMM_WORLD);
31        timestep++;
32    }
33    endLoop(&lr, (int) (n*fd));
34    vSched_finalize(numThrds);
35    MPI_Finalize();
36  }
```

**Fig. 5.** Code transformed to use composed scheduling strategy.

n-body simulation that simulates bio-molecular interactions. The second application code is the CORAL SNAP code [13], regular mesh code which has computation used in the context of heat diffusion. The third application code is the CORAL miniFE code [6], an MPI+OpenMP finite element code involving computation on an unstructured mesh used in the context of earthquake simulations.

We performed the experiments on Cab, an Intel Xeon cluster with 16 cores per node, 2.66 GHz clock speed, a 32 KB L1 data cache, a 256 KB L2 cache, 24 MB shared L3 cache, the TOSS operating system, an InfiniBand interconnect with a fat-tree network topology. We ran each application code with 1 MPI process per node and 16 OpenMP threads per MPI process.

Figure 6 shows the results for the MPI+OpenMP n-body code Rebound [11] run on Cab, with different schedulers applied to this code. In this code, every particle loops through its neighborhood of particles to calculate forces applied to it, identifying the position in the next application timestep; there is geometric locality in this application. This geometric locality is reflected by the order in which the particles are organized in the tree. For example, nearby particles tend to interact with the same sets of particles with a few exceptions. Therefore, the *vSched* strategy of keeping nearby iterations on the same thread in the dynamic section provides performance benefits. The *slackSched* benefits are the generic benefits of reducing the dynamic fraction and its associated overheads. The benefits are not as large for other applications because of its relatively large grain size of each iteration. For Rebound at 1024 nodes, the *comboSched* improves performance 45 % over OpenMP static scheduling. The percent gains of each of the scheduling strategies are significant even at low node counts. Specifically, at 2 nodes, performance improves 35 % over OpenMP static scheduling when we apply only *uSched* to the Rebound code. Using *slackSched* on Rebound gets limited gains of 5.6 % over the *uSched* scheduling strategy. Using *vSched*, performance improves 8.5 % over *uSched*. This is likely because *vSched* can take advantage of the geometric locality in this application. Using the *comboSched* strategy, which combines *slackSched* and *vSched*, the Rebound code gets an overall 44 % performance gain over the OpenMP static scheduled version of Rebound.

Figure 7 shows the results for miniFE [6] run on Cab, with different schedulers applied to miniFE. Here, iteration-to-iteration spatial locality is relatively low because of indirect access caused by the unstructured mesh; for unstructured meshes, the spatial locality across iterations is not as strong as looping over a 1-D array. However, with reasonable variable ordering of mesh elements, there is still a significant amount of spatial locality that *vSched* exploits. Because of imperfect data partitioning of the problem across nodes, moderate load imbalances across nodes exist. Due to the law of large numbers, the imbalances across cores are larger at larger number of nodes. Thus, dynamic or guided scheduling by itself should be able to provide significant performance gains. Consider the results for miniFE running at 1024 nodes of Cab. The *vSched* scheduling strategy gets 15 % performance improvement over OpenMP static scheduling, while the *slackSched* gets 19 % performance gain over OpenMP static scheduling. The *comboStrat* gets 23 % performance improvement over OpenMP static scheduling, and also gets 9.0 % performance improvement over OpenMP guided scheduling. By putting together *vSched* and *slackSched*, we are able to improve performance further, to make our scheduling methodology perform better than *guided*. The benefits of *vSched* and *slackSched* are not completely additive. Composing the scheduling strategies along with tuning of parameters could increase performance benefits, and could yield better performance for the *comboSched*.

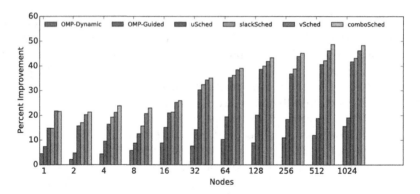

**Fig. 6.** Rebound (n-body): Performance improvement obtained over OpenMP static scheduling.

Figure 8 shows the results for the regular mesh code SNAP [13] run on Cab, with different schedulers applied to the SNAP code. The regular mesh computation has no application load imbalance; the only load imbalance during application execution is that due to noise. Note that the regular mesh computation has inherent spatial locality (because the computation's sweep operation works on contiguous array elements). At 1024 nodes of Cab, performance improves 10 % over OpenMP static with *slackSched*, and we get a reasonable performance gain of 16 % over static scheduling with *vSched*. The *comboSched* scheduler gets 19 % performance improvement over OpenMP static scheduling. This result of *comboSched* specifically helps to show that the optimizations of *vSched* and *slackSched* composed in *comboSched* do not cancel out each other's performance benefits.

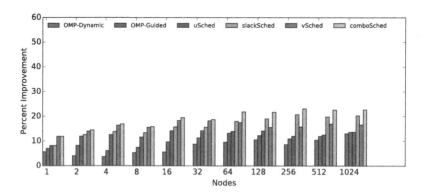

**Fig. 7.** miniFE (finite element): Performance improvement obtained over OpenMP static scheduling.

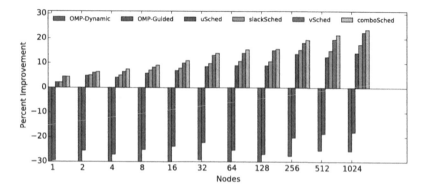

**Fig. 8.** SNAP (regular mesh): Performance improvement obtained over OpenMP static scheduling.

## 6 Related Work

The work in [1, 9, 10] attends to outer iteration locality by dynamically scheduling the loop iterations so that each core tends to get the same inner loop iterations over successive outer iterations. In contrast, our strategy sets aside iterations that are scheduled statically without the locking overhead to maintain outer iteration locality. The problem of amplification and the phenomenon of MPI slack arise only in the context of a cluster of multiprocessors, and are absent from older work which was focused on shared memory machines. Also, hybrid programming with MPI and pthreads/OpenMP did not exist at the time of the work. Zhang and Voss [14] present scheduling techniques based on runtime measurements, but the techniques are designed specifically for the problems arising out of simultaneous multi-threading (hyperthreads). For example, the techniques involve runtime decisions about whether the number of threads should be equal to the number of cores, or equal to the number of hyperthreads.

Loop iterations are a form of independent tasks. Several programming models support creation of independent tasks directly. One of the primary shortcomings of work-stealing [5] is that work-stealing incurs overhead due to the cost of coherence cache misses, which depend on the number of cores and the shared memory interconnect of the node architecture [2]. In contrast, our work focuses on reducing coherence cache misses. Scalable work-stealing [3] can be beneficial in a distributed memory context, but it mainly focuses on steals across a large number of nodes. Our work is focused on within-node scheduling, and to that extent is orthogonal to scalable work stealing.

## 7 Conclusions

In this work, we identified a number of scheduling strategies, each with different features. We expect many of the features of the scheduling strategies to be relevant for running parallel applications on current and future clusters of SMPs.

We then provided a guide for composing these scheduling strategies together. Our results showed on average 31 % performance improvements over static scheduling for three scientific applications.

Many unknown circumstances will likely exist when running applications on next-generation supercomputers, e.g., exascale machines. The composition of existing scheduling strategies, as well as the invention of new scheduling strategies inspired by specific circumstances of current and future clusters of SMPs, could help ensure that the approach remains viable for these next-generation supercomputers.

**Acknowledgements.** This material is based in part upon work supported by the Department of Energy, National Nuclear Security Administration, under Award Number DE-NA0002374. This work was supported in part by the Office of Advanced Scientific Computing Research, Office of Science, U.S. Department of Energy award DE-FG02-13ER26138/DE-SC0010049.

# References

1. Bull, J.M.: Feedback guided dynamic loop scheduling: algorithms and experiments. In: Pritchard, D., Reeve, J.S. (eds.) Euro-Par 1998. LNCS, vol. 1470, p. 377. Springer, Heidelberg (1998)
2. Bull, J.M.: Measuring synchronisation and scheduling overheads in OpenMP. In: Proceedings of First European Workshop on OpenMP, pp. 99–105, Lund, Sweden (1999)
3. Dinan, J., Larkins, D.B., Sadayappan, P., Krishnamoorthy, S., Nieplocha, J.: Scalable work stealing. In: Proceedings of the Conference on High Performance Computing Networking, Storage and Analysis, SC 2009, pp. 53:1–53:11, Portland, OR, USA. ACM (2009)
4. Donfack, S., Grigori, L., Gropp, W.D., Kale, V.: Hybrid static/dynamic scheduling for already optimized dense matrix factorizations. In: IEEE International Parallel and Distributed Processing Symposium, IPDPS 2012, Shanghai, China (2012)
5. Frigo, M., Leiserson, C.E., Randall, K.H.: The implementation of the Cilk-5 multithreaded language. SIGPLAN Not. **33**(5), 212–223 (1998)
6. Heroux, M.: MiniFE documentation. http://www.nersc.gov/users/computational-systems/cori/nersc-8-procurement/trinity-nersc-8-rfp/nersc-8-trinity-bench marks/minife/
7. Kale, V., Gamblin, T., Hoefler, T., de Supinski, B.R., Gropp, W.D.: Abstract: Slack-Conscious Lightweight Loop Scheduling for Improving Scalability of Bulk-synchronous MPI Applications, November 2012
8. Kale, V., Randles, A.P., Kale, V., Gropp, W.D.: Locality-optimized scheduling for improved load balancing on SMPs. In: Proceedings of the 21st European MPI Users' Group Meeting Conference on Recent Advances in the Message Passing Interface, vol. 0, pp. 1063–1074. Association for Computing Machinery (2014)
9. Markatos, E.P., LeBlanc, T.J.: Using processor affinity in loop scheduling on shared-memory multiprocessors. In: Proceedings of the 1992 ACM/IEEE Conference on Supercomputing, Supercomputing 1992, pp. 104–113, Los Alamitos, CA, USA. IEEE Computer Society Press (1992)

10. Olivier, S.L., de Supinski, B.R., Schulz, M., Prins, J.F.: Characterizing and mitigating work time inflation in task parallel programs. In: Proceedings of the International Conference on High Performance Computing, Networking, Storage and Analysis, SC 2012, pp. 65:1–65:12, Salt Lake City, UT, USA. IEEE Computer Society Press (2012)
11. Rein, H., Liu, S.F.: REBOUND: an open-source multi-purpose N-body code for collisional dynamics. Astron. Astrophys. **537**, A128 (2012)
12. Rountree, B., Lowenthal, D.K., de Supinski, B.R., Schulz, M., Freeh, V.W., Bletsch, T.: Adagio: making DVS practical for complex HPC applications. In: Proceedings of the 23rd International Conference on Supercomputing, ICS 2009, pp. 460–469, Yorktown Heights, NY, USA. ACM (2009)
13. Talamo, A.: Numerical solution of the time dependent neutron transport equation by the method of the characteristics. J. Comput. Phys. **240**, 248–267 (2013)
14. Zhang, Y., Voss, M.: Runtime empirical selection of loop schedulers on hyperthreaded SMPs. In: Proceedings of the 19th IEEE International Parallel and Distributed Processing Symposium (IPDPS 2005), vol. 01, pp. 44.2, Washington, DC, USA. IEEE Computer Society (2005)

# Exploiting Fine- and Coarse-Grained Parallelism Using a Directive Based Approach

Arpith C. Jacob[1]([⊠]), Ravi Nair[1], Alexandre E. Eichenberger[1],
Samuel F. Antao[1], Carlo Bertolli[1], Tong Chen[1], Zehra Sura[1],
Kevin O'Brien[1], and Michael Wong[2]

[1] IBM T.J. Watson Research Center, 1101 Kitchawan Rd.,
Yorktown Heights, NY, USA
{acjacob,nair,alexe,cbertol,chentong,zsura,caohmin}@us.ibm.com
[2] IBM Software Group, Toronto, ON, Canada
michaelw@ca.ibm.com

**Abstract.** Modern high-performance machines are challenging to program because of the availability of a wide array of compute resources that often requires low-level, specialized knowledge to exploit. OpenMP is an effective directive-based approach that can effectively exploit shared-memory multicores. The recently introduced OpenMP 4.0 standard extends the directive-based approach to exploit accelerators. However, programming clusters still requires the use of other specialized languages or libraries.

In this work we propose the use of the target offloading constructs to program nodes distributed in a cluster. We introduce an abstract model of a cluster that defines a clique of distinct shared-memory domains that are manipulated with the target constructs. We have implemented this model in the LLVM compiler with an OpenMP runtime that supports transparent offloading to nodes in a cluster using MPI. Our initial results on HMMER, a widely used Bioinformatics tool, show excellent scaling behavior with a small constant-factor overhead as compared to a baseline MPI implementation. Our work raises the intriguing possibility of a natural progression of a program compiled for serial execution, to parallel execution on a multicore, to offloading onto accelerators, and finally extendible with minimal additional effort onto a cluster.

## 1 Introduction

Modern computers are difficult to program because of the use of a broad spectrum of compute resources such as SIMD, SIMT, light and heavyweight multicores, accelerators such as GPUs, clusters, and even rented cloud platforms that may all need to be exploited for high performance. It is difficult and time consuming for the average programmer to reason about fine- and coarse-grained parallelism suitable for these resources and then express this parallelism using low-level language extensions or libraries. Many languages have been introduced to address some of these challenges, including X10 [2], Fortress, Chapel [1], Co-array Fortran [12], and UPC [5], but none have gained widespread acceptance.

© Springer International Publishing Switzerland 2015
C. Terboven et al. (Eds.): IWOMP 2015, LNCS 9342, pp. 30–41, 2015.
DOI: 10.1007/978-3-319-24595-9_3

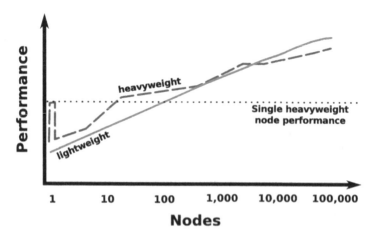

**Fig. 1.** Comparative performance of light and heavyweight nodes on the Graph500 benchmark. The trend lines are extrapolated from Fig. 12 of Koggee [8].

To illustrate why this is a problem Fig. 1 shows performance of the Graph500 breadth-first search benchmark as a function of node count, illustrated as trend lines extrapolated from Fig. 12 of Kogge [8]. Curves for light and heavyweight nodes are depicted. Heavyweight cores provide maximum compute performance in a single node using 16 or more cores clocked at a high rate, sharing coherent, high-bandwidth memory. They are the easiest to program and suitable for a large number of applications. In contrast, lightweight nodes use simpler cores with lower-bandwidth memory that consume less power. As a consequence, they are better able to scale to thousands of nodes in a system.

Figure 1 shows that the best heavyweight single-node implementation is equivalent in performance to a large multiple of lightweight nodes. It is obviously beneficial to first exploit the compute resources and high-bandwidth communication through shared-memory in a single node and only move to a lightweight cluster when the organization's data requirements explode. However, an actor may unnecessarily commit early on to a cluster solution due to perceived "big data" needs or to simply scale early software development investment.

To program clusters, frameworks such as Hadoop using the MapReduce model have become popular but it includes considerable overheads. This may be required for fault-tolerance in large-scale clusters but is inefficient for most users. Indeed, there is evidence that MapReduce is commonly used for datasets less than 100 GB in size [16], and with several times this size available as RAM in a single node[1], it may be prudent to first exhaust single-node solutions. Consequently, what is desired is a software solution that can exploit compute resources in a single node but seamlessly scale to multiple nodes as data size increases.

OpenMP is a directive-based parallel programming standard for shared-memory multicores. The introduction of offloading constructs in the OpenMP 4.0

---

[1] For example, the IBM Power® System E880 is configurable up to 16 TB. See http://www-03.ibm.com/systems/power/hardware/e880/.

standard extends directive-based programming to accelerators within a node that may have non-coherent, disjoint memory. The goal of this work is to extend the offloading model to the wider scope of a cluster so as to avoid the use of low-level libraries like MPI. This raises the intriguing possibility of a single program that may be compiled for serial execution, parallel execution on a multicore, offloaded to accelerators, and finally extended with minimal additional effort to a cluster.

The rest of this paper is organized as follows. Section 2 first discusses past efforts that use OpenMP to program clusters. Section 3 summarizes the offloading model of OpenMP 4.0 and in Sect. 4 we describe our model for using these constructs to program a cluster of nodes. Section 5 describes the implementation of our model in the LLVM compiler and we present preliminary results in Sect. 6. Section 7 discusses extensions to the model and implementation that we plan to explore in the future before we conclude in Sect. 8.

## 2  Related Work

Existing work implements OpenMP 3.1 and prior versions on distributed machines by translating shared-memory programs onto a Software Distributed Shared Memory (SDSM) runtime [7,13] or directly to MPI [11]. An SDSM runtime that transparently keeps memory consistent between nodes was first used in TreadMarks [7] to execute OpenMP programs and was later incorporated into Intel's Cluster OMP [6]. These solutions exploit the relaxed consistency model of OpenMP to cache memory locally and improve performance but problems remain due to memory sharing overheads and frequent global synchronization. Static compiler analyses aim to eliminate barriers and aggressively privatize shared variables but the fine-grained communication pattern of OpenMP 3.1 is a fundamental mismatch for distributed machines.

The distinguishing feature of our work is our abstraction of a machine as a clique of shared-memory domains. Rather than forcing the abstraction of a single shared-memory domain onto a distributed cluster and using compiler analyses to bridge the semantic gap, we rely on an expressive yet simple programming abstraction that is closer to the underlying machine.

Our work is the first to use OpenMP 4.0 offload constructs to program distributed systems. We exploit these constructs to represent our model of disjoint domains of shared memory. Target directives are used to partition a program into distinct regions, each of which can then exploit shared-memory semantics via the standard suite of OpenMP 3.1 constructs. Data mapping clauses allow the user to bridge shared-memory domains via explicit data movement. Our model is easy to comprehend and it allows the user to effectively exploit coarse- and fine-grained parallelism.

## 3  Background: OpenMP Accelerator Model

The OpenMP 4.0 specification [15] significantly extends the capability of a directive based programming approach to exploit coarse-grained parallelism within a node. It introduces an execution and data model for an abstract accelerator that enables a programmer to exploit heterogeneous cores using *device* directives. A node is assumed to contain a host device, typically a multicore processor, attached to one or more accelerators termed *target devices.*

The programming model is host-centric and allows offloading of execution control to the device. Code regions to be offloaded, including functions, are explicitly identified using the *target* directive. The target region accepts standard OpenMP directives and uses the fork-join paradigm to exploit cores within the accelerator.

The accelerator memory model defines a data environment for the host and target devices. To support both shared- and distributed-memory systems the standard specifies that the programmer may not make any assumptions regarding data sharing between devices. The user is required to explicitly migrate data between the two environments and the standard provides the *target data*, *declare target*, and *target update* directives for this purpose.

**Listing 1.1.** Matrix-matrix multiply offloaded to a target device for acceleration.

```
1   double A[P][R], B[R][Q], C[P][Q];
2
3   void main() {
4   // Initialize arrays
5
6   // Offload loop nest for acceleration onto device #1
7   #pragma omp target map(to: A[0:P][0:R], B[0:R][0:Q]) map(tofrom: C[0:P][0:R]) device(1)
8   // Execute iterations of loop i in parallel on 16 accelerator cores
9   #pragma omp parallel for num_threads(16)
10  for (int i=0; i<P; i++)
11    for (int j=0; j<Q; j++)
12      for (int k=0; k<R; k++)
13        C[i][j] += A[i][k] * B[k][j]
14
15  // Computed array C is available on the host
16  }
```

Listing 1.1 shows an OpenMP 4.0 program offloading matrix-matrix multiply onto an accelerator. The *target* directive first establishes a data environment on the device with three arrays $A$, $B$, and $C$ before offloading the computation. Upon completion, the array $C$ is transferred back to the host.

The user is required to guarantee a program free of data races that may otherwise arise due to concurrent execution on devices. These relaxed definitions allow the standard to support a wide spectrum of accelerators including GPUs, FPGAs, DSPs, and PiM devices.

## 4    An Offloading Model for a Cluster

While not originally defined with node-level parallelism in mind, the flexibility of the OpenMP accelerator model raises the intriguing possibility of exploiting coarse-grained parallelism across nodes in a cluster. In particular, the assumption in the model that the device data environments may be distinct allows the possibility of more efficient execution on a cluster. We start by first defining an offloading model to program a cluster.

### 4.1  Definitions

*Shared-Memory Domain.* An implementation defined logical realm with storage accessible through a global address space by one or more processors within it. Data may be cached by processors but the model assumes that caches are kept coherent.

*Host Domain.* The shared-memory domain on which a program starts execution.

*Target Domain.* One or more shared-memory domains other than the Host onto which code and data may be offloaded.

### 4.2  Execution Model

The execution model defines a *clique* of one or more shared-memory domains laid out in a multi-level tree hierarchy. A program begins with a single thread of execution on some implementation defined domain called the Host. All other domains in the clique are inactive at startup and must be expressly activated by the Host.

When the initial thread on the Host encounters a parallel worksharing construct it may spawn additional threads and distribute work for parallel execution on processors within the same shared-memory domain. When a thread on a domain encounters a target construct (or in general, a target boundary) there is a transfer of data and control from one shared-memory domain to another.

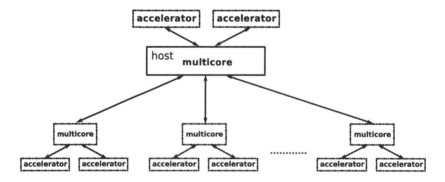

**Fig. 2.** A clique of shared-memory domains laid out on general-purpose microprocessors and accelerators realized as a multi-level tree hierarchy by the offload model. Domains communicate via messages on a hierarchical network and optionally via files on a shared disk.

The thread offloads code and data to the Target domain and program control is transferred to an initial thread on the Target. The original thread waits at the end of the construct until control is returned from the Target. The Target thread executes in its distinct shared-memory domain and may co-opt other threads for parallel execution on the processors within the domain.

### 4.3   Memory Model

As mentioned previously, in our memory model every domain has a distinct data environment with storage coherently addressable by all processors contained within it. Since every domain has an independent address and storage space, variables declared on the Host are only addressable by that domain, and those declared on a Target are only addressable by the Target domain. Domain-private variables are shared across processors within the same domain and follow the relaxed consistency model of traditional OpenMP.

Data sharing between domains is explicitly controlled by the programmer. Any Host variable may be mirrored across domains on one or more Targets through a synchronous operation called "mapping". Mapping creates a distinct Corresponding copy on a particular target for an Original variable on the host. Code within the Host and a Target domain may only access and modify the Original and Corresponding values respectively. Original and Corresponding variables may only be synchronized at target boundaries. Outside the explicit movement of data between domains at target boundaries there is no mechanism to address storage across domains.

Mapping is first and foremost a naming operation that assigns a common identifier to distinct storage locations on the Host and one or more Target domains. In addition, it is a data transfer operation that moves data between the Host and one or more Targets (or vice versa).

Mapping points and the direction of the mirroring are explicitly specified by the user. Host local variables are mapped at these well defined interfaces identified through user-specified directives. For example, data is typically transferred to a Target before its invocation and back to the Host upon completion of work. Host global variables that are explicitly mapped to target domains are mirrored at program startup before any user code executes.

The kinds of programs that work well under these assumptions include those that can partition data (such as an array or a set of files) into distinct subsets across target domains.

## 5   Implementation

We have implemented our offloading model for clusters within LLVM [10], a powerful open-source intermediate representation and optimizer, coupled with Clang [3], a frontend for C/C++ based languages. A recent joint effort by several players has been adding full OpenMP support in Clang [14]. We have extended this implementation to provide offloading support for the accelerator model.

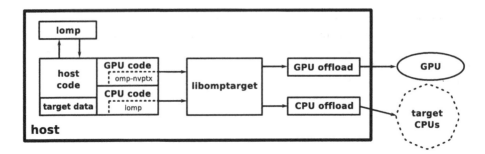

**Fig. 3.** Compiler generated fat binary containing offloaded code for a GPU and a Cluster (labeled CPU) target. Offloading support is provided by a generic target library and device-specific modules. Non-offloaded OpenMP code is supported by our *lomp* library.

Briefly, support for the offloading directives are added in the parser and semantic analyzer. Each target region is outlined into a standalone function. Next, the driver calls the host and one or more target toolchains to obtain distinct object files. Finally, the linker links the host object file into the executable and embeds the target object "as is", resulting in a fat binary.

Figure 3 illustrates the fat binary with included offloading code generated for the GPU and a cluster node.

## 5.1    Runtime Support

In order to generate the behavior defined in the OpenMP specification, the compiler interfaces with a series of runtime libraries for host and target regions. The design provides distinct support for offloading and non-offloading OpenMP directives. We use the IBM lightweight OpenMP (*lomp*) runtime [4] for parallelization of the non-offloaded host code. Offloading support is provided by a target agnostic library coupled with low-level device-specific plugins. The former is labeled *libomptarget* in Fig. 3, while the plugins for the two targets shown in the figure are labeled *GPU* and *CPU offload*.

**Target Agnostic Offloading Library.** The offloading runtime library is completely target agnostic allowing Clang to move the complexity of offloading away from the compiler. This library calls low-level functions in the plugins to allocate memory on a device and transfer data between the host and the target. It also manages the address mapping between Original and Corresponding variables and tracks data references for safe de-allocation. Finally, the library initializes a target device with offloaded code using the plugins, prepares parameters, and initiates execution of the kernel.

**Target Specific Plugins.** The target agnostic library triggers actions on target devices supported by a set of device-specific plugins. These plugins have a pre-determined interface and are located and loaded at runtime by the target agnostic component. They are used to drive low-level actions on the device.

We have implemented a plugin for clusters on top of MPI. Upon program startup every shared-memory domain is activated and all target domains enter an event loop awaiting communication from the host via MPI messages. The host can direct each domain to allocate, de-allocate, and transfer data via MPI.

Recall that a target regions are outlined in functions and linked together into an elf object embedded in the fat binary. At program startup the host transfers the object to every potential device and is immediately loaded by the event loop on the target domains. When the host encounters a target region it sets up the data environment on the specified device and directs the event loop to execute the function.

Since multiple threads on the host may concurrently offload to distinct targets, the plugin requires an MPI library that supports thread safe execution.

**Target Specific Runtime Libraries.** The offloaded device code will itself have OpenMP directives and therefore requires runtime library support implemented for the device. Since we are offloading to general-purpose CPUs, standard *lomp* is sufficient for this purpose.

## 6   Preliminary Results

To illustrate the application of our programming model we have accelerated an important Bioinformatics application, HMMER[2], on a cluster. The application finds homologs of a protein family by comparing its Hidden Markov Model (HMM) representation against a database of protein sequences. A typical search compares tens of thousands of HMMs against tens of millions of sequences and is a compute-intensive task. In this work we offload this search to nodes within a cluster. This benchmark exhibits the typical master-slave programming pattern.

The latest release of HMMER includes code to parallelize the search across nodes within a cluster using traditional MPI. We have summarized the code and illustrated the flow of control initiated via MPI messages in Fig. 4. The master and the worker nodes iterate over each query HMM in lock step. For each query, the database is partitioned into blocks that are offloaded to the next available worker dynamically to avoid load imbalance. Once the entire database is processed the master implements a barrier to synchronize across all workers, before finally requesting and receiving their results. The code is low level and the control flow is fairly involved.

Our implementation of this same search routine is illustrated in Fig. 5. A master thread on the host iterates over each query HMM sequentially. We use the *parallel for* directive to start *num_devices* threads on the host multicore, one for each node in the cluster. Each of these threads operates in parallel, offloading data and execution control to its associated node. Unlike traditional OpenMP where threads are used for compute, we are using them as I/O threads to facilitate parallel offloading. Another approach is to use asynchronous target

---

[2] HMMER 3.1b2: http://hmmer.org.

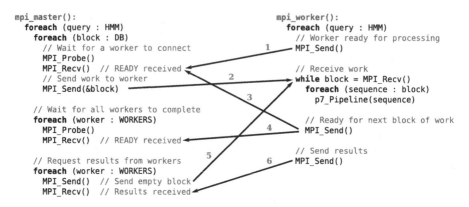

**Fig. 4.** Pseudocode illustrating a search procedure from HMMER that is currently implemented using traditional MPI.

```
target():
  foreach (query : HMM)
    // In parallel, activate a dedicated thread for each device
    // and schedule work dynamically
    #pragma omp parallel for schedule(dynamic) \
                num_threads(num_devices)
    foreach (block : DB)
      device = omp_get_thread_num()
      // Thread sends work to its device and waits for results
      #pragma omp target device(device) map(to:block, query) \
                map(from: results) {
        foreach (sequence : block)
          p7_Pipeline(sequence)
      }
```

**Fig. 5.** HMMER search pseudocode implemented using our proposed abstraction.

offloading with the *nowait* clause of OpenMP 4.1, in which case only a single host thread is necessary.

The worksharing construct implicitly partitions the database across nodes by distributing iterations of the DB loop across host threads. The OpenMP *dynamic* schedule transparently achieves the desired load balancing. Data movement is achieved using map clauses and implicit barrier after the *parallel* pragma transparently synchronizes across all workers. The combination of the 3.1 parallelization pragma with the cluster enabled offloading construct helps realize a much simpler program.

We note that our current implementation is more involved due to a known limitation of the map clause. The standard does not specify the handling of deep copy of structures with pointers, which is required to map the *query* structure onto the target device. Deep copy is necessary to map the variable in the map clause and all data referenced by fields within the variable (it is being considered for addition to the Accelerator model). One way around this limitation is to manually pack and unpack the structure across the device boundary. Our current implementation instead maps a query identifier to each target, which then reads the query data from a shared disk.

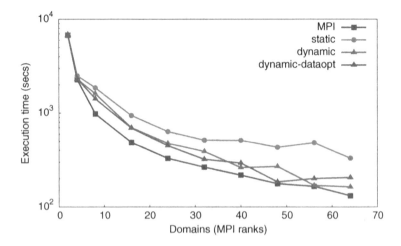

**Fig. 6.** Comparison of HMMER with stock MPI against the implementation in this work.

To measure performance we run our experiments on a four-node IBM Power 8® S824 cluster. A node has four sockets, each with six cores and eight hardware threads per core running at a maximum clock frequency of 3.3 GHz. We use the Open MPI 1.8.5 library compiled with multithreaded support and the LSF cluster management tool to closely pack MPI ranks, 16 per node.

We compiled HMMER for this cluster, enabling stock MPI support, disabling multithreaded execution, and without SIMD. In our experiment we use HMMER to compare a single query HMM against a database of 3.9 M sequences. We selected an appropriate database block size to ensure repeated invocation of target devices to simulate realistic conditions. In our experiments we vary the number of MPI ranks from 2 to 64. We run each experiment several times and select the minimum execution time.

Figure 6 compares execution time (log scale) using HMMER+MPI against our implementation. We see good scaling behavior that is comparable to the low-level MPI implementation. Using a dynamic instead of a static schedule to offload the database consistently gives superior performance, reducing runtime by over 50 % in some cases. We are able to achieve this performance using simple directives applied to a serial program. The complexity of balanced work scheduling across worker nodes, message passing to transfer data, manage control flow, and synchronize across nodes is completely hidden behind high-level OpenMP abstractions.

We observe a constant factor overhead in our implementation beyond 4 ranks. Currently we have not optimized data communication between the host and target devices. For example, if there are repeated invocations of a target device it may be possible for the runtime to reuse memory on the device that was previously allocated. As shown by the curve labeled *dynamic-dataopt*, we can eliminate some of this overhead by establishing a persistent device data environment using the *target data* directive.

We are investigating the reason for the performance degradation of *dynamic-dataopt* with 56 and 64 ranks. We believe this may be due to unbalanced workload partitioning of coarser database partitions that was selected to reduce offloading overhead.

## 7    Discussion

*Rich and efficient data sharing.* The standard accelerator model in OpenMP 4.0 implies that data sharing between the host and a device is specified exclusively via the map clause. While this is likely to be the only method for co-processors like GPUs, in our case we can also exploit a networked filesystem to share data. This also allows the programmer to exploit the bandwidth of a large number of distributed disks.

*Exploiting cores in a node.* It is possible to naturally extend the implementation in Fig. 5 to exploit multicores in a target node. We may use a nested *parallel for* worksharing directive to dynamically distribute database sequences in the block assigned to a target across its cores.

*Nested target regions.* The current standard does not define the semantics of nested target regions. These may be useful, however, to model a co-processor such as a GPU within a node in a cluster. Additional semantics, for example, the scope of "global" variables will have to be clarified. Compiling nested target regions is also more challenging, likely requiring recursive calls in the driver and nested containers within the generated fat binary.

*Exploiting resources in a cloud.* There is no requirement in our model that the clique of shared-memory domains be on the same homogeneous cluster. Our model can be used to offload computation onto rented nodes on one or more cloud platforms to seamlessly scale compute and data requirements from a personal device such as a mobile phone or a laptop, to an organization's cluster, and finally a large-scale cloud platform.

*Beyond offloading.* Our proposed model uses well-defined offloading semantics that are easy to reason about for a programmer. However, more powerful extensions may be desired. In particular, arbitrary communication between any two target devices may be useful for the expert programmer but this is unlikely to be generally friendly.

One direction we plan to explore is the asynchronous update of variables on the host (and the target) initiated by the device. This will allow the support of the parameter-server model [9], which tolerates asynchronous updates of parameter variables for efficient execution of many machine learning algorithms.

# 8   Conclusions

In this work we have introduced an abstract model to represent a cluster, and OpenMP 4.0 target directives to implement a simple directive-based approach to programming a distributed machine. We have implemented this idea in the LLVM compiler with a runtime that transparently offloads execution via MPI.

Initial results on a bioinformatics application shows good scaling behavior. Compared to an MPI based approach, high-level OpenMP abstractions in our implementation completely hide the complexity of balanced work scheduling across worker nodes, message passing for data transfer, control flow management, and synchronization across nodes. We have identified a number of possible optimizations to improve performance and directions to extend the presented model.

The application we have considered for acceleration is fully data parallel, though it requires dynamic workload balancing. In the future it would be interesting to study applications that require more frequent communication and synchronization with the host.

# References

1. Chamberlain, B., Callahan, D., Zima, H.: Parallel programmability and the chapel language. J. High Perf. Comput. Appl. **21**(3), 291–312 (2007)
2. Charles, P., et al.: X10: An object-oriented approach to non-uniform cluster computing. In: Conference on Object-Oriented Programming, Systems, Languages, and Applications, pp. 519–538 (2005)
3. Clang: A C language family frontend for LLVM. http://clang.llvm.org
4. Eichenberger, A.E., O'Brien, K.: Experimenting with low-overhead OpenMP runtime on IBM Blue Gene/Q. IBM J. Res. Dev. **57**(1/2), 8:1–8:8 (2013)
5. El-Ghazawi, T., Smith, L.: UPC: Unified parallel C. In: Supercomputing (2006)
6. Hoeflinger, J.P.: Extending OpenMP to clusters (2006)
7. Hu, Y., Lu, H., Cox, A.L., Zwaenepoel, W.: OpenMP for networks of SMPs. J. Parallel Distrib. Comput. **60**(12), 1512–1530 (2000)
8. Kogge, P.M.: Performance analysis of a large memory application on multiple architectures. In: Conference on Partitioned Global Address Space Programming Models (2013)
9. Li, M., et al.: Scaling distributed machine learning with the parameter server. In: Operating Systems Design and Implementation, pp. 583–598, October 2014
10. The LLVM Compiler Infrastructure. http://llvm.org
11. Millot, D., Muller, A., Parrot, C., Silber-Chaussumier, F.: STEP: a distributed OpenMP for coarse-grain parallelism tool. In: Eigenmann, R., de Supinski, B.R. (eds.) IWOMP 2008. LNCS, vol. 5004, pp. 83–99. Springer, Heidelberg (2008)
12. Numrich, R.W., Reid, J.: Co-array fortran for parallel programming. SIGPLAN Fortran Forum **17**(2), 1–31 (1998)
13. Ojima, Y., Sato, M., Harada, H., Ishikawa, Y.: Performance of cluster-enabled OpenMP for the SCASH software distributed shared memory system. In: Cluster Computing and the Grid, pp. 450–456, May 2003
14. OpenMP Application Program Interface. http://www.openmp.org/
15. OpenMP, A.R.B.: OpenMP version 4.0, May 2013
16. Rowstron, A., et al.: Nobody ever got fired for using hadoop on a cluster. In: Workshop on Hot Topics in Cloud Data Processing, pp. 2:1–2:5 (2012)

# Accelerator Applications

# Experiences of Using the OpenMP Accelerator Model to Port DOE Stencil Applications

Pei-Hung Lin[1]($\boxtimes$), Chunhua Liao[1], Daniel J. Quinlan[1], and Stephen Guzik[2]

[1] Center for Applied Scientific Computing, Lawrence Livermore National Laboratory,
Livermore, USA
{lin32,liao6,dquinlan}@llnl.gov

[2] Mechanical Engineering Department, Colorado State University, Fort Collins, USA
stephen.guzik@colostate.edu

**Abstract.** The Department of Energy has a wide range of large-scale, parallel scientific applications running on cutting-edge high-performance computing systems to support its mission and tackle critical science challenges. A recent trend in these high-performance computing systems is to add commodity accelerators, such as Nvidia GPUs and Intel Xeon Phi coprocessors, into computer nodes so we can achieve increased performance without exceeding the limited power budget. However, it is well-known in the high-performance computing community that porting existing applications to accelerators is a difficult task given the numerous set of unique hardware features and the general complexity of software. In this paper, we share our experiences of using the OpenMP Accelerator Model to port two stencil applications to exploit Nvidia GPUs. Introduced as part of the OpenMP 4.0 specification, the OpenMP accelerator model provides a set of directives for users to specify semantics related to accelerators so that compilers and runtime systems can automatically handle repetitive and error-prone accelerator programming tasks, including code transformations, work scheduling, data management, reduction, and so on. Using a prototype compiler implementation based on the ROSE source-to-source compiler framework, we report the problems we encountered during the porting process, our solutions, and the obtained performance. Productivity is also evaluated. Our experience shows that the existing OpenMP Accelerator Model can effectively help programmers leverage accelerators. However, complex data types and non-canonical control structures can pose challenges for programmers to productively apply accelerator directives.

LLNL-CONF-670941. This work was performed under the auspices of the U.S. Department of Energy by Lawrence Livermore National Laboratory under Contract DE-AC52-07NA27344. This work was also supported by the National Science Foundations Computer Research Infrastructure program under Award No. CNS-1205708. The rights of this work are transferred to the extent transferable according to title 17 §105 U.S.C.

C. Terboven et al. (Eds.): IWOMP 2015, LNCS 9342, pp. 45–59, 2015.
DOI: 10.1007/978-3-319-24595-9_4

# 1    Introduction

The Department of Energy (DOE) has a wide range of large-scale, parallel scientific applications to support its mission and tackle critical research and development challenges in multiple science disciplines. Many of these scientific applications have a lifespan of multiple decades so it is essential to port them to current mainstream high-performance computing (HPC) systems deployed in DOE in a timely fashion. A recent trend in the HPC systems is to add commodity accelerators, such as Nvidia GPUs and Intel Xeon Phi coprocessors, into computer nodes so we can achieve increased performance within a limited power budget. However, it is well-known in the HPC community that porting existing applications to accelerators is a difficult task given the numerous unique set of hardware features of accelerators and the complexity of software.

Although low-level programming models, such as CUDA [2] and OpenCL [10], can often help deliver competitive performance for certain applications, they are not productive porting solutions for large-scale parallel applications due to the extreme and comprehensive changes required in the original source code. On the other hand, high-level programming models such as OpenMP 4.0 [14] and OpenACC [4] provide language annotations in the form of directives and clauses for users to incrementally specify the semantics for porting to an accelerator. Compilers and runtime systems then automatically take care of repetitive and error-prone code transformations, thread scheduling, data management, and so on. Therefore, it is more productive for users to use high-level directive-based programming models to test the feasibility and profitability of using accelerators.

The OpenMP Accelerator Model, introduced as part of the OpenMP 4.0 specification, is a representative high-level directive-based programming model aimed to simplify the programming for accelerators. In a previous study [12], we created a prototype compiler for the OpenMP Accelerator Model and obtained an early assessment. We extend our work by applying the model to port two non-trivial DOE scientific applications: lattice-Boltzmann method and Compressible Navies-Stokes equation. Both applications conduct a stencil computation, an important category of scientific computing done in DOE facilities. However, they have very different stencil sizes so they represent a spectrum of stencil applications. However, they represent a spectrum of stencil applications by their difference in stencil sizes. Our goal is to discover problems developers may face when using the OpenMP Accelerator Model to port real applications. We also share our solutions to the problems, including suggestions to improve the programming model itself. Our contributions include: (1) providing the first study using the OpenMP Accelerator Model in OpenMP 4.0 to port non-trivial scientific applications, (2) illustrating the obstacles for porting real applications and possible solutions and workarounds, and (3) suggesting improvements, including new language features, of the OpenMP Accelerator Model to increase expressiveness and performance for accelerators.

The remainder of this paper is organized as follows. Section 2 gives an overview of the accelerator support in the OpenMP 4.0 specification. Section 3 describes the two applications. Porting experiences and performance results are given in Sect. 4. Section 5 summarizes related work and Sect. 6 presents the conclusion and future work.

## 2   OpenMP 4.0's Accelerator Support

OpenMP is a representative high-level directive-based programming model originally designed to address shared-memory programming. Starting from OpenMP 4.0, it has a set of language directives and runtime routines aimed at simplifying the programming for accelerators. Collectively, the accelerator support is often called the OpenMP Accelerator Model. The OpenMP accelerator model assumes that a computation node has a host device connected with one or multiple target devices. A target device, which can be any logical execution engine defined by an implementation, has threads that behave almost the same as threads on the host device. The OpenMP memory model is extended so that the code region has its own data environment. A device appears to have an independent memory, although it is allowed to share memory among devices.

The execution model is host-centric: a host device "offloads" data and code regions to accelerators for execution. In particular, the target construct is introduced for specifying a computation and the associated data to be offloaded to a device. Initially, only a single thread starts on a device to run an implicit task region. This single thread can fork more threads later when it encounters parallel constructs. Data-mapping attributes, specified using the map clause, define how variables are handled for the device data environments. Data mapping often involves data movement as host and device are commonly in different memory spaces in modern accelerator architectures. To avoid repetitive creation and cancellation of device data environments, the target data directive defines a device data region, in which multiple target regions can share the same device data.

Accelerators are often massively parallel architecture devices that support many concurrent threads with a hierarchical organization. OpenMP 4.0 provides the teams and distribute constructs to manage a two-level thread hierarchy. teams creates a league of thread teams, and the master thread of each team executes the region. distribute is closely nested in a teams region to share work among master threads of teams. Other features in the OpenMP accelerator model include a target update directive to make specified items in the device data environment consistent with their original list items, a target declare directive to specify the variables or functions to be mapped to a device, some combined constructs to simplify the programming, and an environment variable (OMP_DEFAULT_DEVICE) to indicate the default device number, and a set of runtime library routines to set and detect information related to accelerators.

## 3   Applications

Stencil computations are used in many large DOE scientific applications to solve partial differential equations on structured grids. In this paper, we chose two stencil applications, one using the lattice-Boltzmann method (LBM) and the other solving the compressible Navier-Stokes equation (CNS), to represent non-trivial scientific applications. The chosen LBM and CNS algorithms have very different stencil sizes (0-point vs. 25-point) leading to different computational characteristics. The LBM method operates in a *streaming* mode; memory is read once to perform the computation in the 0-point grid site. In the CNS method, memory from a grid site is repeatedly used in all the stencils that include that grid site. Hence, effective caching is extremely important. With effective caching, the arithmetic intensity (FLOPS per unit byte) can be quite high. The performance of the LBM algorithm is often limited by bandwidth whereas the performance of the CNS algorithm is often limited by arithmetic resources. These different characteristics can lead to different implementation strategies when porting the applications to a GPU device. We list a high level comparison between two applications in Table 1.

**Table 1.** Comparison between LBM and CNS applications

|     | Language | AMR library | Stencil | Components | Lines in codes |
|-----|----------|-------------|---------|-----------|----------------|
| LBM | C++ | Chombo | 0-point | 19 | 4670 (12879 w/Chombo code) |
| CNS | Fortran90 | BoxLib | 1D: 9-point | 11 | 1242 (25967 w/BoxLib code) |
|     |          |             | 3D: 25-point |    |                |

In the LBM, hydrodynamics are described by a discrete kinetic equation for a single-particle distribution function [5].

$$\underbrace{f_i(\boldsymbol{j} + \boldsymbol{e}_i\Delta t, t + \Delta t) = \hat{f}_i(\boldsymbol{j}, t)}_{\text{Streaming}} = \underbrace{f_i(\boldsymbol{j}, t) + \mathcal{L}_{ik}\left(f_k(\boldsymbol{j}, t) - f_k^{\text{eq}}(\boldsymbol{j}, t)\right)}_{\text{Collision}}. \tag{1}$$

The chosen LBM application uses Chombo [6], a parallel adaptive mesh refinement (AMR) library used to solve partial differential equations. The domain size selected in the experiment is a $64^3$ Cartesian grid structure partitioned into *boxes*, each of size $32^3$. A total of 8 boxes cover the problem domain and 8000 time steps are performed in a single experiment. Figure 1 shows the pseudo code for the LBM computation. In the experimental setup, a loop in the application iterates over 8 boxes and performs computations to update the grid cells in each box (represented in line 8). Parallelization can be applied to the loop over boxes (line 8) or loops over grid cells (line 11 and line 16). Multi-level parallelization is feasible only if it is supported in the implementation.

The CNS algorithm is based on finite-difference methods and the equations are:

$$\frac{\partial \rho}{\partial t} + \nabla \cdot (\rho \boldsymbol{u}) = 0, \tag{2}$$

$$\frac{\partial \rho \boldsymbol{u}}{\partial t} + \nabla \cdot (\rho \boldsymbol{u}\boldsymbol{u}) + \nabla p = \nabla \cdot \boldsymbol{\tau}, \tag{3}$$

$$\frac{\partial \rho E}{\partial t} + \nabla \cdot [(\rho E + p)\boldsymbol{u}] = \nabla \cdot (\lambda \nabla T) + \nabla \cdot (\boldsymbol{\tau} \cdot \boldsymbol{u}), \tag{4}$$

where $\rho$ is the density, $\boldsymbol{u}$ is the velocity, $p$ is the pressure, $E$ is the specific energy density (kinetic energy plus internal energy), $\boldsymbol{\tau}$ is the viscous stress tensor, $\lambda$ is the thermal conductivity, and $T$ is the temperature. The problem domain in CNS is represented by BoxLib [1], an AMR library very similar to Chombo. The domain size of the CNS experiment is $64^3$ and partitioned into "Fabs" (Fortran array boxes), each of size $32^3$. 50 time steps are performed and 5 output files are

```
 1  fi(cells, 19, boxes) = initial data;
 2  fiUpdate(cells, 19, boxes) = 0;
 3  U(grid, 4, boxes);
 4  Macroscopic(U, fi);
 5  for (int iTS = 0; iTS != nTimeStep; ++iTS)
 6  {
 7    int iBox;
 8    for (every box)
 9    {
10      {  // Advance function
11        for (every cell)
12          Collision(fi, U);
13        Exchange(fi);
14        BC(fi);
15        Stream(fiUpdate, fi);
16        for (every cell)
17          Macroscopic(U, fiUpdate);
18        swap(fi, fiUpdate);
19      }
20    }
21  }
```

```
 1  fi(cells, 19, boxes) = initial data;
 2  fiUpdate(cells, 19, boxes) = 0;
 3  U(grid, 4, boxes);
 4  Macroscopic(U, fi);
 5  for (int iTS = 0; iTS != nTimeStep; ++iTS)
 6  {
 7    int iBox;
 8    for (every box)
 9    {
10      {  // Advance function
11        for (every cell)
12          Collision(fi, U);
13        Exchange(fi);
14        BC(fi);
15        Stream(fiUpdate, fi);
16        for (every cell)
17          Macroscopic(U, fiUpdate);
18        swap(fi, fiUpdate);
19      }
20    }
21  }
```

**Fig. 1.** LBM algorithm pseudo-code      **Fig. 2.** CNS application pseudo-code

generated during the computation. An outer loop iterates over all available Fabs in the "multi-Fab" data structure (shown in line 5 in Fig. 2). Similar to the LBM, multi-level parallelization is applicable if it is supported in the implementation.

## 4    Porting to GPUs

Our porting process starts with obtaining baseline performance of OpenMP versions of the applications. We incrementally add additional accelerator directives and clauses to show the programming effort and performance impact. In particular, we experiment with directives and clauses for data reuse, loop collapsing, loop scheduling and hierarchical thread mapping.

The hardware platform has 132 GB memory, two 8-core Intel E5-2670 CPUs, and two Nvidia K20x GPUs. We use a prototype implementation of the OpenMP Accelerator Model, HOMP (Heterogeneous OpenMP) [12], which is built on the ROSE source-to-source compiler infrastructure [15] developed at Lawrence Livermore National Laboratory. The built-in OpenMP implementation in ROSE supports OpenMP 3.0 directives for C, C++ and a subset of Fortran. Leveraging ROSE's flexibility to experiment with new language extensions, HOMP adds the OpenMP accelerator support [12], including parsing and code transformations for target, target data, map and so on. HOMP generates CUDA code for the growing demands in GPU programming. The original OpenMP runtime library (referred to as XOMP) for ROSE has been extended to support thread configuration, loop scheduling, data management, reduction and many other required operations on GPUs. We use the GNU Compiler Collection (gcc-4.4.6), Nvidia 6.0 SDK, nvcc compiler, and the Nvidia Visual Profiler [3] in this study.

### 4.1    Baseline Performance on CPU and GPU

The default setup in the LBM application has OpenMP directives inserted into the loop for boxes (line 8 in Fig. 1). The OMP_NUM_THREADS environment variable

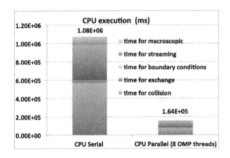

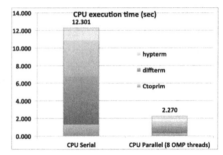

**Fig. 3.** LBM CPU baseline performance     **Fig. 4.** CNS CPU baseline performance

is set to 8 to assign at most 8 OpenMP threads to update the 8 boxes in the loop. We assign at most 8 OpenMP threads to update the 8 boxes in the loop. Each OpenMP thread will then update $32^3$ cells inside a box, a strategy that works well for boxes of this size [13]. The OpenMP parallel region terminates at the end of the loop to form an implicit synchronous barrier between time steps. Figure 3 shows the CPU's serial and parallel performance. The parallel execution with 8 OpenMP threads delivers a 6.76× speedup compared to the serial execution on the testing system.

The CNS application by default has OpenMP directives at the loops for grid cells (line 9, 11, and 13 in Fig. 2). These loops are 3-level nested loops that iterate through the cubical structure in a Fab. The whole application consists of 14 such OpenMP parallel loops. In the configured testing case, loop iterations in the outermost loop are evenly distributed into 8 OpenMP threads for 8 boxes. Figure 4 shows the comparison between serial and parallel execution using 8 threads. The parallel execution delivers a 5.42× speedup on the testing machine.

Before the porting, we discovered a few obstacles to adding OpenMP accelerator directives. We had to modify a subset of code from both applications to make the porting feasible. For example, the current HOMP only supports C/C++ input code to generate CUDA code for the GPU. We used a Fortran-to-C translator implemented in ROSE to translate the functions in the CNS into C language versions for the porting. In the LBM application, several variables used in the target loops were not mappable by the OpenMP 4.0 specification because they are part of other C++ class objects. We copied those variables to temporary variables and mapped the temporary variables as a workaround. The baseline implementations on the GPU simply reuse the OpenMP parallel directives without any optimization involved. Minimal OMP target and OMP map directives are used to identify the target region and data to be mapped onto the device.

For the LBM application, the location of OpenMP directives in the CPU implementation is not an ideal start location for the GPU implementation since it contains multiple kernels in the loop body. Using an incremental approach, we ported individual kernels first and moved the OpenMP directives to the locations of loops to the grid cells inside Collision, Macroscopic and Stream functions (shown at line 11, 15 and 16 in Fig. 1). These three functions consume the majority of execution time (47 % in Collision, 40 % in Stream and 7 % in Macroscopic)

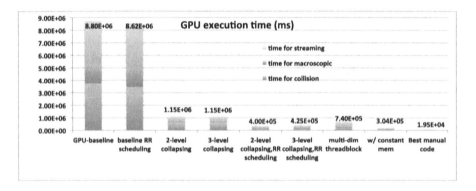

**Fig. 5.** LBM performance on GPU

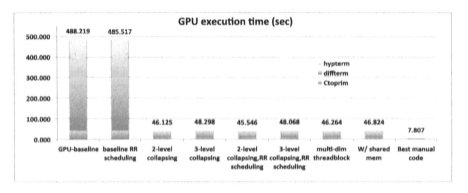

**Fig. 6.** CNS performance on GPU

on the parallel CPU execution. The GPU baseline implementation for the CNS application has OpenMP directives inserted into 1 loop in the ctoprim function, 3 loops in the hyperm function, and 7 loops in the diffterm function. Those are the same locations that have OpenMP directives in the parallel CPU implementation. Diffterm function takes the greatest portion (34%) portion of total execution in the CNS application. Hyperm and ctoprim take 24% and 13%, respectively.

The baseline GPU performance in both applications were not competitive compared to their corresponding CPU version performance (shown in Figs. 5 and 6). After inspection with the Nvidia Visual Profiler [3], we found that the baseline GPU implementations have extremely low achieved GPU occupancy (<2%). The baseline GPU implementations have extremely low achieved GPU occupancy (<2%). This is due to the nested loops, identified by the OpenMP directives, which have only small loop iteration sizes in their outermost loop. The translated CUDA codes exploit at most 40 GPU threads to perform the computation and result in low parallelism and performance. The next step in porting was to improve the GPU utilization by increasing the parallelism.

## 4.2   Increasing Parallelism

Achieving high parallelism is the key for a GPU device to get high computing performance. In addition to optimizing applications for high parallelism, the porting process needs to take into account that the maximum parallelism in the real execution is subject to certain CUDA limitations. These are the limitations for K20X GPU used in this paper:

– At most 1024 threads in a thread block.
– At most 64 warps (32 threads/warp) in a SMX.
– A thread can have up to a 63 register usage.
– Each SM has up to 48 KB shared memory shared by multiple thread blocks.

We describe two feasible approaches to increasing parallelism for the chosen applications.

The first approach is loop collapsing. Loop collapsing is a transformation that converts multiple perfectly nested loops into a single loop. Compared to the original outermost loop, the collapsed loop has a larger iteration size with potential to expose higher parallelism. We apply the directive #pragma omp for collapse (n) to perform loop collapsing. However, loop structure in the LBM application has statements between the nested loops and does not form a perfectly nested loop. Collapsing non-perfectly nested loops is not allowed by the OpenMP specification. After reviewing the nested loop structure, we manually moved statements between loops in LBM application into the innermost loop body since this change causes no side effect and can form a perfectly nested loop. After collapsing, we could exploit more GPU threads to perform parallel execution on the collapsed loop. Therefore, more GPU threads could be assigned to perform parallel execution on the collapsed loop. The XOMP runtime incorporates the CUDA runtime to maximize the utilization of the GPU threads. Compared with the baseline GPU implementations, there are about 5× and 10× speedups delivered for the LBM and CNS applications respectively (shown in Figs. 5 and 6).

The second option to increase parallelism is to use the multi-dimensional thread structure supported in CUDA. In the LBM application, we can seamlessly allocate 32 × 32 threads to a thread block and have 32 thread blocks mapped to the outermost loop. This can achieve 100 % occupancy in the execution if only 32 registers are given to each GPU thread. But there are only two concurrent thread blocks in the setup due to the limitation in the allowed warp number. In the CNS application, we can have the same allocation if ghost cells are not involved in the computation. Otherwise, the loop iteration size becomes 40 (32 and 4 ghost cells on both sides) in the three-level nested loop. To fulfill the CUDA limitation discussed earlier, we allocate only 40 threads in a thread block and have multiple thread blocks mapped to the loop iteration space. 16 concurrent thread block are allowed in executions, and it is also the maximum allowed number in this GPU model. This configuration has lower theoretical occupancy (50 %) and the computation is inefficient due to the usage of partial-warp. The performance is reported in histograms marked with multi-dim threadblock in Figs. 5 and 6. Compared with the collapsing variants, a 1.5× speedup is achieved in the LBM application but a marginal difference is shown for the CNS application.

## 4.3   Loop Scheduling

OpenMP supports multiple loop scheduling policies, including static, dynamic, guided, auto, and runtime. For regular loops running on CPUs, statically and evenly dividing loop iterations among threads using a schedule(static) clause (referred to as static-even schedule in this paper) often leads to the best performance with minimal scheduling overhead. On the GPU, we need to perform coalesced memory access for high performance. The static-even schedule will have one GPU thread accessing multiple successive words in memory and lead to multiple memory transactions. A round-robin scheduling using schedule(static,1) will fulfill the need to perform coalesced memory access on the GPU device. We apply the round-robin schedule and compare only the kernel execution times in the CNS application. Round-robin scheduling delivers the highest (76 %) improvement in one kernel in the hypterm function and an average of 26.4 % improvement for all kernels. Performance reports show modest improvement for total execution time in the CNS application (1 %) and a larger improvement in the the LBM application (2.8×). The performance analysis reports high overhead due to memory movement between the host and device memories.

## 4.4   Exploiting Memory Hierarchy

Nvidia GPUs provide multiple specialized memories, including on-chip software controllable cache shared within a thread block (referred to as shared memory) and constant memory accessible by all threads for read-only global data. The current OpenMP 4.0 lacks support to exploit the specialized memories. We propose to extend the OpenMP Accelerator Model to have a cache clause to allow users to hint such opportunities. The clause has a form of cache (var_list), in which each variable listed can be further prepended by an optional const modifier. For example cache (array1[0:10], const array2[5:10]) tells the compiler that there are two arrays which should be cached in the memory hierarchy of the accelerator. One of the arrays is a read-only subarray. Similar to the map clause, the cache clause can only be used with target or target data directives. Variables shown in the cache clause must also show up in the map clause affecting the same code region. With this clause, compilers translate the code to exploit either the shared memory or the constant memory of GPUs.

   After evaluating the two applications, the LBM gained more benefits from the constant memory than the shared memory. We can store many constant coefficients, stride distances, and an array storing discrete velocity directions and an array storing weights in the constant memory space. Figure 7 extracts the comparison (execution time includes memory copying overhead) with only two kernels in the LBM application to demonstrate the performance with constant memory usage. A 1.32× speedup is achieved for the overall execution time from the implementation with constant memory. Higher speedups, from 1.74× to 2.44×, were observed in the execution times for these three functions individually.

   On the other hand, the CNS has relatively low constant data referenced by multiple functions. But the CNS application uses a 25-point stencil in the 3D

**Table 2.** Shared memory usage and GPU occupancy

| Shared memory report | | | |
|---|---|---|---|
| Kernel | Size/block (byte) | Threads/block | Occupancy |
| Hypterm original | 1920 | 40 | 50 % |
| Tiled 2 iterations | 3840 | 80 | 56 % |
| Tiled 3 iterations | 5760 | 120 | 50 % |
| Tiled 4 iterations | 7680 | 160 | 47 % |
| Diffterm original | 3520 | 40 | 41 % |
| Tiled 2 iterations | 7040 | 80 | 28 % |
| Tiled 3 iterations | 10620 | 120 | 25 % |
| Tiled 4 iterations | 14080 | 160 | 23 % |

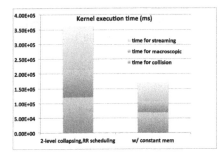

**Fig. 7.** LBM with constant memory     **Fig. 8.** CNS with shared memory

computation. Stencil data can therefore be stored in the shared memory space
to gain the benefit of the fast memory. We used shared memory for six kernels
(3 in Hypterm and 3 in Diffterm) in the GPU implementation for the CNS application. Table 2 shows the details of the required shared memory size, thread
assignment and the achievable highest GPU occupancy. This implementation
doesn't deliver higher performance compared to our earlier implementation with
the best performance (shown in Fig. 8) due to a much lower GPU occupancy.
To increase the active thread number in each thread block, loop tiling can be
performed in the loop for the second dimension in the 3D nested loop. We can
exploit more GPU threads after loop tiling but it also proportionally increases
the required shared memory size for each thread block. Table 2 also shows the
changes in GPU occupancy by tiling both kernels with different tiled sizes.
The GPU occupancy will be limited by the allowed 48KB shared memory size.
We conclude that exploiting shared memory in our implementation for the CNS
application does not improve performance. It would require other optimizations
to achieve efficient shared memory usage.

## 4.5   Reducing Memory Movement Between Host and Device

We observed several variables and arrays are copied repetitively to the GPU's memory in different kernels. Using target data directives with map clauses can usually reduce repetitive memory allocations and transferring. However, we found that this is not a trivial task for the two chosen applications due to language restrictions. OpenMP 4.0 defines a set of restrictions for variables listed in the map clause, such as (1) data must have a complete type for C/C++, (2) a variable that is part of another variable (e.g. a field of a struct) is not allowed unless it is an array element or array section, (3) C++ class types mapped must not contain static data or virtual members, and (4) pointer types are allowed but the memory block to which the pointer refers to is not mapped. Chombo (used in the LBM application) and BoxLib (used in the CNS application) share a data structure called Fortran array box (Fab). Fab is a structure of arrays that can store multiple components and it provides a high-level data abstraction. Information, such as loop bounds, stencil size, and a data pointer to the component array, is packaged inside the Fab. Members in Fab contain primitive arrays, scalar variables, and some static data. An ideal strategy in the porting process is to copy the entire Fab structure to the GPU's memory space. However, the Fab structure is not mappable according to OpenMP 4.0. A workaround task is to extract and store all the members of Fab in primitive arrays. Then the temporary arrays can be mapped and copied to the GPU memory. This will involve a significant code modification in the porting process.

## 4.6   Manual Tuning for GPU Performance

We provide manual implementations for both applications to evaluate the achievable performance through manual performance tuning. We manually implement the chosen applications with the CUDA language and consider the possibilities to involve OpenMP 4.0 standards and compiler transformations to automate the process. The manual implementations serve as a reference to study the transformation obstacles in the design of the OpenMP accelerator model. Several manual optimizations require good understanding in the application design to perform code modifications and they are not implemented as automatic transformations in this study.

The manually-tuned GPU implementation for the LBM application significantly simplifies the Fab structure, restructures the code, and consolidates all the memory copying. Other optimizations include hand-tuned kernels (including BoxLib's exchange function), exploiting constant memory, and several code modifications specifically for the GPU implementation. A simplified Fab structure on GPU code is designed to store only the essential data members in the CPU's Fab structure. Data is allocated and copied to GPU memory once and reused by all the kernels listed in the pseudo code in Fig. 1. This optimized implementation delivers the best performance between the CPU's and GPU's implementations (shown in Fig. 5).

The manual tuning processes for the CNS application minimize memory copying between the host and device, exploit efficient usage of shared memory, and maximize GPU occupancy. A $4^3$ thread block is chosen based on the ghost cell size in the computation to avoid the partial warp usage. The code was modified to have only minimal memory transfers between host memory and device memory. All initialized data stored in the Fab data structure is copied to the device memory before the computation. There are infrequent data movements which send only a subset of computed data back to the host memory for boundary exchange performed by the BoxLib library and visualization dumps. The manual code delivers the best GPU performance with about 6× speedup compared to the best implementation with the OpenMP accelerator model (shown in Fig. 6). However, the delivered performance is not superior to the performance on the CPU due to overheads in allocating, copying and freeing memory on the GPU. Eliminating that overhead for the CNS application, the GPU execution time for the three kernels is at a comparable level to the CPU execution time.

## 4.7   Productivity

We briefly discuss the productivity benefit by using the OpenMP accelerator model. We choose the line number as the metric to evaluate the gain in productivity. Table 3 lists the essential information for the study. The number of accelerator directives inserted, lines in source code being ported, lines in the transformed code on the CPU (host code), and the line of the generated CUDA code on the GPU (device code), are collected in the table. Besides the code generated by the HOMP compiler, each runtime function packs a series of low-level CUDA function calls and additional codes to perform the designated task. Without the runtime support, manual implementation needs to perform the same series of CUDA function calls repetitively. For both transformed host and device codes, Table 3 lists two counts with and without including the line numbers packaged by the runtime functions. The count with lines performed in the runtime functions provides an estimation for the code size in a manual implementation. As shown in the table, using a few lines of directives can essentially save the efforts of writing hundreds or even thousands of lines of generated code. Accelerator

**Table 3.** Productivity study using lines of code (LOC)

| Functions | Source LOC | Directives | Host LOC | | Device LOC | | Ratio (LOC/directives) | |
|---|---|---|---|---|---|---|---|---|
| | | | A | B | A | B | A | B |
| LB collision | 45 | 2 | 57 | 464 | 48 | 58 | 52.5 | 261.0 |
| LB macroscopic | 46 | 2 | 52 | 421 | 45 | 55 | 48.5 | 238.0 |
| LB stream | 21 | 2 | 53 | 460 | 35 | 45 | 44.0 | 252.5 |
| CNS ctoprim | 14 | 2 | 27 | 205 | 30 | 40 | 28.5 | 122.5 |
| CNS hypterm | 57 | 6 | 81 | 793 | 123 | 153 | 34.0 | 157.7 |
| CNS diffterm | 82 | 14 | 335 | 2647 | 206 | 276 | 38.6 | 208.8 |

A: Lines of code without counting in runtime;
B: Line sof code with counting in runtime

directives supported by the OpenMP 4.0 can greatly simplify the porting process and improve productivity. On the other hand, programming using the OpenMP accelerator model does require additional domain knowledge, analysis, or optimization to achieve high performance on the target platform. Occasional manual code changes are needed also to workaround some language restrictions or expose more parallelism. However, the efforts of learning low-level CUDA or OpenCL would be more significant.

## 5   Related Work

Many previous studies [8,9,11,17] have evaluated the performance and productivity of OpenACC using a range of kernels or applications. For example, Wienke et al. [17] presented their experiences with OpenACC using two real-world applications. OpenACC helped them reach 80 % of the best-effort OpenCL version in a moderately complex simulation kernel. They reported that the inability to exploit local memory of the GPUs could contribute to the loss of performance of other complex OpenACC applications. Herdman et al. [8] used a hydrodynamics mini-application to compare OpenACC, OpenCL and CUDA. They found that OpenACC was extremely viable but their OpenCL and CUDA versions were not optimized. Hoshino et al. [9] used both kernels and a real-world computational fluid dynamics applications to compare CUDA and OpenACC. They reported that some complex Fortran data types such as arrays of derived types and derived types with variable-length arrays are not supported by OpenACC, but extensively used in the code.

The application experience of using the OpenMP accelerator support is rare due to the lack of compiler support. Dietrich et al. [7] presented an approach to measure the performance of applications utilizing OpenMP offloadings. Their focus is at performance analysis on the Intel Xeon Phi coprocessor. Silva et al. [18] compared OpenACC and OpenMP for accelerator computing. A set of parallel programming patterns, not real applications, were used to compare language features. No performance experiments were done due to the lack of compiler support. Unat et al. [16] presented a domain-specific OpenMP-like programming model for stencil methods. For small kernels, they realized up to 80 % of the performance of optimized CUDA versions. Our work provides the first study of the performance and programmability of the OpenMP accelerator model using the HOMP compiler [12]. OpenACC [4] provides a cache (var_list) directive to support cache memory on accelerators. However, this directive may only appear inside loops. By contrast, our proposed cache() is a clause which can be used with one or multiple code regions. Besides leveraging the highest level of cache, the additional const modifier in our design can support the read-only semantics to exploit constant memory.

## 6   Discussion and Future Work

We have found that the OpenMP Accelerator Model is a productive approach for porting existing applications to GPUs. The porting strategy can be straightforward. Users should prepare a baseline OpenMP version running on CPUs.

Then the target directive can be inserted around parallel regions. There are only a limited set of accelerator directives and clauses in OpenMP 4.0 to improve parallelism, scheduling, and data reuse, among others. So a strategy is to incrementally apply them and check the effect by performance analysis tools.

However, real applications pose unique challenges to effectively apply directive-based programming models. (1) A scientific application often has complex data types which may not be supported by the language specifications. A common workaround is to manually copy a portion of the complex data object into a variable of a simpler, supported type. (2) An application may have non-perfectly nested loops, which can be a candidate for collapsing after simple transformations. One possible way to improve productivity is to extend the collapse(n) clause to accept a flag, like collapse(n:force), to force collapsing across multiple non-perfectly nested loops when applicable. Compilers could enforce a transformation to form a perfectly nested loop, but users have to ensure the correctness of the code movements. (3) Large-scale DOE applications usually leverage many third-party libraries to increase productivity. Porting such an application may involve a challenging task to port the underlying libraries. (4) In an ideal world, users should be able to simply insert directives into existing codes to port to new platforms. However, non-trivial code restructuring may be needed to expose the right granularity of parallelism. (5) Our attempt to exploit special caches on GPUs generated some interesting results. Using constant memory for LBM resulted in significant performance improvements. On the other hand, using shared memory for CNS does not deliver higher performance in our study. The intuitive implementation to exploit special caches on GPUs may degrade the performance. Additional analysis and optimization support will be helpful to achieve good performance on GPU devices.

Our future research directions are in the following: (1) testing extensions to port complex data types and non-canonical control structures (e.g. non-perfectly nested loops). (2) using more scientific applications to find improvements to the directive-based programming models, (3) further investigation of ways of exploiting shared memory for better performance in real applications, and (4) exploring extensions to express semantics related to managing multiple accelerator devices.

# References

1. BoxLib. https://ccse.lbl.gov/BoxLib/
2. CUDA Zone - The resource for CUDA developers. http://www.nvidia.com/cuda
3. Nvidia visual profiler. https://developer.nvidia.com/nvidia-visual-profiler
4. OpenACC: Directives for Accelerators. http://www.openacc-standard.org/
5. Chen, S., Doolen, G.D.: Lattice Boltzmann method for fluid flows. Annu. Rev. Fluid Mech. **30**, 329–364 (1998)
6. Colella, P., Graves, D.T., Keen, N., Ligocki, T.J., Martin, D.F., McCorquodale, P., Modiano, D., Schwartz, P., Sternberg, T., Straalen, B.V.: Chombo software package for amr applications - design document. Technical report, Lawrence Berkeley National Laboratory (2009)

7. Dietrich, R., Schmitt, F., Grund, A., Schmidl, D.: Performance measurement for the OpenMP 4.0 offloading model. In: Lopes, L., Žilinskas, J., Costan, A., Cascella, R.G., Kecskemeti, G., Jeannot, E., Cannataro, M., Ricci, L., Benkner, S., Petit, S., Scarano, V., Gracia, J., Hunold, S., Scott, S.L., Lankes, S., Lengauer, C., Carretero, J., Breitbart, J., Alexander, M. (eds.) Euro-Par 2014, Part II. LNCS, vol. 8806, pp. 291–301. Springer, Heidelberg (2014)

8. Herdman, J., Gaudin, W., McIntosh-Smith, S., Boulton, M., Beckingsale, D., Mallinson, A., Jarvis, S.: Accelerating hydrocodes with OpenACC, OpeCL and CUDA. In: 2012 SC Companion: High Performance Computing, Networking, Storage and Analysis (SCC), pp. 465–471, November 2012

9. Hoshino, T., Maruyama, N., Matsuoka, S., Takaki, R.: CUDA vs OpenACC: performance case studies with Kernel benchmarks and a memory-bound CFD application. In: 2013 13th IEEE/ACM International Symposium on Cluster, Cloud and Grid Computing (CCGrid), pp. 136–143, May 2013

10. Khronos OpenCL Working Group: The OpenCL Specification - Version 1.0. Technical report, The Khronos Group (2009)

11. Levesque, J.M., Sankaran, R., Grout, R.: Hybridizing S3D into an exascale application using OpenACC: an approach for moving to multi-petaflops and beyond. In: Proceedings of the International Conference on High Performance Computing, Networking, Storage and Analysis, SC 2012, pp. 15:1–15:11. IEEE Computer Society Press, Los Alamitos, CA, USA (2012)

12. Liao, C., Yan, Y., de Supinski, B.R., Quinlan, D.J., Chapman, B.: Early experiences with the OpenMP accelerator model. In: Rendell, A.P., Chapman, B.M., Müller, M.S. (eds.) IWOMP 2013. LNCS, vol. 8122, pp. 84–98. Springer, Heidelberg (2013)

13. Olschanowsky, C., Guzik, S.M.J., Loffeld, J., Hittinger, J., Strout, M.M.: A study on balancing parallelism, data locality, and recomputation in existing PDE solvers. In: The International Conference for High Performance Computing, Networking, Storage and Analysis (2014)

14. OpenMP Architecture Review Board: The OpenMP API Specification for Parallel Programming. http://www.openmp.org/

15. Quinlan, D.J., et al.: ROSE compiler project. http://www.rosecompiler.org/

16. Unat, D., Cai, X., Baden, S.B.: Mint: realizing CUDA performance in 3D stencil methods with annotated C. In: Proceedings of the International Conference on Supercomputing, ICS 2011, pp. 214–224. ACM, New York, NY, USA (2011)

17. Wienke, S., Springer, P., Terboven, C., an Mey, D.: OpenACC — first experiences with real-world applications. In: Kaklamanis, C., Papatheodorou, T., Spirakis, P.G. (eds.) Euro-Par 2012. LNCS, vol. 7484, pp. 859–870. Springer, Heidelberg (2012)

18. Wienke, S., Terboven, C., Beyer, J.C., Müller, M.S.: A pattern-based comparison of OpenACC and OpenMP for accelerator computing. In: Silva, F., Dutra, I., Santos Costa, V. (eds.) Euro-Par 2014 Parallel Processing. LNCS, vol. 8632, pp. 812–823. Springer, Heidelberg (2014)

# Evaluating the Impact of OpenMP 4.0 Extensions on Relevant Parallel Workloads

Raul Vidal, Marc Casas[✉], Miquel Moretó, Dimitrios Chasapis, Roger Ferrer, Xavier Martorell, Eduard Ayguadé, Jesús Labarta, and Mateo Valero

Barcelona Supercomputing Center (BSC),
Universitat Politècnica de Catalunya (UPC), Barcelona, Spain
`marc.casas@bsc.es`

**Abstract.** OpenMP has been for many years the most widely used programming model for shared memory architectures. Periodically, new features are proposed and some of them are finally selected for inclusion in the OpenMP standard. The OmpSs programming model developed at the Barcelona Supercomputing Center (BSC) aims to be an OpenMP forerunner that handles the main OpenMP constructs plus some extra features not included in the OpenMP standard. In this paper we show the usefulness of three OmpSs features not currently handled by OpenMP 4.0 by deploying them over three applications of the PARSEC benchmark suite and showing the performance benefits. This paper also shows performance trade-offs between the OmpSs/OpenMP tasking and loop parallelism constructs and shows how a hybrid implementation that combines both approaches is sometimes the best option.

## 1 Introduction and Motivation

OpenMP has been for many years the most popular programming model for shared memory architectures. The OmpSs programming model [5] developed at the Barcelona Supercomputing Center aims to be an OpenMP forerunner that handles the main OpenMP constructs plus other features not included in the OpenMP standard. OmpSs is based on `#pragma` annotations and its semantics are almost identical to the OpenMP standard. For these reasons, a code in OmpSs that uses only the features included in the OpenMP standard is equivalent to its OpenMP counterpart. It is not straightforward to make the choice on which OmpSs features should be adopted by the OpenMP standard and how these new features would interact with the already existing ones.

This paper brings some light to the above mentioned dilemmas by pursuing two goals: The first is to show the usefulness of three OmpSs features not currently handled by OpenMP 4.0 by using them to accelerate three well known applications of the PARSEC benchmark suite [3,4]. Secondly, this paper shows performance trade-offs between the OmpSs/OpenMP tasking and loop parallelism constructs (e.g. `#pragma omp for`) and proposes a hybrid implementation that combines both kinds of constructs to maximize performance. More precisely, this paper deploys the following OmpSs features:

© Springer International Publishing Switzerland 2015
C. Terboven et al. (Eds.): IWOMP 2015, LNCS 9342, pp. 60–72, 2015.
DOI: 10.1007/978-3-319-24595-9_5

- the multi-dependencies feature, which allows to specify different data-dependence scenarios in a single `#pragma` annotation, significantly increasing programmability.
- runtime support for NUMA-aware scheduling of tasks, which schedules them on the cores closest to the data the task accesses.
- the concurrent clause, which relaxes task synchronization and allows increased overlap of task creation with remaining computations.

Three applications of the PARSEC benchmark suite are considered in this paper: Facesim, Fluidanimate and Streamcluster. New OmpSs versions of these applications are used to show the potential of the new features. The concurrent clause is applied to Facesim and Fluidanimate to reduce synchronization penalties. The multi-dependencies clause is deployed in the Fluidanimate code to express complex data-dependencies that allow barrier removal without increasing the programming burden. Runtime support for NUMA-aware scheduling is deployed in the Streamcluster code. Finally, the performance trade-offs between tasking constructs and simpler forms of loop parallelism are analyzed in the Facesim code.

The rest of this paper is organized as follows: Sect. 2 describes the three applications studied in this paper and the proposed parallelization strategies, Sect. 3 presents the evaluation in terms of performance and programmability, while Sect. 4 describes the related work. Finally, Sect. 5 summarizes the main conclusions of this work.

## 2    Application Parallelization

### 2.1    Facesim

**Description.** Facesim animates a human face by simulating its movements. It employs a 3D model composed of a tetrahedral mesh representing the flesh of the face and two triangulated surfaces which model the bones of the head: the cranium and the jaw. The physical forces and motions in the model are computed frame by frame to produce the animation. Facesim uses the Newton's method for solving the system of equations that models the motion. The system is stored in a sparse matrix formed by two one-dimensional arrays: `dX_full` and `R_full`, defining the left-hand and right-hand sides of the equation system, respectively. The total number of nodes is equivalent to the arrays' size. The nodes are the vertices of the tetrahedrons the mesh is composed of. Each tetrahedron shares the nodes with its neighbors and for each node the force contributions are computed. A parallel conjugate gradient method is used in each step of the Newton's method to solve its associated linear system and find the displacement of the nodes in the current frame which is added to a separate array storing the current positions of the nodes.

**PARSEC Pthreads Parallelization.** In the Pthreads parallelization provided by the PARSEC benchmark suite, the mesh is split into a number of partitions

**Fig. 1.** Facesim UPBS, UCPF, AFD and AVIF parallel execution using the same time scale. Beginning of a frame. The OmpSs trace (top) exhibits no barriers. The original Pthreads trace (bottom) makes extensive use of barriers and UCPF routine is serialized.

equal to the number of threads available. It has a queuing system in which work units are queued to be processed by the team of threads the system spawns upon initialization. There is a master thread which executes the code of the application. When it reaches a parallel region, it calls the queuing system to create work units in a loop and waits in a barrier outside of the loop for the team of threads to finish. The work units are created by means of an ad-hoc scheduling library written in C which manages the team of threads.

Facesim's parallel computations are grouped in three major parallel kernels. Two of them generate the linear system associated with each iteration of Newton's method and the third one solves it.

– *Update State*: Updates velocities, force directions and material properties which depend on the current positions of the mesh. Update State is computed with two functions: Update Position Based State (UPBS) and Update Collision Penalty Forces (UCPF).
– *Add Forces*: Comes after Update State. Computes force contributions for each node. This kernel is actually computed with two functions: Add Velocity Independent Forces (AVIF) and Add Force Differential (AFD).
– *Conjugate Gradient (CG)*: This iterative method is set up to do a maximum of 200 iterations. The CG methods performs two reduction operation per iteration.

UPBS and CG are the most time consuming routines. There are several barriers in this application per iteration of Newton's method: One at the end of *Update State*, two from *Add Forces* and three within each *CG* iteration.

**Taskification Strategy.** With respect to Facesim we consider three different approaches. The first one exclusively uses tasking clauses with dependencies when necessary. The second one uses loop parallelism clauses, like the omp for construct. Finally, the third combines task and loop parallelism.

```
for each partition
#pragma omp task depend(in:variable)
    taskfunction1();

#pragma omp task depend(inout:variable)
    faketask();

for each partition
#pragma omp task depend(in:variable)
    taskfunction2();
```

**Fig. 2.** An additional task is used to create an anti-dependency. This is in fact a synchronization point since the `taskfunction2` tasks run after all the `taskfunction1` finish.

```
for each partition
#pragma omp task concurrent(variable)
    taskfunction1();

for each partition
#pragma omp task in(variable)
    taskfunction2();
```

**Fig. 3.** The `concurrent` clause is equivalent to an `inout` dependency on *variable*, but allows the tasks to operate concurrently on it.

The taskification concerning the first two phases of Facesim, *Update State* and *Add Forces*, is achieved by removing barriers and expressing control dependencies between the different subroutines. Such control dependencies are expressed by using a data dependency on a sentinel variable. As such, once the task that has the sentinel as an output parameter finishes, it passes the control flow to tasks that have the same sentinel as an input. In the *Update State* phase, UPBS and UCPF subroutines run concurrently and a task is generated per domain partition. With respect to the *Add Forces* phase, AFD and AVIF subroutines concerning a particular partition start right after the UPBS task operating over that same partition has finished. This is expressed by using task dependency semantics in OmpSs/OpenMP 4.0, removing a barrier synchronization from the original code. With respect to the implementation that uses the `#pragma omp for` construct, it mimics the Pthreads parallelization and uses barrier synchronization to handle parallelism. Figure 1 compares the parallel execution of these two phases in the original code (trace at the bottom) and the taskified code (top). All barriers are removed in the latter case, allowing subroutines to overlap and, as a consequence, the CG iteration starts much earlier. Also, thanks to specifying data dependencies, the UCPF routine is not serialized in the taskified version of the code.

With respect to the third phase of Facesim, *CG*, the tasking OmpSs/OpenMP versions contain specific code to relax the synchronization points and allow some degree of overlap between task creation and computation. In case of OpenMP, we add an additional task to create an anti-dependency to make sure the synchronization is respected while task creation is overlapped with it. In Fig. 2 we show how this approach is implemented. Although there are features in OpenMP 4.0

that allow alternative implementations, like the `taskgroup` construct, they can be used to implement a synchronization point but not to overlap task creation with synchronization. In the case of OmpSs we use the `concurrent` clause which is equivalent to an `inout` dependency, but allows tasks to operate concurrently on this data dependency. Figure 3 shows how the `concurrent` clause is used. Tasks that have an input or output dependency on *variable* respect it and do not overlap their execution with the concurrent tasks.

The implementation that uses loop parallelism adds the corresponding `#pragma omp parallel for` construct and uses `static` scheduling. A global parallel region for the CG iterations wraps the external loop. Inside of it, a `single` construct is used to update variables after the three parallel loops of each CG iteration.

Finally, in the hybrid approach, loop parallelism is used to handle the fine grain parallelism required by the *CG* phase, while the parallelism required by other routines is expressed in terms of tasks, as this combination showed the best performance results. Each one of these three approaches is implemented using OpenMP 4.0 and OmpSs, which means that we have 6 different version of Facesim in addition to the baseline Pthreads code.

## 2.2   Fluidanimate

**Description.** This application simulates incompressible fluid interactive animation, using the Smoothed Particle Hydrodynamics (SPH) method [11]. Each iteration of Fluidanimate involves running 8 different routines which are responsible for actions like rebuilding the spatial index, computing fluid densities and forces at given points, handling fluid collisions or updating particle locations.

**Original Parallelization.** The fluid surface is partitioned into $N$ segments and there is one thread per segment. $N$ is equal to the number of cores the application runs on. The kernels are parallelized and separated by barriers. When a particular thread runs a particular kernel, it takes care of all the computations involving its grid segment. For each iteration of the algorithm, the Pthreads implementation requires 8 barriers to make sure the execution of each kernel starts once the previous kernel computations have finished. That is required because each thread needs the previous kernels' computations on its grid segment and its neighbors to be finished once the execution of the new kernel finishes. Threads may have to update values belonging to neighbor segments, which requires the use of locks to avoid data races.

**Taskification Strategy.** Several different taskification strategies are considered: *OmpSs Trivial, OmpSs Finer Task, OmpSs Multi-Dependencies* and *OmpSs without Barriers*.

The *OmpSs Trivial* task-based implementation follows the same approach as Pthreads. Every time the application starts a new iteration, a task is created for each kernel and segment. Since the kernels are separated by barriers, only tasks related to the same kernel are allowed to run concurrently. Accesses to foreign grid segments are controlled by locks.

*OmpSs Finer Tasks:* The main difference between this strategy and the *OmpSs Trivial* consists in the number of tasks created. In the trivial version, a single task is created for each kernel and segment, meaning that a maximum of $N$ tasks, $N$ being the number of partitions, can run concurrently. For the *OmpSs trivial* version, $N$ is equal to the number of cores the application runs on. In case of the *OmpSs Finer Tasks* implementation, we increase the number of segments to four times the number of cores. By doing this, we split the work into four times more pieces than the previously presented versions, which implies that the OmpSs runtime has more flexibility to balance the load between two barriers.

```
if (segment in corner)
#pragma omp task in( neighborhood[0], ..., neighborhood[3] )
//Task Code
else if (segment in boundary)
#pragma omp task in( neighborhood[0], ..., neighborhood[5] )
//Task Code
else if (internal segment)
#pragma omp task in( neighborhood[0], ..., neighborhood[8] )
//Task Code
```

**Fig. 4.** Fluidanimate code handling multiple dependency scenarios by using one #pragma per scenario.

```
#pragma omp task in( { neighborhood[j] , j=0:neighborhood.size() } )
//Task Code
```

**Fig. 5.** Fluidanimate code where multiple dependency scenarios are handled by a single #pragma annotation.

```
#pragma omp task dependence_type ( { item_list[j], j=0:item_list.size() } )
//Task Code
```

**Fig. 6.** Generic #pragma annotation with multi-dependencies. The dependencies are defined over a list of items, which has a dynamically defined size.

*OmpSs multi-dependencies:* This strategy consists of removing all barriers between the 8 different routines of each iteration. For each routine and partition we generate a set of tasks and we specify dependencies between them to make sure the previous routine has finished its pass over a segment and its neighbors when a task starts operating over this particular segment. The number of task dependencies is defined by its segment's position over the grid. If the segment is located on one of the four corners of the square grid, the total number of task input dependencies is 4. If the segment is located at the border, the dependencies are 6 and if it is an internal segment, its corresponding task has 9 input dependencies. Figure 4 shows the code required in OpenMP 4.0 to handle this scenario where the number of dependencies is variable. Of course, a **#pragma omp task** annotation is required in each case, implying that 3 different annotations are required for each of the 8 different routines each iteration of Fluidanimate is composed of, which ends up increasing the number of pragma annotations to 24.

To avoid such programming hardship, OmpSs has support to handle this complexity using a single high-level pragma annotation. In Fig. 6 there is generic #pragma annotation with multi-dependencies in OmpSs. The dependencies are defined over a list of items, which has a dynamically defined size. Figure 5 illustrates how the multi-dependency feature is used in the Fluidanimate source code. The only requirement is to generate a data-structure for each segment that lists all the neighbors. The size of this data structure changes depending on the number of neighbors and it is used to figure out the number of dependencies at runtime. The number of tasks considered by the *OmpSs multi-dependencies* strategy is the same as *OmpSs Finer Tasks*.

*OmpSs without Barriers:* This strategy includes all the improvements of the *OmpSs Finer Tasks* and the *OmpSs multi-dependencies* techniques plus the removal of the barrier between different iterations. Since computations of different iterations cannot be overlapped, the barrier between iterations is replaced by a `concurrent` clause, as is done in Facesim between the different CG iterations.

### 2.3  Streamcluster

**Description.** Streamcluster solves an online clustering problem. It takes a stream of points and then groups them in a predetermined number of centers. The program spends up to 90 % of the time in a function called `Pgain`, where points are assigned to existing centers using the Euclidean distance. Also `Pgain` calculates whether opening a new center is advantageous or not. If opening the new center lowers the cost of the current clustering, then the center is opened and points that are closer to this center than to previously created centers are reassigned to the new center. `Pgain` is executed a predefined number of iterations, obtaining new centers.

**Original Parallelization.** The Pthreads parallelization is very simple: the large array containing all the points to cluster is broken into chunks of constant size (200,000 points in our experiments). Each chunk is then processed in parallel in a number of partitions equal to the number of threads. A barrier synchronization is added to make sure that all threads finished processing all the points before a new chunk is processed. Streamcluster provides its own barrier implementation to synchronize threads. Once all the chunks of the stream of points are processed, a final pass to cluster the centers found on the different chunks is done. Streamcluster is a memory intensive application as it continuously reads data from memory. In the original parallelization, the data structures that store these points are allocated before creating the different threads and reused in each chunk processing. As a consequence, this application suffers scalability difficulties in NUMA machines.

**Taskification Strategy.** In the case of Streamcluster we develop two tasking versions, one in OmpSs and the other in OpenMP. We focus on the function

**Pgain** of this code as the program spends the majority of its execution time in it. While the Pthreads version of **Pgain** makes use of a dynamically allocated array per thread to store the partial cost computations and performs a reduction of all these costs over a global array after the parallel work, the tasking implementation does not need the global array and uses a local one per task. With atomic synchronization the local arrays of costs are updated. These changes simplify the code and minimize the time spent in index table computations.

Also, additional changes are made in the OmpSs code to taskify memory allocation and exploit the NUMA aware scheduling that the OmpSs runtime system performs for systems with multiple sockets. This scheduler tries to ensure that tasks execute in the sockets where their data structures have been allocated, reducing the cost of accessing memory. To do so, a few API calls to schedule tasks in specified NUMA spaces are added to the code. Figure 7 depicts how to use this API. OpenMP 4.0 has some environment variables to specify either on which cores the threads should be placed (OMP_PLACES) or whether threads can be moved between cores (OMP_PROC_BIND), however it does not have the feature of doing that in a per task basis.

```
for each partition p
{
nanos_current_socket(socket of partition p) ; //API call
#pragma omp task out(dest[k1:k2],points[k1:k2])
//initialization task
nanos_current_socket(socket of partition p); //API call
#pragma omp task in(points[k1:k2])
//task accessing a Point
}
```

**Fig. 7.** The NUMA-aware scheduling API specifies the socket where tasks run. In this way, the programmer can force tasks to run in the socket where the data they access is allocated.

## 3    Evaluation

The evaluation is performed on an IBM System X server iDataPlex dx360 M4, composed of two 8-core Intel Xeon E5-2670 processors at 2.6 GHz with 20 MB of shared last-level cache and with hyperthreading disabled. There is 32 GB of DDR3 RAM at 1.6 GHz.

The OpenMP implementation used is the GNU OpenMP (GOMP) included with gcc 4.9.1. We also used the OmpSs programming model [5] and its associated toolflow: Nanos++ runtime system (version 0.7.5), Mercurium source-to-source compiler (version 1.99.6), and gcc 4.9.1 as the back-end compiler. To analyze the behavior of the benchmarks, we used the Extrae instrumentation package (version 2.5) and the Paraver trace viewer (version 4.5) [10].

### 3.1    Performance Evaluation

While the PARSEC benchmark suite provides different input sets, the experiments shown in this paper make use of the largest set, the 'native' input. All the benchmarks are executed with 1, 2, 4, 8 and 16 threads, mapping one thread per core. Figure 8 shows the measured speedups of all the applications and strategies considered. The speedups are computed taking the execution time of the Pthreads implementations of Facesim, Fluidanimate and Streamcluster available in the PARSEC benchmark suite running on 1 thread. The left hand side of Fig. 8 shows the speedups of each one of the 7 parallelization strategies considered for Facesim: Pthreads, loop parallelism using OpenMP and OmpSs, tasking using OpenMP and OmpSs and the hybrid approaches combining tasking and loop parallelism. The best performing version is OmpSs Hybrid, which shows a speedup of 11.4x when run on 16 cores, closely followed by OpenMP Hybrid and the OmpSs and OpenMP loop parallelism strategies which have a speedup of 10.7x, 10.7x and 10.9x. The two parallel strategies that exclusively use a tasking approach show a speedup of 9.8x and 9.4x when run on 16 cores, significantly less than the hybrid and loop parallelism approaches. The hybrid approaches are the most well suited as they combine the benefits of barrier substitution by task dependencies, the low overheads of loop parallelism when tasking provides no benefit and the locality of the static scheduling performed by the CG routine.

In case of Fluidanimate, results are shown at the center of Fig. 8. The Pthreads and the *OmpSs trivial* versions have identically poor performance, achieving speedups below 8x when they run on 16 cores. If the granularity of the tasks is reduced, the speedup reaches 8x when run on 16 cores. The *OmpSs Multidependencies* strategy of removing all the barriers that separate the 8 internal routines of each iteration and replacing them by task dependencies provides significant benefits and allows the speedup to be slightly above 9x when 16 cores are used. Finally, if the barrier that separates the different iterations is removed, the application scales up to 10.1x on 16 cores.

Streamcluster performs similarly on all of its versions when 1, 2, 4 and 8 cores are considered. When the two 8-cores sockets are used, NUMA effects bring load

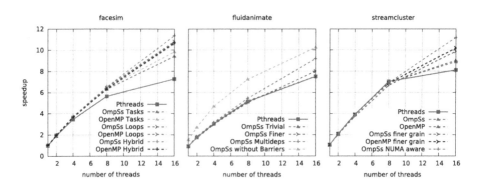

**Fig. 8.** Speedups of the different benchmarks and their tested versions

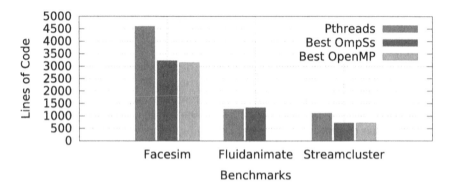

**Fig. 9.** Lines of code of the different benchmarks and their different versions

imbalance, which undermines the performance of the Pthreads implementation. The OpenMP and OmpSs implementations partially correct this load imbalance and achieve a speedup close to 9x on 16 cores. These load balancing benefits increase if finer grain tasks are considered, achieving scalabilities close to 10x on 16 cores. The fine grain versions make use of 5 tasks per thread, while the original OpenMP/OmpSs version use just 1 task per thread. Finally, the NUMA aware scheduling feature of the OmpSs runtime system provides further improvements reaching a speedup of 11.1x.

### 3.2 Programmability

Ease of use, portability and versatility are of paramount importance when deciding whether to use a programming model or not. It is difficult to quantify the above statement, but we can provide some insight on how easy it is to use such task-based models compared to Pthreads in terms of lines of code (LOC). LOC for the selected benchmarks is as follows: Facesim has 35,000 LOC, Fluidanimate 3,000 LOC, and Streamcluster 1,500 LOC.

Figure 9 shows the LOC of our task-based implementations compared to the original Pthreads implementations considering only files that are relevant to the parallel implementation, i.e. files that contain calls to Pthreads or task invocations, atomic primitives, etc. In this case, we only show the LOC of the best performing version of our OmpSs and OpenMP codes. The other versions have very similar number of LOC, with less than 3.5 % variation with respect to the best performing one.

On one hand, using OpenMP/OmpSs to parallelize applications allowed to reduce the size of the original code base in the case of Facesim (25 % less LOC) and Streamcluster (20 % less LOC). This is achieved by means of removing unnecessary barrier implementations and thread scheduling facilities. It also allowed to express more parallelism in all applications, whether allowing to parallelize originally sequential sections or by allowing more tasks to run concurrently.

This is the case with Fluidanimate, where a more advanced parallelization strategy is performed without significantly increasing the number of LOC (less than 4 %).

On the other hand, sometimes specifying dependencies might not be easy depending on the accessed data structure. For example, irregular and dynamic data structures are difficult to handle with current data dependencies. Also, very fine-grain tasks and an excess of dependency annotations can cause performance degradation due to runtime overheads. Designing future architectures driven by the runtime of the target parallel applications can be a suitable solution to reduce some of these overheads [12].

## 4 Related Work

In this paper we apply several parallelization strategies available in OpenMP 4.0 and OmpSs to three applications of the PARSEC benchmark suite. Similarly, the KASTORS suite [13] uses the OpenMP 4.0 task dependency constructs to extend the Cholesky and QR decompositions from the PLASMA library [9]. Also, the KASTORS suite provides a parallelized Poisson equation based kernel and extends the SparseLU and Strassen benchmarks from the Barcelona OpenMP Tasks Suite [6]. The main improvement of the work presented in this paper is that we do not only use the tasking features available in OpenMP 4.0 but also suggest and evaluate new ones. In contrast, the mentioned KASTORS approach [13] suggests new features, different from the ones proposed in this paper, but does not evaluate them.

Besides OpenMP 4.0 and OmpSs, other programming models and runtime system handle task-based parallelism. For example, the StarPU task programming library [2] provides a runtime system and an API to handle task-level parallelism. StarPU has been successfully used to implement important numerical routines [1] on heterogeneous environments, although its capabilites do not outperform OpenMP 4.0. Other approaches reproduce the OmpSs vision to target specific research issues, like the Distributed asyncHronous Adaptive Resilient Management of Applications (DHARMA) [8]. DHARMA is a task programming model designed with resilience as a primary focus. It is a data-flow approach that uses work-over-decomposition. Also, the Open Community Runtime (OCR) [7] initiative aims at creating a standard task-based runtime system. Very simple micro-kernels are publicly available to validate this approach.

## 5 Conclusions

In this paper we demonstrate the usefulness of three OmpSs features not currently available in the OpenMP 4.0 specification. The first one is the concurrent clause, which can be used to relax synchronization by overlapping task creation with computation. The second is the possibility to handle multiple dependency scenarios in a single #pragma annotation and the third one is the NUMA-aware scheduling feature available in the OmpSs runtime system. Each one of these three features provides significant improvements in terms of scalability and programmability. Additionally, this paper provides a comparison in terms of performance of task parallelism against loop parallelism and shows how combining them is sometimes the best option. We expect to provide more examples in the future to further motivate the need for OpenMP extensions and to strengthen the position of OmpSs as an OpenMP forerunner.

The importance of features like the ones discussed in this paper and, in general, of the task parallelism provided by OpenMP and OmpSs is increasing with the emergence of massivelly parallel and heterogeneous hardware, which will certanly require task clauses to allow programmers to handle large amounts of concurrency.

**Acknowledgments.** This work has been partially supported by the European Research Council under the European Union's 7th FP, ERC Grant Agreement number 321253, by the Spanish Ministry of Science and Innovation under grant TIN2012-34557 and by the HiPEAC Network of Excellence. It has been also supported by the Severo Ochoa Program awarded by the Spanish Government (grant SEV-2011-00067) M. Moreto has been partially supported by the Ministry of Economy and Competitiveness under Juan de la Cierva postdoctoral fellowship number JCI-2012-15047. M. Casas is supported by the Secretary for Universities and Research of the Ministry of Economy and Knowledge of the Government of Catalonia and the Co-fund programme of the Marie Curie Actions of the 7th R&D Framework Programme of the European Union (Contract 2013 BP_B 00243).

# References

1. Agullo, E., Augonnet, C., Dongarra, J., Ltaief, H., Namyst, R., Roman, J., Thibault, S., Tomov, S.: Dynamically scheduled Cholesky factorization on multicore architectures with GPU accelerators. In: Symposium on Application Accelerators in High Performance Computing (SAAHPC), Knoxville, USA (2010)
2. Augonnet, C., Thibault, S., Namyst, R., Wacrenier, P.-A.: STARPU: a unified platform for task scheduling on heterogeneous multicore architectures. In: Sips, H., Epema, D., Lin, H.-X. (eds.) Euro-Par 2009. LNCS, vol. 5704, pp. 863–874. Springer, Heidelberg (2009)
3. Bienia, C., Kumar, S., Singh, J.P., Li, K.: The PARSEC benchmark suite: characterization and architectural implications. In: The 17th International Conference on Parallel Architectures and Compilation Techniques (PACT), pp. 72–81 (2008)
4. Bienia, C., Li, K.: Parsec 2.0: a new benchmark suite for chip-multiprocessors. In: Proceedings of the 5th Annual Workshop on Modeling, Benchmarking and Simulation, June 2009
5. Duran, A., Ayguad, E., Badia, R.M., Labarta, J., Martinell, L., Martorell, X., Planas, J.: OmpSs: a proposal for programming heterogeneous multi-core architectures. Parallel Process. Lett. **21**(02), 173–193 (2011)
6. Duran, A., Teruel, X., Ferrer, R., Martorell, X., Ayguade, E.: Barcelona OpenMP tasks suite: a set of benchmarks targeting the exploitation of task parallelism in OpenMP. In: International Conference on Parallel Processing (ICPP), pp. 124–131 (2009)

7. Knauerhase, R., Sarkar, V.: The open community runtime and its use in systems research. In: Tutorial: International Conference on Architectural Support for Programming Languagues and Operating Systems (ASPLOS) (2013)
8. Kolla, H., et al.: DHARMA: distributed asynchronous adaptive resilient management of applications. In: Minisymposia on Resilience in Numerical Simulations and Algorithms at Extreme Scale. SIAM Conference on Computational Science and Engineering (2015)
9. Kurzak, J., Luszczek, P., YarKhan, A., Faverge, M., Langou, J., Bouwmeester, H., Dongarra, J.: Multithreading in the plasma library. In: Multicore Computing: Algorithms, Architectures, and Applications, p. 119 (2013)
10. Labarta, J., Gimenez, J.: Performance analysis: from art to science. In: Parallel Processing for Scientific Computing, Chap. 2, pp. 9–32. SIAM (2006)
11. Müller, M., Charypar, D., Gross, M.: Particle-based fluid simulation for interactive applications. In: Proceedings of the 2003 ACM SIGGRAPH/Eurographics Symposium on Computer Animation (SCA), pp. 154–159 (2003)
12. Valero, M., Moreto, M., Casas, M., Ayguade, E., Labarta, J.: Runtime-aware architectures: a first approach. Int. J. Supercomput. Frontiers Innovations 1(1), 29–44 (2014)
13. Virouleau, P., Brunet, P., Broquedis, F., Furmento, N., Thibault, S., Aumage, O., Gautier, T.: Evaluation of OpenMP dependent tasks with the KASTORS benchmark suite. In: DeRose, L., de Supinski, B.R., Olivier, S.L., Chapman, B.M., Müller, M.S. (eds.) IWOMP 2014. LNCS, vol. 8766, pp. 16–29. Springer, Heidelberg (2014)

# First Experiences Porting a Parallel Application to a Hybrid Supercomputer with OpenMP 4.0 Device Constructs

Alistair Hart[✉]

Cray Exascale Research Initiative Europe, JCMB, King's Buildings,
Edinburgh EH9 3FD, UK
ahart@cray.com

**Abstract.** In this paper we describe the process of porting the Nek-Bone mini-application to run on a Cray XC30 hybrid supercomputer using OpenMP device constructs, as introduced in version 4.0 of the OpenMP standard and implemented in a pre-release version of the Cray Compilation Environment (CCE) compiler. We document the process of porting and show how the performance evolves during the addition on the 66 constructs needed to accelerate the application. In doing so, we provide a user-centric introduction to the device constructs and an overview of the approach needed to port a parallel application using these. Some contrasts with OpenACC are also drawn to aid those wishing to either implement both programming models or to migrate from one to the other.

## 1 Introduction

High Performance Computing (HPC) node architectures are becoming increasingly complex as systems evolve towards exascale performance. There are many more cores (processors) per node, more threads per processor and a return in the use of wide "single instruction multiple data" (SIMD) vectors.

Heterogeneous (or "hybrid") node designs are also now common, as evidenced by the biannual Top500 listing of the world's fastest supercomputers: 75 systems on the November 2014 list used accelerators[1] [1].

It is difficult to program hybrid nodes to achieve an acceptable fraction of the available performance. More importantly, it is also difficult to develop (and then maintain) applications that are performance portable. By this, we mean that the application can be built and then executed on a wide variety of HPC architectures with only minimal changes. This is important, given that large applications are, at a given time, typically run on a variety of HPC platforms, and that these applications often outlive many generations of HPC procurements (and even, sometimes, developers).

---

[1] We use the term "accelerator" generically to cover technologies including GPUs (e.g. from Nvidia or AMD) and coprocessors (such as the Intel Xeon Phi "Knights Corner" coprocessor).

© Springer International Publishing Switzerland 2015
C. Terboven et al. (Eds.): IWOMP 2015, LNCS 9342, pp. 73–85, 2015.
DOI: 10.1007/978-3-319-24595-9_6

Heterogeneous node architectures offer two significant challenges. First, developers must use a bespoke programming model that allows the use of the accelerator. Secondly, hybrid nodes introduce a diverse memory space with, typically, the CPU and accelerator(s) on a node having separate memory spaces. Given the relatively slow (high latency, low bandwidth) connection between the memory spaces and the (consequent) lack of automatic synchronisation between them, developers are forced to explicitly manage the memory spaces and data transfers.

The OpenACC standard introduced a high-level, directive-based programming models for accelerators [2]. This has been very successfully used for some large production-quality applications, e.g. the turbulent combustion code S3D [3] and the numerical weather prediction code COSMO [4]. The OpenMP standard [5] now offers a comparable programming model, through the device constructs introduced in version 4.0 of the standard.

Directive-based programming models are attractive as developers do not need to re-write their code in a low-level language. The existing code (written in Fortran, C or C++) is augmented through directives and, optionally, calls to a runtime Application Program Interface (API). The directives are non-executable comments or pragmas that instruct a suitably-enabled compiler to offload certain computational tasks to the accelerator and to manage the data synchronisation between the diverse memory spaces. Alternatively, if support for the directives is disabled (or a non-accelerating compiler is used), the code can be built and executed on the CPU.

Given the relative newness of the OpenMP4.0 standard, there are currently no widely-available compilers that offer support for the device constructs. There is thus a lack of experience in the HPC community in using this programming model. In this paper, we have access to a pre-release version of the Cray Compilation Environment that supports use of the OpenMP constructs. We use this to port a parallel application to run almost entirely on the accelerator.

The aim of this paper is not to demonstrate the performance that can be achieved with accelerators and we only discuss performance tuning briefly. Rather, we seek to document the process of porting a representative application to act as a *vademecum* for developers as and when the device constructs are supported in released compilers.

A good programming environment is key to a successful port to accelerators. In addition to the compiler, this should include runtime information systems and profiling tools. As part of the documentation in this paper, we present information gained from a selection of these and show how it guides the application development work.

The application we consider in this paper is the NekBone mini-application, which seeks to capture the computational workload of the Nek5000 computational fluid dynamics (CFD) application originally developed by Paul Fisher from Argonne National Laboratory [6]. The code uses the spectral element method. The simulated problem is divided into a set of "elements". The physical quantities in each element are represented as a set of spectral modes (akin to a Fourier decomposition), with the number of modes in the set being $N$. This is fixed for the duration of the simulation and is typically between 8 and 20, depending on the level of accuracy required.

The computational workload is dominated by combinations of these spectral modes. This translates to matrix-matrix combinations, where the rank of the matrix is $N$. These combinations are repeated independently for every element. Whilst optimised Basic Linear Algebra Subroutines (BLAS) libraries exist, these are typically optimised for large-rank matrices and do not provide an API that will perform a (large) number of independent (small) multiplications simultaneously. For this reason, neither NekBone nor Nek5000 make use of these libraries.

Like Nek5000, NekBone is parallelised using domain decomposition, dividing the set of elements across a set of processing elements. Message passing is then used to ensure that the elements on each domain boundary remain consistent with their neighbours at each timestep of the simulation.

The NekBone code is written in Fortran and contains roughly 11,000 lines, of which 80 % are executable code (i.e. not comments, blank lines nor directives). The domain decomposition is carried out using the Message Passing Interface (MPI) API. For this work, we use a simplified version of the communication layer [7] that was developed as part of the EPiGRAM project [8]. An OpenACC port of the NekBone code was developed as part of the CRESTA project [9]. As this paper aimed to document the porting process "from scratch", we did not refer to this during this work. In general, however, porting from OpenACC to OpenMP device constructs is quite straightforward and we highlight the similarities and difference between the programming models in this paper.

The work described in this paper was carried out on a Cray XC30 hybrid computer. Each node comprised a single 12-core Intel Xeon E5-2695v2 (Ivybridge) CPU (with a clock frequency of 2.4 GHz and turbo enabled) and an Nvidia K40s GPU. The nodes were integrated together using the Cray Aries interconnect.

A pre-release version of the Cray Compilation Environment (CCE) compiler was used for this work, which provided preliminary support for the OpenMP4.0 device constructs. The performance results in this paper should therefore be seen as indicative and liable to change when a suitable released version of the compiler becomes available. This does not affect the conclusions of this paper.

The structure of this paper is as follows. In Sect. 2, we give an overview of the OpenMP device constructs. We give a high-level overview of the porting process in Sect. 3, before applying this to the NekBone code in Sect. 4. Finally, we draw some conclusions in Sect. 5.

## 2   OpenMP Device Constructs

Device constructs were introduced in OpenMP4.0 and are described in Sect. 2.9 of the Standard. They provide a mechanism for offloading (i.e. accelerating) computational tasks ("kernels") from the "host" (typically a CPU) to one or more "devices" (usually locally attached accelerators). In this Section, we give a brief introduction to the device constructs from the perspective of an application developer.

```
!$omp target                          !$omp target map(to:a,b)
!$omp teams                           !$omp&          map(from:c)
!$omp distribute                      !$omp teams
DO j = 1,n3                           !$omp distribute
  DO i = 1,n1                         DO j = 1,n3
    c(i,j) = 0                          DO i = 1,n1
    DO k = 1,n2                           c(i,j) = 0
      c(i,j)=c(i,j)+a(i,k)*b(k,j)         DO k = 1,n2
    ENDDO                                   c(i,j)=c(i,j)+a(i,k)*b(k,j)
  ENDDO                                   ENDDO
ENDDO                                    ENDDO
!$omp end distribute                   ENDDO
!$omp end teams                        !$omp end distribute
!$omp end target                       !$omp end teams
                                       !$omp end target
```

(a) Automatic array scoping.          (b) Explicit array scoping.

**Fig. 1.** Accelerating a matrix-matrix multiplication loopnest with the target construct. Optionally, map clauses may be used to scope arrays in the data environment.

The computational tasks to be executed on the device are typically loopnests. As a start, three nested directives are required, as shown in Fig. 1.

The **target** construct indicates that the loopnest should be offloaded to the device. It also creates a device data environment, that we discuss in Sect. 2.1.

The **teams** construct creates a "league" of threadteams and the master thread of each team executes the region. The combination of **target** and **teams** is broadly equivalent to the **parallel** directive in OpenACC (up to a few technical details), and shares the same prescriptive behaviour; the region will always be offloaded (unlike the more descriptive **kernels** directive in OpenACC). The "league of threadteams" is analogous to the "gangs of workers" in OpenACC and to the "grid of threadblocks" in CUDA.

Finally, the **distribute** construct arranges the distribution ("scheduling") of the loop iterations over the threads. This role is played by the **loop** directive in OpenACC.

All three constructs have optional clauses. We will discuss those for **target** in Sect. 2.1. The main use of clauses on the **teams** construct is to declare **private** and **reduction** variables for this loopnest. The use of these is identical to that in "traditional" OpenMP or, indeed, in OpenACC. Developers familiar with OpenACC should note that scalars within a loopnest are **shared** by default in OpenMP, compared to **private** in OpenACC. The **num_teams** and **thread_limit** clauses are primarily used for performance tuning and are generally not used during early application porting.

The **private** clause can be added to the **distribute** construct to give finer-grained control over privatisation of variables within a loopnest. The **collapse** and **dist_schedule** clauses can also be used for tuning, but we do not address them here.

## 2.1   Data Regions

When a loopnest is offloaded to the device, it will require data to process. In the first instance, this data will reside in the host memory. Before the offloaded kernel is executed, memory will need to be allocated in the device memory and (as necessary) data copied from the host to the device. After the kernel finishes executing, data may need to be transferred back to the host before the device memory is freed.

The `target` construct defines a "data region" (also known as "data environment") that implements this. By default, the OpenMP-enabled runtime will allocate and free appropriate device memory on the boundaries of the construct. The compiler will also examine the data use within the kernel and arrange appropriate data movements at the construct boundaries. For example, a shared array that is used in a read-only fashion will be copied to the device before the kernel executes, but need not be copied back afterwards.

The user can replicate or alter the default behaviour using explicit `map` clauses on the `target` construct, with "map-types" used to specify the data movements. Read-only arrays use map-type `to`, and write-only arrays `from`. Arrays that read and written have map-type `tofrom`. Finally, scratch arrays that are only used within the loopnest require no data movement and use map-type `alloc`.

It is, of course, very inefficient to move data at the boundaries of every `target` construct. Instead, we should seek to hold the data on the device for as long as possible, processing it with multiple kernels. The `target data` construct provides a mechanism for this, allowing users to define a region of their application. Specified arrays will be resident on the device for the entirety of this region, with `map` clauses used to specify the data movement at the construct boundaries.

The `target data` construct does not accelerate any code within the specified region, so it is usual that the region will contain one or (usually) more `target` constructs. It may also span unaccelerated code that executes on the host, which may include calls to subprograms.

Users should note that, unlike with the `target` construct, the compiler will not automatically scope any shared arrays present in a `target data` construct. All relevant arrays must be explicitly specified using `map` clauses (as in OpenACC).

Within a data region, there are separate copies of the shared arrays in the host and device memories with no automatic synchronisation of data. If synchronisation is required (e.g. to move buffers to the CPU for MPI exchange, or to print values for debugging), this is done using the `target update` construct. To move data from the host memory to that of the device, the `device` clause is used; to move in the opposite direction, the `host` clause is used. The clauses take arguments that are either whole arrays or array slices.

Data regions can be nested, either within a single routine or further down the calltree. When entering an inner data region, if relevant shared variables are already present in the device memory then this version will be used and no further memory allocation or data transfer will occur. Similarly, the memory will remain allocated on exiting the inner data region without data transfers.

```
Time% |      Time |      Imb. |  Imb. |    Calls |Group
      |           |      Time | Time% |          | Function
|-----------------------------------------------------------------
| 100.0% | 0.118094 |        -- |    -- | 173121.0 |USER
||-----------------------------------------------------------------
||   34.0% | 0.040187 | 0.000630 |  1.8% |  76800.0 |mxmf2_generic_
||   12.1% | 0.014332 | 0.000201 |  1.6% |  76800.0 |mxm_
||    8.3% | 0.009745 | 0.000194 |  2.2% |   3200.0 |ax_e_
||    5.8% | 0.006881 | 0.000110 |  1.8% |    301.0 |glsc3_
||    5.0% | 0.005956 | 0.000161 |  3.0% |   3200.0 |local_grad3_t_
|=================================================================
```

**Fig. 2.** Traced profile of NekBone executing on the CPU, showing routines taking 5 % or more of the runtime.

The OpenMP map-types therefore behave like the OpenACC data clauses that start with present_or_. There is no equivalent of the OpenACC present clause. The OpenMP runtime system maintains a table of memory addresses that are resident on the device. It is not expected that there is any significant overhead in checking the present table, so developers can employ multiple levels of data region nesting if it aids the porting process.

## 3  A High Level View of the Porting Method

Having described the relevant constructs in Sect. 2, it is useful to sketch out a method for applying them to an application, as we do for NekBone in Sect. 4.

It is important to work incrementally, adding one directive construct at a time and testing the code. Correctness checks should be implemented in the code wherever possible, e.g. residual values in solvers or array checksums. It is advisable that these are double precision, even if the relevant parts of the code are single precision. These should be compared at every stage, but noting that it is impossible to always have bit-wise identical answers when executing the code on different architectures (e.g. CPU and GPU).

As the code may need to be run many times, it is useful to work with a small testcase. This should, however, exercise all parts of the code that are needed in the production-sized problem. It is very likely that the performance of the code will decline during the early stages of porting, due to the data movements between the separate memory spaces. Performance should then increase once significant parts of the application calltree are ported and data locality is improved.

It is advisable to use a version control system (VCS) that allows the application developer to archive the source code at each stage of the porting process. Application output and basic performance information can then be included in each commit message. If the code then executes incorrectly with a new testcase, it is easy to "wind back" the porting process to see where the error was first introduced.

Given this incremental approach, the user should start at the "leaves" of the application calltree, i.e. routines that do not call any further routines. Where there are many leaf routines, the user should begin with those that take significant time in the application profile. As porting proceeds, minimisation of data movement may well require the acceleration of further leaf routines, but these should be addressed as the need arises.

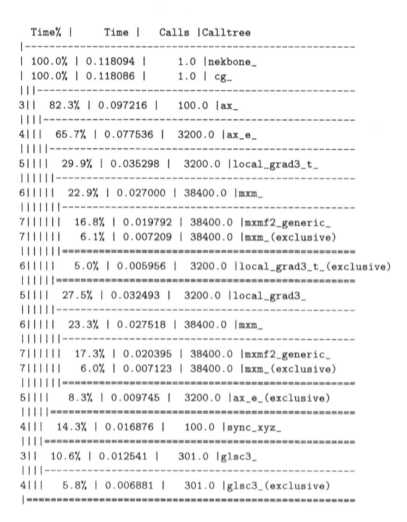

```
Time% |      Time |    Calls |Calltree
|-------------------------------------------------------
| 100.0% | 0.118094 |      1.0 |nekbone_
| 100.0% | 0.118086 |      1.0 | cg_
|||-----------------------------------------------------
3||   82.3% | 0.097216 |    100.0 |ax_
||||----------------------------------------------------
4|||   65.7% | 0.077536 |   3200.0 |ax_e_
|||||---------------------------------------------------
5||||   29.9% | 0.035298 |   3200.0 |local_grad3_t_
||||||--------------------------------------------------
6|||||   22.9% | 0.027000 |  38400.0 |mxm_
|||||||-------------------------------------------------
7||||||   16.8% | 0.019792 |  38400.0 |mxmf2_generic_
7||||||    6.1% | 0.007209 |  38400.0 |mxm_(exclusive)
|||||||===========================================
6|||||    5.0% | 0.005956 |   3200.0 |local_grad3_t_(exclusive)
||||||=============================================
5||||   27.5% | 0.032493 |   3200.0 |local_grad3_
||||||--------------------------------------------------
6|||||   23.3% | 0.027518 |  38400.0 |mxm_
|||||||-------------------------------------------------
7||||||   17.3% | 0.020395 |  38400.0 |mxmf2_generic_
7||||||    6.0% | 0.007123 |  38400.0 |mxm_(exclusive)
|||||||===========================================
5||||    8.3% | 0.009745 |   3200.0 |ax_e_(exclusive)
|||||==============================================
4|||   14.3% | 0.016876 |    100.0 |sync_xyz_
||||=================================================
3||   10.6% | 0.012541 |    301.0 |glsc3_
||||-------------------------------------------------
4|||    5.8% | 0.006881 |    301.0 |glsc3_(exclusive)
|==================================================
```

**Fig. 3.** Function Calltree View of the profile of NekBone executing on the host, showing routines taking 5% or more of the runtime. The indentation levels on the left hand side show the depth of the calltree.

Each of the selected leaf routines should be addressed in turn. Within a given leaf routine, each loopnest should generally be accelerated using a target

construct. Exceptions are loopnests that do not reference large data arrays or
loopnests that must be executed serially. Serial loopnests must remain on the
CPU and are likely to be a serious bar to performance, given the associated data
synchronisation costs. Where possible, these loops should be rewritten using a
parallelisable algorithm and then accelerated.

When introducing target constructs, the compiler can be left to automatically scope the arrays and determine the appropriate map clauses. This information is reported in the compiler feedback. It is very useful for what follows,
however, if the user introduces explicit map clauses for the most-significant (usually the largest) data arrays. This scoping (i.e. selecting the correct map-type
for a given array) can either be done by hand, or based on the compiler feedback
before the map clauses are introduced, as shown in Fig. 1.

### 3.1   Fusing Local Data Regions

As described before, most of the effort in a successful accelerator port is spent
in ensuring data locality. This is done by introducing progressively-larger data
regions that span increasing amounts of the application calltree.

The first stage in this is to work within a given leaf routine. Each target
construct has an implicit data region. The aim is (usually) to introduce a single,
explicit data region that spans all the executable code in this routine. This data
region is incrementally constructed by fusing neighbouring data regions (implicit
or explicit).

```
Loop  |     Loop  |   Time  | Loop Hit  |   Loop  |  Loop  |  Loop  |Function=/.LOOP[.]
Incl  |     Incl  |  (Loop  |           |   Trips  | Trips  | Trips  | PE=HIDE
Time% |     Time  |  Adj.)  |           |   Avg  |  Min  |   Max  |
|-----------------------------------------------------------------------------------
| 105.5% | 0.676522 | 0.000211 |        1 |   100.0 |  100 |   100 |cg_.LOOP.1.li.56
|  98.8% | 0.633409 | 0.000447 |      100 |    32.0 |   32 |    32 |ax_.LOOP.1.li.141
|  81.9% | 0.524856 | 0.014328 |    76800 |    17.5 |   10 |   100 |mxmf2_generic_.LOOP.1.li.69
|  79.6% | 0.510528 | 0.263983 |  1344000 |    14.3 |   10 |   100 |mxmf2_generic_.LOOP.2.li.70
|  38.5% | 0.246545 | 0.246545 | 19200000 |    10.0 |   10 |    10 |mxmf2_generic_.LOOP.3.li.72
|  19.5% | 0.124745 | 0.004068 |     3200 |    10.0 |   10 |    10 |local_grad3_t_.LOOP.1.li.258
|  19.4% | 0.124372 | 0.004076 |     3200 |    10.0 |   10 |    10 |local_grad3_.LOOP.1.li.236
|===================================================================================
```

**Fig. 4.** Inclusive and exclusive time in loops, as measured by CrayPAT

Once the significant leaf routines have been accelerated, the developer should
now move up the calltree one level and establish data regions in the parent
routines that call these leaves.

The first step is to establish a data region around each call to an accelerated
leaf routine. The map clauses for this are easily constructed from those on the
single data region inside the leaf routine. If the parent routine calls further leaf
routines (which reference the most-significant data arrays), these should also be
accelerated as above. Even if the calls to these routines take little time, they

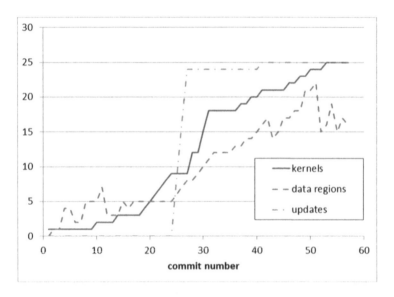

**Fig. 5.** The number of device constructs present in the code as a function of VCS commit number.

should still process the device-resident copies of the arrays to maintain data locality and avoid data synchronisation overheads.

If the parent routine contains additional loopnests, these should be accelerated wherever possible. Finally, the same process of data region fusing should be repeated until a single data region spans the entire parent routine. Once this is achieved, the developer can now take a further step up the calltree and repeat the process.

This process should continue until the application port is complete. This might be when the entire application is executing on the accelerator(s). Alternatively, it might be when the outermost data region is outside the main computational structure in the code, for instance the timestep loop. In some cases it might be when all accelerator-suitable code is ported, and data movement costs are minimised but perhaps not eliminated.

## 4  Porting NekBone

The method described in Sect. 3 was used to port the NekBone application. The porting was carried out on a Cray XC30 system using a pre-release version of the Cray Compilation Environment (CCE).

The NekBone source code supplies some testcases. Testcase "example1" was used to test the code during the porting process. This simulates a problem with 32 elements per MPI rank and a spectral order of $N = 10$. Both of these numbers are relatively small, which will make it hard to gain full performance from the targetted GPU architecture. Production-sized problems will, however,

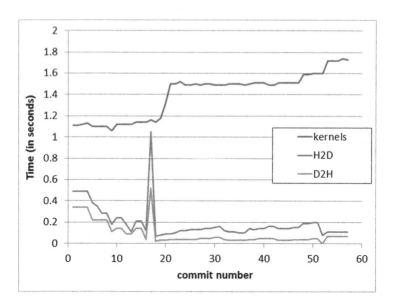

**Fig. 6.** The time spent in accelerator kernels and data synchronisation as a function of VCS commit number.

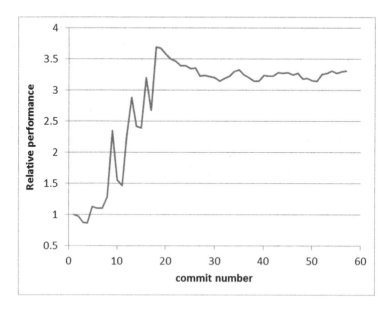

**Fig. 7.** The relative performance of the application as a function of VCS commit number. The baseline is that for after introducing the first target construct.

have many more elements. This problem was run using 8 MPI ranks, distributed as one rank per node (giving a ratio of one MPI rank per GPU).

The `git` VCS was used, with around 60 separate commits as device constructs were progressively added to the code. The commit log messages included the program runtime output and basic profiling information to track progress.

The first task was to generate an application profile and calltree for the application to identify the most significant leaf nodes. This was done using the Cray Performance Analysis Toolkit (CrayPAT). The code was instrumented to trace all the user routines using the command `pat_build -u`. The profile in Fig. 2 shows that routine `mxmf2_generic()` dominates the runtime, implementing matrix-matrix multiplication for the spectral decomposition. Command `pat_report -O calltree` was then used to generate the calltree view of the profile, seen in Fig. 3, providing a plan for accelerating the application. In both cases, the CrayPAT API has been used to restrict profiling to the timestep loop.

Porting thus began in `mxmf2_generic()` a single `target` construct as shown in Fig. 1.

As noted before, the multiplied matrices are small. This can be confirmed through loop-level profiling of the application. With CCE, the code is recompiled with flag `-h profile_generate` and profiled with CrayPAT as before. The results in Fig. 4 show a mean tripcount of only 14 to 18 for these loops.

Porting then proceeded as described in Sect. 3. A single data region was easily added and tested) around the call to the ported routine in `mxm()`. Further data regions were then established in `local_grad3()` and `local_grad3_t()`. The latter routine also called `add2s2()`, so this also had to be ported. The advantage of the `map` clause `present_or` semantic is that this is correct even for calls to this routine from other, so far unported, parts of the application calltree. If the OpenACC `present` clause were used, by contrast, the routine would need to be cloned before acceleration.

Extending the data regions into routine `ax()` required porting `sync_xyz()` and its child routines. These implement the MPI halo exchange. With OpenMP4.0, calls to MPI routines must reference buffers in host memory, so `update` clauses were required to synchronise these buffers between host and device after packing (and before unpacking) on the device. We would hope that future versions of the OpenMP standard would support an equivalent of the OpenACC `host_data` directive that allows direct MPI transfers between device memories on different nodes (as well as interoperability with CUDA libraries).

In porting routine `maskit()`, a loopnest was encountered that was not easily parallelised. To proceed with the port, the decision was made to temporarily execute it on the host, with `update` constructs needed to synchronise the data. This impacted performance, as shown by the runtime commentary, which in CCE is activated (without recompilation) using the `CRAY_ACC_DEBUG` environment variable. Setting this to 2, we see a transfers of the form:

```
ACC:        copy to host 'w' (8000 bytes)
```

This is done 32 times per timestep. This, and the associated transfer of another array accounted for 64 % of the data transfers.

The total porting process took around 3 days, and around 60 commits to the VCS. The number of constructs added to the code is shown as a function of the commit number in Fig. 5. The fluctuations downward indicate the removal of some redundant inner data regions. In Fig. 6 we show how the time spent per node in accelerator kernels increases as the port proceeds and more `target` constructs are introduced. The time spent in data transfers generally reduces as data regions are widened. The upward spike corresponds to the first stage in porting the halo transfer leaf routines.

Finally, in Fig. 7 we show how the performance of the application improves as the port proceeds (relative to that when we add the first `target` construct). The plateau does not indicate wasted effort, but rather that the chosen testcase is too small to properly exercise the accelerator. If the process was repeated with a larger local problem size, we would expect to see an upward trend.

## 5    Conclusions

In this paper, we have presented some first experiences in porting a parallel application to run on accelerated nodes of an HPC system using the OpenMP device constructs.

As well as introducing the constructs, we have described an algorithm for porting a real application, showing the steps that a developer should follow and indicating how appropriate tools can be used to provide feedback to guide the porting process.

We have demonstrated this method by porting the parallel NekBone application, applying 66 device construct structures to accelerate around 11,000 lines of Fortran code. This average rate of 1 construct per 170 lines fits with anecdotal experience using OpenACC, where large codes typically required 1 directive per 150 to 250 lines of code. Of these 66 constructs, 25 were used to define offloaded kernels, and the remainder to define and synchronise the data environment.

The development process took around three days and was split into approximately 60 incremental stages. Each stage usually involved adding or modifying one device construct. We showed how application evolved over these stages, both in terms of performance and number of constructs.

The port of NekBone is by no means complete, with one final, tricky loopnest to parallelise and accelerate. There is also substantial room for performance tuning, although the fundamental multiplication of $10 \times 10$ matrices does not fit well with the warp size of 32 on current Nvidia GPUs.

As the OpenMP standard evolves, further performance improvements should be possible, such as the use of direct MPI communications between device memory spaces on different nodes.

In conclusion, however, the OpenMP device constructs provide a rich and relatively complete programming model for porting large scale applications to accelerators in a performance-portable manner. Compiler development is in progress and, at least with the Cray Compilation Environment, already offer a robust and efficient implementation of the constructs.

**Acknowledgments.** This work was supported in part by the European Commission through the EPiGRAM project (grant agreement no. 610598).

# References

1. The Top500 list. http://www.top500.org
2. The OpenACC standard. http://www.openacc.org
3. Levesque, J.M., Sankaran, R., Grout, R.: Hybridizing S3D into an exascale application using OpenACC: an approach for moving to multi-petaflops and beyond. In: Proceedings of the International Conference on High Performance Computing, Networking, Storage and Analysis (SC 2012), Article 15, p. 11. IEEE Computer Society Press, Los Alamitos, CA, USA (2012)
4. Fuhrer, O.: Proceedings of CUG2014 (May 2014, Lugano, Switzerland). https://cug.org/proceedings/cug2014_proceedings/includes/files/inv108.pdf
5. The OpenMP standard. http://www.openmp.org
6. The Nek5000 project. https://nek5000.mcs.anl.gov/index.php/Main_Page
7. Markidis, S., Ivanov, I., Akhmetova, D., Laure, E., Gong, J., Schlatter, P., Henningson, D., Fischer, P.: Proceedings of EASC2015 (April 2015, Edinburgh, UK). http://www.easc2015.ed.ac.uk/program-archive/slides/s18Ivanov.pdf
8. The EPiGRAM project. http://www.epigram-project.eu
9. The CRESTA project. http://www.cresta-project.eu

# Tools

# Lessons Learned from Implementing OMPD: A Debugging Interface for OpenMP

Joachim Protze[1,2,3], Ignacio Laguna[3(✉)], Dong H. Ahn[3], John Del Signore[4],
Ariel Burton[4], Martin Schulz[3], and Matthias S. Müller[1,2]

[1] RWTH Aachen University, 52056 Aachen, Germany
[2] JARA – High-Performance Computing, 52062 Aachen, Germany
{protze,mueller}@itc.rwth-aachen.de
[3] Lawrence Livermore National Laboratory, Livermore, CA 94550, USA
{lagunaperalt1,ahn1,schulzm}@llnl.gov
[4] Rogue Wave Software, Bolder, CO 80301, USA
{ariel.burton,john.delsignore}@roguewave.com

**Abstract.** With complex codes moving to systems of increasing on-node parallelism using OpenMP, debugging these codes is becoming increasingly challenging. While debuggers can significantly aid programmers, existing ones support OpenMP at a low system-thread level, reducing their effectiveness. The previously published draft for a standard OpenMP debugging interface (OMPD) is supposed to enable the debuggers to raise their debugging abstraction to the conceptual levels of OpenMP by mediating the tools and OpenMP runtime library. In this paper, we present our experiences and the issues that we have found on implementing an OMPD library prototyp for a commonly used OpenMP runtime and a parallel debugger.

## 1 Introduction

OpenMP is becoming increasingly popular as a portable programming model for *on-node parallelism* as programmers desire to port their codes to its simple directive-based API. This trend, however, is presenting great challenges to debugging. As OpenMP enables easy mapping of tasks to a wide range of resources—more cores, wider simultaneous multithreading (SMT), single-instruction/multiple-data (SIMD) units and accelerators like GPUs and co-processors—reasoning about the OpenMP program's state when debugging can quickly overwhelm programmers.

A parallel debugger is an effective aid to guide programmers in inspecting the state of parallel programs. Programmers can follow through source lines and easily examine the state of key variables at arbitrary points in execution. While

---

Part of this work was performed under the auspices of the U.S. Department of Energy by Lawrence Livermore National Laboratory under Contract DE-AC52-07NA27344. (LLNL-CONF-671193).

C. Terboven et al. (Eds.): IWOMP 2015, LNCS 9342, pp. 89–101, 2015.
DOI: 10.1007/978-3-319-24595-9_7

today's debuggers support debugging of OpenMP programs at a low system-thread level, they do not allow debugging at the level that programmers conceive the high-level programming model abstractions. For example, no existing debugger provides support, such as stepping a logically-related group of threads together (which requires identifying the teams of threads that are at the same OpenMP parallel nesting level), displaying the conceptual stack trace of a thread (e.g., by splicing the trace of a thread to that of the master thread and to identify and omit the trace belonging to the OpenMP runtime itself), and showing the state in which an OpenMP thread could be in.

To effectively aid programmers, debuggers must raise their debugging abstraction to the conceptual level of OpenMP. Constructing the conceptual state requires, however, that the debuggers are able to extract at runtime relevant information from the OpenMP's runtime system. An existing approach that is used in commercial debuggers, such as TotalView [6] or Allinea DDT [1], is to build the knowledge necessary to interact with each runtime directly into the debugger. While useful, it has led to limited support in terms of use cases and of compiler and runtime implementations of the OpenMP language. A standard interface approach, in which debuggers can extract the relevant state from *any* OpenMP runtime system, can lead to a much better solution.

In this paper, we report on our early analysis and experiences with OMPD, the standard OpenMP debug interface recently proposed by the OpenMP Tools Committee [4]. As much as we desire OMPD to serve as the general interface, we have found that it presents obstacles and challenges as we implement it for the Intel OpenMP Runtime, a popular OpenMP runtime library, as well as for TotalView and GDB, widely used debuggers. Thus, we discuss modifications to the current specification needed to overcome our issues. We hope that our experiences will shed light on the effective OpenMP debugging path to other debugger and OpenMP runtime implementers.

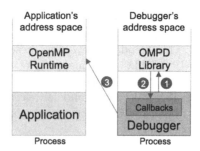

**Fig. 1.** Overview of the workflow of OMPD: (1) the debugger requests information about OpenMP (e.g., the state of an OpenMP thread, parallel region, task, etc.) via an OMPD API function call; (2) OMPD calls back the debugger to request information of the OpenMP runtime (e.g., the value of a symbol in the runtime); (3) the debugger gets this information from the runtime.

In the rest of the paper, we first summarize prior work, and then describe the OMPD interface and its functional architecture. Next, we illustrate some of the important use cases that OMPD can enable. Then, we discuss the problems that we have encountered with the current specification of OMPD and propose our suggested modifications. Finally, we describe future challenges and conclude.

## 2   Prior Work

Previous work has proposed portable debugging interfaces for parallel runtime libraries, such as for MPI [3] and threads [7]. The key mechanism to providing portability is the encapsulation of the debugging API in a loadable library, which forms the bridge between debuggers and runtime systems. This library is dependent on the internal implementation details of a particular runtime and is loaded by the debugger to request information from that runtime. Upon initialization, the debugger registers hooks with this library to provide the necessary functionality to access the target process (e.g., using the trace interface). When the debugger then calls the debugging API implemented by this library, it uses these hooks to extract information from the target process and then uses its knowledge about internal information to interpret it and return it to the debugger. This decouples debugging functionality implemented by the debugger from implementation dependent runtime information.

Crownie and Gropp used this design to implement an interface that allows a debugger to obtain the information necessary to display the contents of MPI message queues [3]. The same concept has been used in the `libthread_db` library [7], an interface for monitoring and inspecting thread-related aspects of multithreaded programs. Similar thread debugging interfaces have been implemented on other systems such as Tru64, IRIX, AIX and Linux.

Crownie et al. proposed `DMPL` [2], an interface to help a debugger understand the internals of the OpenMP runtime using the aforementioned library-based design. The focus of this interface is to allow a debugger obtain information about *shared* and *private* variables of OpenMP parallel regions.

More recently, the OpenMP Tools Committee proposed `OMPD` [4], a general interface to debug OpenMP programs. `OMPD` extends the functionality proposed in `DMPL` and covers a wider range of debugging use cases—from examining the state of OpenMP threads and tasks, to allowing the debugger to place breakpoints at the beginning and end of parallel regions. We describe these use cases later in this paper.

## 3   The OpenMP Debugging Interface

Tools targeting OpenMP need access to state information within the OpenMP runtime to improve their ability to deal with OpenMP abstractions and to provide information to users at that level of abstraction. This is true for both performance and debugging tools, although, different requirements apply.

## 3.1   OMPT: A Runtime Interface for OpenMP Tools

The standard way to provide state information from a runtime is a set of additional API functions exposed by the runtime. The recently proposed OMPT interface [5], which has also been published by the OpenMP ARB as an official white paper, takes this approach and offers both state query functions and callback functionality for relevant events. This can be used by performance tools to examine the state of the runtime, identify parallel regions and tasks, and to assemble call stacks to offer users a view without interwoven runtime stack frames.

## 3.2   Why Distinguish OMPD from OMPT?

In general, the information offered by OMPT is also required by debuggers. However, debuggers access information in a fundamentally different way: they access and debug a process externally from a different process. This is commonly referred to as "third-party access", which makes a pure runtime library API approach difficult. In particular, calling a function in the target process's runtime has the following problems:

– It may not be possible at all, for example, it is not possible to call a function in a target core file. Some target architectures, such as GPUs, may not permit the debugger to call functions at all.
– It is unreliable since the target process or thread may have corrupted itself to the point where calling a function causes a crash (e.g., a SIGSEGV). Also, it assumes that the function being called in the target is asynchronously reentrant.
– It may change the process and thread state and may have unintended side effects.
– It is relatively expensive and may scale poorly, as each call requires many low-level operations to read/write target memory and registers, continue execution, handle breakpoint traps, and cleanup the process.

OMPD therefore intends to expose the same information as available from OMPT or from the OpenMP APIs directly, but without the need to run in the process of the application and the runtime. As shown in Fig. 1, the OMPD runtime is loaded by the debugger and resides in the debugger process. The OMPD library supports the debugger in getting the right information out of the runtime library.

Note that an OpenMP library does not necessarily need to implement OMPT to provide OMPD. We therefore propose to use a distinct namespace for each of the two interfaces and do not reuse type names from the OMPT interface for OMPD (even if they offer similar or identical semantics). For example, the header file ompd.h should not depend on ompt.h. Nevertheless, OpenMP runtime implementers may choose to implement a common internal state tracking for OMPT and OMPD.

### 3.3   The OMPD Architecture

As illustrated in Fig. 1, the OMPD library is loaded by the debugger. Whenever the debugger calls an OMPD API function, the library needs to get information from the OpenMP runtime library (e.g., reading values from the runtime library's memory). To maintain a clear separation of concerns, this functionality is not provided (i.e., reimplemented) by the OMPD library; rather the debugger exposes functions for the OMPD library to access the address space of the target process. As the debugger loads the OMPD library, the debugger registers these functions as callback functions with the OMPD library, so the library can access the functions. Using these debugger callback functions, the OMPD library accesses the memory space of the target process, which contains the needed OpenMP state information. It then uses its constructed knowledge of the runtime system and OpenMP objects to return the requested information to the debugger. Section 5 focuses on the set of callback functions defined for OMPD.

Special issues emerge when the debugger process runs on an architecture different from where the target application with the OpenMP runtime library is run. Examples for this situation include debugging on a system like IBM Blue Gene/Q or Cray systems, where the compute nodes have a different architecture from the front-end nodes, or in a hybrid system combining CPUs with accelerators such as GPUs. We will address some of these issues in Sects. 6 and 7.

## 4   Use Cases of OMPD

OpenMP-aware debuggers must enable a programmer to debug the program at the level of OpenMP programming abstractions. Tools must be capable of making the relevant program state visible without revealing unnecessary implementation details. OMPD must be designed and implemented to empower tools to serve this purpose. In this section, we present some of the capabilities that an OpenMP-aware debugger can provide and how OMPD can be used to help the debugger provide these capabilities. They are the representative use cases that cannot easily be supported without the help of a standard runtime debug interface.

### 4.1   OpenMP-Aware Stack Trace

One of the most important debugging views of a thread is its stack trace. For OpenMP programs, however, the raw stack trace of a thread has proven to be inadequate because it often contains too much detail on the underlying OpenMP runtime implementation while not fully capturing its high-level semantics.

Let's take an example of a basic construct in OpenMP: a parallel region. Listing 1.1 shows a minimal code example. For each thread that arrives at the begin of the parallel region, a team of threads are created, which will execute in parallel the block following the omp parallel pragma. Listing 1.2 shows how

```
1  {
2  // code before parallel region
3  #pragma omp parallel
4    {
5      // parallel region code
6    }
7  // code after parallel region
8  }
```

**Listing 1.1.** Parallel region is the basic OpenMP constuct

```
1  void parallel_region_block()
2  {
3    // parallel region code
4  }
5  [...]
6  {
7  // code before parallel region
8  omprt_run_parallel(parallel_region_block);
9  // code after parallel region
10 }
```

**Listing 1.2.** Simplified source-to-source translation of pragma omp parallel

this omp parallel pragma can be translated. This source-to-source translation represents how a compiler could realize the occurrence of this high-level OpenMP pragma into a low-level mechanism.

The function omprt_run_parallel in this example is implemented within the OpenMP runtime library and is responsible for creating the team of threads and for making these threads execute the function being passed as a function argument. This is a commonly used technique although each runtime may use a distinct function name for omprt_run_parallel: main._omp_fn is used in GNU OpenMP while .omp_microtask. is used in the Intel OpenMP Runtime.

For an execution of the code that has been translated according to this scheme, at least two distinct stack traces can result. The master thread, which is the thread that created the team, will have a stack trace shown in Listing 1.3. A stack trace for any other team member (or slave) thread is shown in Listing 1.4. Note that this is a simplified example for illustration purpose only. Depending on the runtime implementation, the stack trace might appear much more obfuscated.

There are two main problems with the representation shown in this example. First, the slave thread stack trace lacks the history about the parallel-region context. Listing 1.4 provides no clue that parallel_region_block originated

```
in parallel_region_block () from file:3
in omprt_internal () from libopenmp
in omprt_run_parallel () from libopenmp
in block () from file:8
```

**Listing 1.3.** Stack trace of the master thread pausing at a breakpoint on line 3 of Listing 1.2

```
in parallel_region_block () from file:3
in omprt_internal () from libopenmp
in start_thread () from libpthread
in clone () from libc
```

**Listing 1.4.** Stack trace for a team member pausing at a breakpoint on line 3 of Listing 1.2

```
in #omp parallel from file:5 @ T3
in block () from file:3 @ T1
```

**Listing 1.5.** Stack trace as it shoud be provided for team member thread 3

from the parallel region or called from within `block`. Even if the raw stack trace of a system-level thread includes a thread creation history, often this would not help either. Most runtime implementations manage thread pools and reuse threads across teams so the history information could be mixed up.

More importantly, from a programmer's perspective, this raw representation of a stack trace is inadequate: most programmers do not want to see all the runtime internal indirections in the stack trace. Instead, an abstraction at the conceptual level of the programmer's model, as shown in Listing 1.5, is more insightful. To provide such a high-level representation, however, the debugger needs to fetch the following information from a runtime debug interface: (1) the hierarchy of parallel contexts; (2) the entry and exit points of the runtime to unroll the parallel-region creation of the master thread and to remove runtime library functions from the stack trace.

For this purpose, OMPD provides the function `ompd_get_enclosing_parallel_handle`, which allows a debugger to unroll the hierarchy of parallel contexts. We will describe this OMPD function in details in Sect. 6, and a modification to the current specification, which we need to improve this workflow.

### 4.2  Stepping in and Out of a Parallel Region

Another common use case when working with a debugger is stepping through the execution, entering, and leaving functions. For the example in Listing 1.1 the user would expect to reach line 5 when stepping in, and line 7 when stepping out of the parallel region. This is the behavior when the code is compiled without OpenMP enabled. However, with OpenMP and without special handling by the debugger, a single step would end up in the OpenMP runtime library. Instead, the debugger must again hide the implementation details of the runtime library, moving forward to the reentry point in the application.

To enable this, OMPD must supply entry point information at the right place. When entering the parallel region, the region is not created yet, so the information is unavailable. The expectation is that, at some point between entering the runtime and leaving the runtime, the information about the entry point to the application is available. The debugger then needs to stop the execution of the target only when this information becomes available, extract the information and continue to the entry point. Thus, OMPD must provide breakpoint information to the debugger so that it can be notified via a breakpoint event only when the information is available. We will discuss in Sect. 6 how OMPD should provide the breakpoint information.

## 5   OMPD Callback Interface

Here we describe the callback functions that a debugger needs to provide to the OMPD library to enable the library to gather information from the application. We carefully reduce the set of callback functions to a minimum and discuss where we see issues with the set provided by the current OMPD document [4].

### 5.1   Functions for Operating System Interaction

A lesson learned from prior debugging libraries is that a library that is loaded by a debugger should not rely on system memory management, but instead use debugger-provided memory management. Using the primitive memory management callback functions `ompd_alloc_memory` and `ompd_free_memory`, the library gives the debugger control over its memory management. This allows the debugger to use its own custom implementation of memory management (e.g., malloc/free vs. new/delete).

Similarly it is best practice to use the debugger's output routines for output that is produced by the library. This way the debugger can redirect the output in its usual way, for example to `stderr` or to a log file. The callback function `ompd_print_string` provides a simple interface to print strings using the debugger's output stream.

The current OMPD proposal defines a function to resolve an error code to a string. As the error codes are specified in the interface, the string should be constant and well defined. Consequently, there is no reason why the error string should be provided by the debugger. Thus we propose to remove this callback function.

### 5.2   Resolving Structures for Target Architecture

In general, we cannot assume that the OMPD library and the OpenMP runtime operate on the same architecture. On the other hand, we do not want to see multiple OMPD libraries that are specialized built for each target architecture. For these reasons, the library needs a way to get the sizes of target types at runtime. The debugger knows about the target architecture, so we assume a debugger should be able to provide size information for primitive types that are defined in the C standard with an architecture and compiler dependent size. The OMPD callback function `ompd_sizeof_prim_ttype` is defined to return a vector of sizes for the types `char`, `short`, `int`, `long`, `long long`, and the pointer type `void *`.

The draft of the OMPD interface suggests functions to resolve application specific structs and functions to get sizes and offsets for structure elements. This approach is in general not applicable as most runtime libraries are delivered in a stripped format with removed type information. On the other hand, the information about structure sizes and member offsets cannot be calculated within the OMPD library when the application is executed on a different architecture. Further, an OMPD library should be able to handle OpenMP runtime libraries built for different architectures, so the OMPD library needs to get the information about structure sizes and offsets from the targeted runtime library.

The pthread debugging interface [7] does not use callbacks for resolving types either. The approach for the pthread library is to include all necessary sizes and offsets in the runtime library—they can be calculated during initialization of the library and can be fetched by reading the value of integer global symbols. For the pthread library, this is implemented using preprocessor macros to transparently provide and access the sizes when new symbols are added to structures. An OMPD library implementation might use a similar macro approach or just put all the needed offsets in the code. While our proposed change to OMPD does not specify *how* structure offsets and sizes are calculated by OMPD, it omits the callbacks for structure type and member lookups.

### 5.3   Access Application Memory

The API function `ompd_tsymbol_addr_lookup` is used to identify the base address for any basic symbol in the address space of the application respectively the OpenMP runtime library. We will discuss implications of the access to thread local or accelerator address space in Sect. 5.4.

Based on the address of a symbol and offsets for elements, the OMPD library will use the memory access functions `ompd_read_tmemory` and `ompd_write_tmemory` to read and write values in target memory. We propose to use an additional argument to specify the primitive type for the access and replace the size argument with a count argument that specifies the number of array items. With this information, the debugger might perform endianness conversion for a memory access.

The current OMPD callback interface suggests a function to convert the endianness of memory, which is read from the target memory before. This function misses an argument to specify the primitive type for the conversion or misses the argument to express the count of values. A reason for having a dedicated function for read and type conversion is that reading from the target memory can have a quite high latency. Reads of multiple values from a struct in the target memory would have the latency for every read. The debugger might cache the memory page and reduce the latency. On the other hand, we expect just the read of single values or vectors of values since this is the amount of information returned in the API functions.

We propose to specify the primitive type instead of a size, to give the debugger the possibility to distinguish pointer from integer values. The return type for pointer reads should be `ompd_taddr_t`.

### 5.4  Debugger's Context Argument

Most API and callback functions include a context pointer. For the debugger the context pointer identifies on which target process, thread, or address space the callback function is supposed to operate. The debugger provides the context pointer when calling an API function. The OMPD library must pass the context pointer back to the debugger as an argument to most of the callback functions.

In general, the OMPD library should not assume that a context pointer is valid after the API call returned. The state of the target application might change or the debugger might use the handle in another way. The key question is: where does an OpenMP implementation store the values to answer the OMPD API function call? Thus, what context is needed to answer the question?

For OMPT, the answer is simple: the API function is called in a thread context, thus the function must be answered with information available in this thread's context. For SMP systems, an OMPD library should be able to answer API function calls with knowledge from the corresponding thread. Thus, the debugger must provide the right thread context with each API function call.

The current version of the tools interface did not consider the target construct and the use of OpenMP with accelerators. The information might be stored on the thread that initiated the `target` region or in the thread on the accelerator. The debugger cannot know where the information is stored. Nevertheless, the debugger needs to provide the context pointer to interact with the right address space. OMPD needs a callback function to request the right context, so that for example, it can navigate from an accelerator context to a process context in search for accelerator-thread information.

## 6  OMPD API Function Specifications

In this section, we describe high-level problems we expect with the OMPD API specification as proposed in the first technical report on OMPT [4].

### 6.1  Providing Information on Compatible Runtime Library

The technical report does not specify a way to tell the debugger how to find a compatible OMPD library for a runtime library. It suggests that the OpenMP runtime might provide a list of filename strings that identify the locations of all the compatible OMPD library implementations. This approach will fail when we think of heterogeneous systems with running the application on one architecture and operation system, and debugging on another platform. For example, we cannot expect that the runtime library on the compute nodes would carry the OMPD path information on the login nodes. Our proposal is to give a unique name to each OMPD library in terms of the version and optional architecture information corresponding to the runtime library. The debugger would then attempt to find this OMPD library in the systems library path.

## 6.2   API Specification for Breakpoints

As described in Sect. 4.2, OMPD needs to provide breakpoint information for all the cases where control gets transferred to the OpenMP runtime, especially for entering and leaving parallel regions and tasks.

The current OMPD specification has a structure containing four pointers to code locations where the debugger might set breakpoints to get notified of the entering and leaving event of parallel regions and tasks. However, the four locations might be insufficient to cover general cases. A runtime library might have multiple implementations of handling parallel regions for various corner cases; or an OpenMP implementation does not outline the parallel region as shown in our Listing 1.2 but inlines the runtime code. In the latter case, a breakpoint for every parallel region is necessary.

Another fundamental issue is that this approach is not extensible. For example, there might be a need for a new breakpoint for the **target** construct. Changing this **struct**, however, will break compatibility between interface versions.

From the debugging perspective, it's more scalable to have a constant symbol for all parallel processes and threads than collecting addresses from all processes to place breakpoints.

For all these reasons, we propose to specify the names of dummy breakpoint functions, which need to be called by the OpenMP runtime to trigger the events. The dummy function is an empty function, but the runtime library needs to make sure that the compiler does not optimize out the function call. The debugger then sets the breakpoints to these functions within the runtime whenever needed:

```
1   void ompd_break_pre_parallel(){}
2   void ompd_break_post_parallel(){}
3   void ompd_break_pre_task(){}
4   void ompd_break_post_task(){}
```

Extending this list would not break compatibility with the previous interface.

## 6.3   Missing Function to Identify Master

When creating a stack trace as described in Sect. 4.1, the debugger needs to resolve the parent thread for a parallel region. The OpenMP standard has the function ompd_get_anchestor_thread_num to get the parent thread for the parallel region.

We propose to add the function ompd_get_anchestor_thread with a signature like in Listing 1.6 to the OMPD API. The signature is aligned to the API functions currently in the interface. We think, using the thread handle instead of the thread number is more consistent in case of the OMPD API.

## 7   Future Challenges

Although the OMPD API currently supports OpenMP 3.0 specification, when extended for the current 4.0 version of OpenMP, it will face a new set of challenges. In particular, the **target** construct whereby the application outsources

```
1  EXTERN ompd_rc_t ompd_get_anchestor_thread(
2      ompd_context_t *context, /* IN: debugger handle for the target */
3      ompd_parallel_handle_t parallel_handle, /* IN: handle for a parallel
           region */
4      ompd_thread_handle_t *parent_thread_handle /* OUT: handle for parent
           thread */
5  );
```

**Listing 1.6.** Proposed signature for `ompd_get_anchestor_thread`

its calculations to an accelerator will present technical challenges. In this section, we discuss how we prepare the current OMPD interface for the necessary future accelerators' support.

### 7.1    Context Pointer for Accelerators

In Sect. 5.4, we touched upon the topic of the meaning of a context pointer with respect to accelerators. We already discussed the need for a callback function to switch the context to the right location. When this callback is provided, an OMPD API function for an accelerator will first use this callback to switch the context from the accelerator thread context to the process thread context. As such switching would be necessary for each API call, it might be more efficient and cleaner to introduce a single API call thereby the OMPD library can specify the required context.

### 7.2    Addressing Accelerator Threads

Another potential issue is the specification of `ompd_osthread_handle`. The handle is important to build a mutual understanding on the low-level thread between the debugger and the OMPD library. The handle can be used when OMPD cannot determine whether or not a thread is an OpenMP thread by fetching a thread-local-storage (TLS) variable. On a runtime system that provides OpenMP thread personality through a TLS variable, we do not believe this handle is necessary. With accelerators, it is unlikely that all of the OpenMP runtimes will provide OpenMP personality via TLS. In many cases, the OpenMP thread running on an accelerator will be identified using the `osthread` handle. However, the current specification of the `osthread` handle will break compatibility if extended with accelerator support. Thus, we propose to use a flat struct that contains only an `int` to specify the kind of thread and an `uint64_t` for the specific thread handle. The values for the kinds of threads need to be defined in the interface.

### 7.3    Return Codes

All API and callback functions are specified to return an error code. The current specification provides one common set of error codes. If a callback function returns an error, and the API function fails, the debugger is interested in this error code. The set of error codes for callback functions should be a subset of error codes for API function calls.

# 8   Conclusions

In this paper, we described some of the issues that we experienced during implementing an OMPD library prototype. We proposed some changes to the OMPD technical report for both the callback and the API interface. The changes on the callback interface affect the ability of endianness conversion and type lookup. The proposed changes on the API interface concern the matching of compatible OpenMP runtime library and OMPD library versions and the specification of debugger breakpoints. We proposed to add a function to get the master thread in a parallel region. Finally, we highlighted certain aspects of the interface which will likely break compatibility between interface versions when extended for accelerator support in the future.

# References

1. Allinea Software: Allinea DDT. http://www.allinea.com/products/ddt. Accessed 16 May 2015
2. Cownie, J., Del Signore, J., de Supinski, B.R., Warren, K.: DMPL: an OpenMP DLL debugging interface. In: Voss, M.J. (ed.) WOMPAT 2003. LNCS, vol. 2716, pp. 137–146. Springer, Heidelberg (2003)
3. Cownie, J., Gropp, W.D.: A standard interface for debugger access to message queue information in MPI. In: Margalef, T., Dongarra, J., Luque, E. (eds.) PVM/MPI 1999. LNCS, vol. 1697, pp. 51–58. Springer, Heidelberg (1999)
4. Eichenberger, A., et al.: OMPT and OMPD: OpenMP Tools Application Programming Interfaces for Performance Analysis and Debugging. Technical report, OpenMP.org, May 2013. http://openmp.org/mp-documents/ompt-tr.pdf. Accessed 15 May 2015
5. Eichenberger, A., et al.: OpenMP Technical Report 2 on the OMPT Interface. Technical report, OpenMP.org, March 2014. http://openmp.org/mp-documents/ompt-tr2.pdf. Accessed 15 May 2015
6. Rogue Wave Software: TotalView® Graphical Debugger (2015). http://www.roguewave.com/products/totalview.aspx. Accessed 16 May 2015
7. Inc., Sun Microsystems. man pages section 3: Threads and realtime library functions. User documentation, May 2002. https://docs.oracle.com/cd/E19683-01/816-0216/816-0216.pdf. Accessed 15 May 2015

# False Sharing Detection in OpenMP Applications Using OMPT API

Millad Ghane, Abid M. Malik$^{(\boxtimes)}$, Barbara Chapman, and Ahmad Qawasmeh

Computer Science Department, University of Houston, Houston, TX, USA
{mghane2,ammalik3,bchapman,arqawasm}@uh.edu
http://www2.cs.uh.edu/~hpctools

**Abstract.** Writing a parallel shared memory application that scales well on the future multi-core processors is a challenging task. The contention among shared resources increases as the number of threads increases. This may cause a false sharing problem, which can degrade the performance of an application. OpenMP Tools (OMPT) [2]- a performance tool APIs for OpenMP- enables performance tools to gather useful performance related information from OpenMP applications with lower overhead. In this paper, we propose a light-weight false sharing detection technique for OpenMP programming model using OMPT. We show that the OMPT framework has the ability to detect unique patterns that can be used to build a quality detection model for false sharing in OpenMP programs. In this work, we treat the false sharing detection problem as a binary classification problem. We develop a set of OpenMP programs in which false sharing can be turned on and off. We run these programs both with and without false sharing and collect a set of hardware performance event counts using OMPT. We use the collected data to train a binary classifier. We test the trained classifier using the NAS Parallel Benchmark applications. Our experiments show that the trained classifier can detect false sharing cases with an average accuracy of around 90 %.

**Keywords:** OpenMP · OpenMP Tools API · False sharing · Machine learning · Performance events

## 1 Introduction

With the wide-spread deployment of multi-core processors, many applications are being modified to enable them to utilize the hardware fully. OpenMP is a popular choice for programming shared memory systems. OpenMP offers a simple means to parallelize a computation so that programmers can focus on their algorithm rather than on managing multiple threads. The simplicity of OpenMP also masks some potential problems from the programmer. One of them is a well-known false sharing problem [9]. Current false sharing detection techniques [9,11] rely on tracing the data movement across multiple cores. This requires heavy instrumentation and excessive data gathering and analysis. Thus,

© Springer International Publishing Switzerland 2015
C. Terboven et al. (Eds.): IWOMP 2015, LNCS 9342, pp. 102–114, 2015.
DOI: 10.1007/978-3-319-24595-9_8

they incur a high overhead. This high overhead limits the scalability of these tools which is important for the future exascale computing [11].

In this work, we treat false sharing as a binary classification problem and use a decision tree to build a classifier for detecting false sharing in a given OpenMP code. The performance of a classifier depends on the features that are used to represent instances. For false sharing, memory behaviour is important information. Using OMPT [2], we look for the unique memory signatures within the OpenMP parallel regions generated by the false sharing effect. We use supervised learning to train a decision tree classifier with a set of sample OpenMP kernels - with and without false sharing. We apply our trained classifier to the NAS Parallel Benchmark programs. In more than 90 % of the cases, our light-weight classifier correctly identified the false sharing problems.

Our contributions are as follows:

1. Use of OMPT API for collecting unique dynamic patterns that can be used to build cost models for various OpenMP performance issues. In this work, we use unique memory patterns to detect false sharing problems in OpenMP codes.
2. A light-weight machine learning based methodology that can detect false sharing in a given OpenMP code. The approach is independent of the compiler and OpenMP runtime library.
3. Our experimental results show that our approach is robust and has good accuracy in detecting false sharing in real OpenMP applications.

This paper is organized as follows: Sect. 2 gives an overview of the false sharing problem and motivation behind the work. Section 3 describes the related work in this area. Section 4 briefly talks about the OMPT framework. Section 5 gives our approach and methodology. Section 6 talks about our experimental results and analysis. Section 7 gives the conclusion and future line of action.

## 2    Motivation

When a core on a multicore processor modifies data that is currently shared by the other cores, the cache coherence mechanism has to invalidate all copies in the other cores. An attempt to read this data by another core, shortly after the modification, has to wait for the most recent value in order to guarantee the data consistency among cores. This degrades the performance. In false sharing, multiple processor cores access different data elements that reside in the same cache line. A write operation to a data element in the cache line will invalidate all the data in all copies of the cache line stored in other cores. A successive read by another core will incur a cache miss, and it will need to fetch the entire cache line from either the main memory or the updating core's private cache to make sure that it has the up-to-date version of the cache line. Poor scalability of multi-threaded programs can occur if the invalidation and subsequent read to the same cache line happen very frequently. How bad is the scalability? Fig. 1 shows a code snippet of an OpenMP program that exhibits the false sharing problem.

```
int *local_count = (int*)malloc(sizeof(int)*NUM_THREADS*PADDING);
int *vector = (int*)malloc(sizeof(int)*VECTOR_SIZE);
for(i=0;i<COUNT;i++)
{
#pragma omp parallel
    {
        int tid = omp_get_thread_num()*PADDING;
        if(tid < 0) tid = 0;

        #pragma omp for
        for(j = 0; j < VECTOR_SIZE; j++)
            local_count[tid] += vector[j]*2;

        #pragma omp master
        {
            int k;
            for(k = 0; k<NUM_THREADS; k++)
            result += local_count[k];
        }
    }
}
```

**Fig. 1.** OpenMP codelet with false sharing problem

**Table 1.** Execution time of OpenMP code from Fig. 1

| Code version | 1-thread | 2-thread | 4-thread | 8-thread |
|---|---|---|---|---|
| Without padding | 0.503 | 3.763 | 3.961 | 4.432 |
| With padding | 0.503 | 0.263 | 0.137 | 0.078 |

Its performance is inversely proportional to the number of threads as shown in Table 1 because of the false sharing effect. Mitigating the false sharing effect through the **PADDING** variable can lead to an astonishing 57× performance improvement for this code.

## 3   Related Work

Detecting false sharing accurately requires complete information on memory allocation and memory (read and write) operations from each thread. Previous work [3,13] has developed approaches for memory analysis that use memory tracing and cache simulation. The main drawback of this approach is within the memory tracing part, which can incur very large overheads. A memory shadowing technique was used [23] in an attempt to minimize the overhead of tracking the changes to the data state. Work by [12,13] also use information from the hardware performance monitoring unit to support performance analysis. HPCToolkit [12], and Memphis [15] use the sampling result from AMD IBS (Instruction-Based Sampling) to generate data centric information. Intel PTU (Performance Tuning Unit) [4] utilizes event-based sampling to identify the data address and function that is likely to experience false sharing. Several attempts have been made to eliminate the false sharing problem. For example, careful selection of runtime scheduling parameters, such as chunk size and chunk stride, when distributing loop iterations to threads has been used to prevent false sharing [1]. Proposed data layout optimization solutions include array padding [8] and memory alignment methods [20]. A runtime system called SHERIFF [10] performs both detection and elimination of false sharing in C/C++ applications parallelized using the Pthreads library. PREDATOR [11] is a predictive software-based false sharing detector that generalizes from a single execution to precisely predict false sharing that is latent in the current execution. DARWIN [22] introduces a dynamic framework to help application developers detect instances of false sharing as well as identify the data objects in an OpenMP code that cause the problem. Our work is similar to the work [7] which is specific to the Pthreads library. However, our approach is for OpenMP programming model and independent of the compiler and OpenMP runtime library.

## 4   OMPT- Application Programming Interface for Tools

OMPT is an Application Programming Interface (API) that enables portable tools to collect performance analysis information of OpenMP programs. The design of OMPT takes advantage of two prior OpenMP tools APIs: the POMP API [16] and the Collector API [6]; hence OMPT supports trace-based measurements and asynchronous sampling provided in the POMP API and the Collector API respectively, and specifies interfaces for applying blame shifting logic to resource synchronization. The OMPT interface can be implemented either entirely in the compiler or entirely in the OpenMP runtime system, as well as using a hybrid compiler/runtime option. Our implementation of the OMPT API was completely in the OpenMP runtime. Figure 2 describes the interaction of an OpenMP program with a performance analysis tool through the OMPT API.

The basic layout of the OMPT framework is given in Fig. 2(a). The design of the OMPT API consists of mutually exclusive states describing each OpenMP thread, defined callback events representing the entry and exit for commonly used pragmas, and a set of API calls that can be used by tools to acquire information from the OpenMP runtime. A performance tool requests notification of a specific event by passing the name of the event to be tracked as well as a callback function to be invoked by the OpenMP runtime each time the event occurs. Figure 2(b) gives an example of an execution of the OpenMP code shown in the figure, while OMPT is enabled. Two events, *begin_implicit_barrier* and

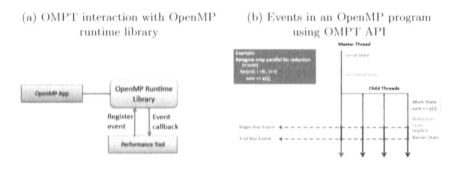

(a) OMPT interaction with OpenMP          (b) Events in an OpenMP program
    runtime library                            using OMPT API

**Fig. 2.** Working of the OMPT framework.

*end_implicit_barrier*, are encountered by each thread in the parallel region. The functionality of the callback functions, associated with these events, is controlled by a performance tool. OMPT also provides data structures, populated by the runtime, that include the parallel region identifier, wait identifiers and stack frame data. For a runtime to comply with the OMPT specification, state support is required along with the mandatory events. Please refer to the work proposed in [2] for complete and detailed information on the OMPT API.

## 5    Our Approach

This section describes our methodology in detail.

### 5.1    OMPT for Capturing Unique Patterns

A parallel region in an OpenMP program can be broken down into different events. For example, a typical OpenMP program may consist of creation of physical threads at the beginning of a parallel region, execution of the job by each thread, and threads waiting at barriers at the end of the parallel region. In Fig. 3(a), Point $A, B, C, D, E$ and $F$ represent OpenMP events that can be captured through OMPT API. Point $A$ is the *Fork Event*, and Point $F$ represents the *Join Event*. Point $B, C, D$ and $E$ can be any event depending upon the OpenMP directive being used to expose parallelism. Previous work does performance modeling by collecting information at the coarse level, i.e., using Point $A$ and $F$ [22]. However, OMPT allows a user to collect information at the fine level with respect to the intermediate events, i.e., using Point $B, C, D$ and $E$. The basic idea behind our approach is that if we can record certain features between the OpenMP events, they can be used as patterns to characterize an OpenMP kernel for various cost modeling techniques. The work [17] by our group shows that such signatures exist for OpenMP kernels for energy and power. Figure 3(b) gives an energy signature (rate of change of energy between the OpenMP events) of the Strassen application. We observe the same behavior in the OpenMP applications similar to the Strassen application. We use the same logic to find the memory signatures that detect false sharing in a given OpenMP program.

Cache invalidation is an important memory behavior. Many tools use it for false sharing detection [22]. Table 2 gives cache invalidation pattern for the code in Fig. 1. Point $A$ and $D$ represent *Fork* and *Join* events respectively. Point $B$ indicates the event when all the threads have been created. Point $C$ represents the event when the first thread hits the synchronization barrier. We observe that there is a pattern in the rate of cache invalidation between these events–*number of cache invalidation between the events divided by the time between the events*– in the OpenMP codes showing false sharing with the same number of threads. We did a statistical analysis on these patterns collected from OpenMP kernels. False sharing was injected manually. We observed low variance in values for these patterns.

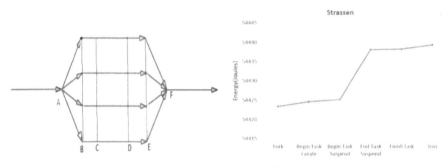

(a) Point $B, C, D$ and $E$ are fine level OpenMP events. Point $A$ and $F$ are coarse level OpenMP events.

(b) Energy pattern for the Strassen application using OMPT [17].

**Fig. 3.** OpenMP Execution Model

**Table 2.** Cache invalidation pattern for the code in Fig. 1

| Code version | 1-thread | 2-thread | 4-thread | 8-thread |
|---|---|---|---|---|
| time (sec.) | 0.503 | 3.763 | 3.961 | 4.432 |
| cache invalidation | 4,284 | 89,466 | 100,884 | 130,013 |
| rate of invalidation→ A and B | - | 2350 | 3561 | 5779 |
| rate of invalidation→ B and C | - | 23870 | 44445 | 57843 |
| rate of invalidation → C and D | - | 4350 | 5521 | 7722 |

## 5.2 Hardware Performance Information

We developed a tool to monitor a group of events within an OpenMP program using OMPT. The tool helps in capturing memory patterns for false sharing.

The data set between the OpenMP events is hardware performance information that is collected by running various OpenMP programs. In modern processors, Performance Monitoring Unit (PMU) can count hardware events per thread. The counter values can be retrieved using performance tools (e.g., Intel PTU, PERF) or APIs (e.g., libpfm, PAPI) [5]. For our work, we use the PAPI library to access these hardware performance counters and extract values. Tools like Intel PTU and PERF analyze the whole program and show the results for the lifetime of a given application. For our work, PAPI is a better choice as we are interested in studying the behavior of a specific section of a given OpenMP code and not the whole program. For information collection, we follow the following steps:

1. After creating physical threads, hardware counters for each event are initiated for each thread.
2. Each time an OpenMP event begins, the current values of related hardware counters are read and stored.

3. Each time an OpenMP event ends, the hardware counter values are read and stored again.
4. The difference in values are calculated and stored.

The above steps are repeated for each parallel region we encounter during our experimentation. All feature values are normalized to make it independent of data and program size. We talk about the data normalization approach in Sect. 6.

### 5.3    Binary Classifier for False Sharing Detection

The basic idea behind our prediction method is to build a binary classifier using a set of hardware performance features collected using OMPT. We collect the data using Source Code Repository (OmpSCR) [18]. OmpSCR consists of OpenMP applications written in C, C++, and Fortran. For our training purpose, we changed the source codes of OpenMP applications in a way that we can have two running modes; (1) with false sharing, and (2) without false sharing. For the false sharing mode, we change the directives and source code of a program to ensure cache invalidation and bad performance. For example, instead of accessing matrices in a row-wise order in a C source code, the for-loops are changed in a way that the accesses are made in a column-wise order. The work [7] adopts the same methodology for building a data set for detecting false sharing in PThread programs using machine learning. To ensure the generality of our approach, we change the input data size (big or small) and the number of threads $(4, 8, 16, 24)$. In short, we run a program in two running modes for each data set and number of threads. This helps us in generating training and testing cases for our classifiers. We build a separate classifier for each number of threads.

### 5.4    Feature Selection

Selecting the best features for a classifier is an important research topic in the area of artificial intelligence. An extensive research literature is available on optimal feature selection problem. In our case, features are hardware-dependent performance events. We have many hardware events for any platform, and not all of them are important or relevant to capture unique patterns for the false sharing detection problem. We collect 227 hardware features that can be categorised into five groups; features related to (1) resource stalls, (2) cache accesses (data and instruction cache), (3) memory accesses, (4) translation lookaside buffers, and (5) intra- and inter-processor communications. Our list contains all the potential events that can help in finding patterns related to false sharing. If all the hardware features are used to build a classifier, it may result in overfitting, i.e., you might have good accuracy during the training phase, but the trained classifier might perform poorly on unseen test cases. Therefore, it is important to select the best or optimal number of features that can give an acceptable performance during the training and testing phases. For our work, we use the $C4.5$ decision tree algorithm [14] for building a binary classifier. The algorithm uses *Information Gain (IG)* criterion to sort the available features. The feature with the highest IG value is selected as the root node. Features with low IG values are adjusted at the lower levels or depths of the tree, i.e., away from the root node. For our work, we first build a tree by using all the available hardware features. This results in a huge tree as the decision tree algorithm tries to improve its performance by reusing the features. We select the features up to certain level or depth to build a new smaller tree with better accuracy and precision. We discuss this in detail in Sect. 6.

# 6  Experimentation and Results

This section discusses our experimentation and results.

## 6.1  Training Phase

We use the J48 Decision Tree from the WEKA Package [14] to build four binary classifiers, i.e., one for each number of threads. The J48 tree is an implementation of the C4.5 decision tree. We use 64-bit Intel Xeon E5-2640 processor working at 2.5GHz on two sockets as our computing framework. Each socket has six cores with two hyper-threading. Therefore, we have a total of 24 threads. The machine has 32KB/core L1 cache, 256KB/core L2 cache, 13MB/CPU L3 cache (as the last level cache), 64GB memory as RAM, and ×86_64 GNU/Linux 3.10.14 as the operating system. We use the Intel Compiler Beta 16 suite as the infrastructure to compile applications. We use the Intel OpenMP Runtime Library that supports OMPT API.

The training data set is collected by running programs from the OmpSCR package. Each program is executed with different number of threads, data sizes and two false sharing modes. During the execution of each program, our tool collects data for all the parallel regions and stores it in a file to be processed after the program is done. The value of each feature is recorded between two consecutive OpenMP events. These values are combined together to build an instance for each program run. Let $V_{XY}$ be a vector that contains all feature values between the two consecutive OpenMP event $X$ and $Y$. For Fig. 3, $< V_{AB}, V_{BC}, V_{CD}, V_{DE}, V_{EF}, CLASS >$ is a complete feature vector for the OpenMP kernel between Point $A$ and $B$. The $CLASS$ variable is true when the kernel is run in the false sharing mode, and its value is false when it is run without the false sharing mode. When a program terminates, there is a file containing data for each number of threads that can be used to build a classifier for each number of threads.

**Limitation of Our Approach:** Nested parallelism is a common situation in real OpenMP applications. Consider a recursive function that uses OpenMP directives. If recursive call happens to be inside a parallel region, you are implicitly executing a parallel region inside another one. We are not covering this condition in this work. For nested parallelism, our tool collects the results for the top-level parallel region, and no performance monitoring is done for the children.

**Feature Selection:** Size of a feature vector plays a significant role in the precision/accuracy of a decision tree. Using more features may lead to a good accuracy but it may result in over-fitting with unseen test cases. Figure 4(a) shows the trade-off between accuracy and number features for the four threads classifier (to detect false sharing in OpenMP code with four number of threads). The horizontal axis represents number of levels traversed down in the decision tree from the root node. The vertical axis shows the precision of the decision tree using the number of features upto the corresponding level. The arrows in the figure represent number of unique features upto that specific level. For example, we have 90 % precision when we use 11 features upto level five of the decision tree. We have a total 227 number of features. With full features, we are able to achieve 95.4 % precision. We get the same accuracy by using 14 features that can be captured upto level six in the decision tree. Figure 4(b) gives the top 14 hardware features upto level six from our work.

**Normalization of Data:** Normalization of features' values plays an important part in defining the accuracy of a classifier. We use two types of normalization: (1) each feature value is divided by the total number of instructions in a given OpenMP kernel, and (2) manually discritization of the feature values. For the second type, we determine the range of each feature value and divide it into five classes. If the feature value is within 20 % of maximum value then it is in Class $A$. If the value is between 20 % and 40 % then it belongs to Class $B$. If the value is between 40 % and 60 %, then it is in Class $C$. If the value is between 60 % and 80 %, then it is in Class $D$. If the value is between 80 % and 100 %, then it is in Class $E$.

We use the 10-fold cross validation to test the performance of classifiers during the training phase. We use 21 and 84 hardware features with both normalization strategies. Figure 5 shows the results. Overall, the accuracy ranges from 50 % to 97 %. The classifiers for four and eight threads have better accuracy than 16 and 24 threads classifiers. Also, manual discritization strategy gives better performance.

## 6.2   Validation of the Approach

We validated our classifier using real applications. For our work, we use OpenMP benchmark applications from the NAS Parallel Benchmark [19]. The NAS Parallel Benchmark is a set of applications designed for performance evaluation of supercomputers. They are maintained by the NASA Advanced Supercomputing Division, and the source codes are developed in the C and Fortran languages. Programs in these benchmarks are highly optimized for less false sharing events. For our experimentation, we manually injected false sharing in the source.

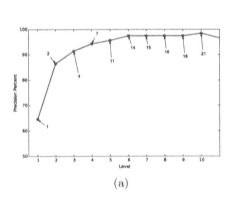

| # | Description |
|---|---|
| 1 | RESOURCE_STALLS:SB |
| 2 | L2_RQSTS:CODE_RD_HIT |
| 3 | PERF_COUNT_HW_STALLED_CYCLES_FRONTEND |
| 4 | RESOURCE_STALLS:LB |
| 5 | OFFCORE_RESPONSE_0:SNP_NOT_NEEDED |
| 6 | L2_RQSTS:ALL_DEMAND_RD_HIT |
| 7 | PERF_COUNT_HW_INSTRUCTIONS |
| 8 | LOAD_HIT_PRE:HW_PF |
| 9 | L2_RQSTS:PF_MISS |
| 10 | LD_BLOCKS:DATA_UNKNOWN |
| 11 | OFFCORE_RESPONSE_1:SNP_NONE |
| 12 | AGU_BYPASS_CANCEL |
| 13 | MEM_LOAD_UOPS_RETIRED:L3_MISS |
| 14 | L2_TRANS:ALL |

(a)                                        (b)

**Fig. 4.** (a) Performance trade-off for the four-thread classifier using different features at different levels. (b) Top 14 hardware features.

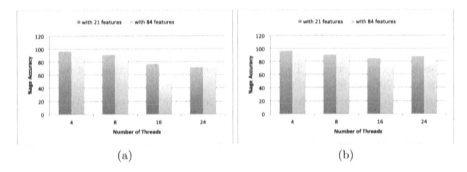

(a)                                        (b)

**Fig. 5.** Performance of the four classifiers. (a) Data set normalization using maximum number of instructions (b) Manual normalization of data set.

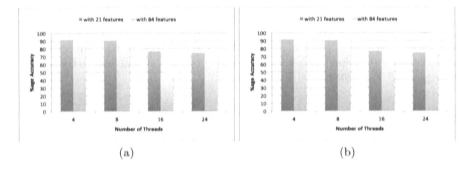

(a)                                        (b)

**Fig. 6.** Performance of the four classifiers using NAS Parallel. (a) Data set normalization using maximum number of instructions (b) Manual normalization of data set.

Figure 6 shows the accuracy of the four classifiers using unseen applications from the NAS Parallel Benchmark. The accuracy ranges from 49 % to 90 % for the classifiers trained on the dataset normalized using maximum instruction size. The accuracy ranges from 77 % to 90 % for the classifiers trained on the data that was discretized manually. The classifiers for four and eight number of threads give good accuracy as compared to the classifiers for 16 and 24 number of threads.

## 7    Conclusion and Future Work

OMPT - a performance tool API for OpenMP- enables performance tools to gather useful performance information from OpenMP applications with low overhead and to map this information back to a user-level view of applications. In this paper, we show that the OMPT API can be used to track unique patterns or signatures in OpenMP kernels. These unique patterns can be used to develop models for OpenMP performance issues. In this paper, we developed a detection model for false sharing by treating it as a binary classification problem. We used the unique signatures collected by OMPT to train a binary classifier. We used J48 decision tree learning approach that trained itself using the information collected using OMPT. We used mini-programs and OpenMP Source Code Repository (Omp-SCR) to build a classifier and tested it using the NAS Parallel Benchmark applications. The results showed that the accuracy of our model ranges from 70 % to 90 %.

For the future work, we are planning to refine the information. We are also planning to look into other classification and regression methods that can be used to build more robust and accurate detection models for false sharing. The main issue with the current dynamic false sharing tools is scalability. These tools use instrumentation technique to collect necessary information for prediction false sharing. This instrumentation phase is responsible for the major overhead. We believe that our machine learning approach can be used to select the appropriate parallel regions for instrumentation and can help in reducing the overhead.

**Acknowledgments.** The authors would like to thank their colleagues in the HPC-Tools group at the University of Houston for their extensive collaboration to make this work a reality. We would also like to thank Nagendra Kaushik Katta for proofreading the final draft of the paper. This work is supported by the National Science Foundation under grant CCF-1148052.

## References

1. Chow, J.-H., Sarkar, V.: False sharing elimination by selection of runtime scheduling parameters. In: Proceedings of the 1997 International Conference on Parallel Processing (1997)

2. Eichenberger, A., Mellor-Crummey, J., Schulz, M., Copty, N., DelSignore, J., Dietrich, R., et al.: OMPT and OMPD: OpenMP tools application programming interfaces for performance analysis and debugging. In: International Workshop on OpenMP (IWOMP 2013) (2013)
3. Gunther, S.M., Weidendorfer, J.: Assessing cache false sharing effects by dynamic binary instrumentation. In: Proceedings of the Workshop on Binary Instrumentation and Applications (WBIA 2009), New York (2009)
4. Intel Corporation.: Avoiding and Identifying False Sharing Among Threads (2010)
5. Intel Corporation.: Intel Performance Tuning Utility 4.0 User Guide (2011)
6. Itzkowitz, M., Mazurov, O., Copty, N., Lin, Y.: An OpenMP runtime API for profiling. Sun Microsystems, Inc., OpenMP ARB White Paper. http://www.compunity.org/futures/omp-api.html
7. Jayasena, S., Amarasinghe, S., Abeyweera, A., Amarasinghe, G., De Silva, H., Rathnayake, S., Meng, X., Liu, Y.: Detection of false sharing using machine learning. In: Proceedings of the International Conference on High Performance Computing, Networking, Storage and Analysis (SC 2013), New York (2013)
8. Jeremiassen, T.E., Eggers, S.J.: Reducing false sharing on shared memory multiprocessors through compile time data transformations. In: SIGPLAN (1995)
9. Liu, T., Berger, E.: SHERIFF: precise detection and automatic mitigation of false sharing. In: Proceedings of the 2011 ACM International Conference on Object Oriented Programming Systems Languages and Applications, pp. 3–18 (2011)
10. Liu, T., Berger, E.: Sheriff: Detecting and Eliminating False Sharing. Technical report, University of Massachusetts, Amherst, Massachusetts (2010)
11. Liu, T., Tian, C., Hu, Z., Berger, E: PREDATOR: predictive false sharing detection. In: Proceedings of the 19th ACM SIGPLAN Symposium on Principles and Practice of Parallel Programming, New York (2014)
12. Liu, X., Mellor-Crummey, J.: Pinpointing data locality problems using datacentric analysis. In: 2011 9th Annual IEEE/ACM International Symposium on Code Generation and Optimization (CGO), pp. 171–180 (2011)
13. Marathe, J., Mueller, F., de Supinski, B.R.: Analysis of cache-coherence bottlenecks with hybrid hardware/software techniques. ACM Trans. Archit. Code Optim. (TACO) **3**, 390–423 (2006). New York
14. Hall, M., Frank, E., Holmes, G., Pfahringer, B., Reutemann, P., Witten, I.H.: The WEKA data mining software: an update. SIGKDD Explor. **11**(1), 10–18 (2009)
15. McCurdy, C., Vetter, J.: Memphis: finding and fixing numa-related performance problems on multi-core platforms. In: 2010 IEEE International Symposium on Performance Analysis of Systems Software (ISPASS), pp. 87–96 (2010)
16. Mohr, B., Malony, A.D., Hoppe, H.-C., Schlimbach, F., Haab, G., Hoeflinger, J., Shah, S.: A performance monitoring interface for OpenMP. In: Proceedings of the Fourth European Workshop on OpenMP, Rome, Italy (2002)
17. Nandamuri, A., Malik, A.M., Qawasmeh, A., Chapman, B.M.: Power and energy footprint of openMP programs using OpenMP runtime API. In: Proceedings of the 2nd International Workshop on Energy Efficient Supercomputing (E2SC 2014), pp. 79–88. IEEE Press, Piscataway (2014)
18. OpenMP Source Code Repository. http://www.pcg.ull.es/ompscr/
19. NAS Parallel Benchmark Applications. http://www.nas.nasa.gov/publications/npb.html#url
20. Torrellas, J., Lam, H.S., Hennessy, J.L.: False sharing and spatial locality in multiprocessor caches. IEEE Trans. Comput. **43**, 651–663 (1994)
21. Weaver, V.: The Unofficial Linux Perf Events Web-Page (2013). http://web.eece.maine.edu/vweaver/projects/perf_events/

22. Wicaksono, B., Tolubaeva, M., Chapman, B.: Detecting false sharing in OpenMP applications using the DARWIN framework. In: Proceedings of International Workshop on Languages and Compilers for Parallel Computing (2011)
23. Zhao, Q., Koh, D., Raza, S., Bruening, D., Wong, W., Amarasinghe, S.: Dynamic cache contention detection in multi-threaded applications. In: Proceedings of the 7th ACM SIGPLAN/SIGOPS International Conference on Virtual Execution Environments (VEE 2011), pp. 27–38 (2011)

# Exception Handling with OpenMP
# in Object-Oriented Languages

Xing Fan[✉], Mostafa Mehrabi, Oliver Sinnen, and Nasser Giacaman

Department of Electrical and Computer Engineering, The University of Auckland,
Auckland, New Zealand
fxin927@aucklanduni.ac.nz

**Abstract.** OpenMP has become increasingly prevalent due to the simplicity it offers to elegantly and incrementally introduce parallelism. However, it still lacks some high-level language features that are essential in object-oriented programming. One such mechanism is that of exception handling. In languages such as Java, the concept of exception handling has been an integral aspect to the language since the first release. For OpenMP to be truly embraced within this object-oriented community, essential object-oriented concepts such as exception handling need to be given some attention. The official OpenMP standard has little specification on error recovery, as the challenges of supporting exception-based error recovery in OpenMP extends to both the semantic specifications and related runtime support. This paper proposes a systematic mechanism for exception handling with the co-use of OpenMP directives, which is based on a Java implementation of OpenMP. The concept of exception handling with OpenMP directives has been formalized and categorized. Hand in hand with this exception handling proposal, a flexible approach to thread cancellation is also proposed (as an extension on OpenMP directives) that supports this exception handling within parallel execution. The runtime support and its implementation are discussed. The evaluation shows that while there is no prominent overhead introduced, the new approach provides a more elegant coding style which increases the parallel development efficiency and software robustness.

## 1   Introduction

Even though the evolution of OpenMP has made it increasingly comprehensive for shared-memory applications, the framework still has some way to go before it is widely used for general software development. In particular, the current OpenMP standard lacks support for essential programming features such as mechanisms for error recovery. As a matter of fact, OpenMP is mainly used for compute-intensive applications that are deterministic and less error-prone, such as batch-like, or numerical and scientific computations. For other kinds of parallel programs (such as server-side applications [10], games [7], desktop and mobile platform software [13]), which are typically interaction-based, handling unexpected situations is essential for robustness.

© Springer International Publishing Switzerland 2015
C. Terboven et al. (Eds.): IWOMP 2015, LNCS 9342, pp. 115–129, 2015.
DOI: 10.1007/978-3-319-24595-9_9

Exception handling is an error recovery mechanism which enables programs to anticipate and recover from abnormal situations and consequently avoid any abrupt termination of applications. Compared with other error handling approaches (e.g. error code based, callback function based [4]), exception-based recovery is more compliant with object-oriented principles, due to its support for user-defined exceptions. In object-oriented languages, useful information about an error is typically stored in an instance of an Exception class. Moreover, it is lexically clearer and more flexible to directly surround code that could potentially throw exceptions in *try-catch-finally* blocks. OpenMP does not provide rich support for object-oriented exception handling in parallel environments. If anything, considering that a parallelized application is likely to introduce more potential problems than that in a sequential application, this lack of support for exception handling makes it especially difficult to write robust object-oriented parallel code using the OpenMP approach. This is especially important to recognize in an object-oriented language such as Java, where exception handling is an integral part of the language. As Android and multi-core mobile devices continue their dominance, the relevance of parallel programming is evermore relevant and presents another opportunity for OpenMP to embrace this community of developers.

In this paper, an in-depth examination for exception handling in an OpenMP environment has been proposed. The contributions of this paper can be divided into three parts. First, the categorization and formalization of object-oriented exception handling in OpenMP parallel regions. Second, the concept of flexible thread cancellation is proposed, which provides a better approach for managing the control flow of a program, as well as facilitating exception handling on threads. Finally, the usability and performance are evaluated through an OpenMP implementation for Java [12].

## 2   Related Work

Although the official OpenMP standard does not have a comprehensive error handling mechanism at the moment, several error handling models have been proposed for OpenMP. Gatlin [4] initially classifies error handling into three categories based on exception, callback function and error-code. Exception-based error handling is widely used in object-oriented languages such as C++ and Java, but combining this mechanism with parallelization approaches in OpenMP has not been studied in depth so far. On the contrary, error recovery models that are based on callback functions are widely used in different domains, but they seem to be too complicated to use. Low level languages such as C and Fortran mainly use this approach to handle errors, as these languages lack proper exception handling mechanisms. For this category, Duran et al. [3] introduces a model for error recovery in OpenMP that is based on callback functions. The model proposes a mechanism for registering callback functions using the onerror clause to specify a function that is called in case of a specific error. Moreover, Wong et al. [14] discussed the necessity of error-handling models in OpenMP. However they argue that the model must support exception-unaware languages (e.g. C and Fortran), thus their model does not include the semantics of exception throwing and *try-catch* blocks.

## 3  Problem Overview

In this section, we itemize the obstacles towards efficient and robust exception handling programming with the help of some code snippet examples.

### 3.1  Current Situation

Although it may be possible to handle exceptions thrown within OpenMP parallel regions, it is rather counter-intuitive, demanding and confusing to correctly implement since the semantics are evaded in the OpenMP standard. According to the specifications of OpenMP 4.0 [1], when an exception is thrown inside a parallel region, the only restriction is that the exception should be caught and handled within the same region and by the same thread. Therefore, a parallel region surrounded by a *try-catch* block does not comply with OpenMP specifications (see Fig. 1a). Moreover, we also cannot guarantee that a *try-catch* block within a parallel region will function as it is expected, due to some semantic defects within OpenMP specifications [8]. For example, Fig. 1b shows a *try-catch* block embedded inside an OpenMP parallel region. Although this syntax may get through an OpenMP compiler, it has a potential runtime bug. In this particular case, when an exception occurs before the barrier, the control flow of the encountering thread will jump to the catch block. This jump will skip the barrier directive, while the other threads that do not encounter an exception end up halting indefinitely at the barrier synchronization. This is similar to the reason why OpenMP standard strictly follows the Single Entry, Single Exit (SESE) principle as [8] indicated. Although there are already some static analysis techniques proposed such as [9] which is designed for checking the validation of barriers, it still lacks the consideration onto exception handling semantics.

### 3.2  Problem Definition

The current situation of using *try-catch* blocks suggests that programmers encounter difficulties due to programming inconveniences and pitfalls of OpenMP error handling. Lacking a standard and consistent error handling mechanism in OpenMP makes programmers struggle in writing robust and efficient OpenMP code. The major consequence of the lack of exception handling mechanisms in OpenMP hinders the widespread use of OpenMP in object-oriented languages, since there is no clear OpenMP conformity with contemporary software design paradigms. Generally, error handling in OpenMP needs to be improved in three major aspects: (a) The semantics for checking whether catching an exception can cause other problems. (b) Convenient and flexible mechanisms for controlling or canceling execution within parallel environments. (c) A reliable runtime support for the default behavior of parallel executions when they encounter uncaught exceptions.

```
try{                                   #pragma omp parallel{
  #pragma omp parallel for               try{
  for (int i=0; i<4; i++)                  phase1_cause_exception();
  {                                        #pragma omp barrier
    cause_exception();                     phase2();
  }                                      }catch(Exception e){
}catch(Exception e){                       //handling exception
  //handling exception                   }
}                                      }
```

(a)                                    (b)

Fig. 1. (a) *Try-catch* mechanism that does not syntactically and semantically conform with the OpenMP specification; (b) Syntactically conforms with OpenMP specification, but semantically it has a defect.

## 4  Cancellations

Before discussing exception handling within OpenMP parallel regions, it is help-ful to discuss the significance of cancellation in a parallel context. In sequential programming, canceling execution at a certain part in the code is easily achieved by using the supported programming language keywords (e.g., **break** to cancel a loop, or **return** to cancel execution within a method). Because there is only one control flow, cancellation in sequential code simply means canceling the current scope of execution. In an OpenMP parallel region, such a cancellation keyword is lexically in a sequential program but semantically executing in par-allel (the OpenMP philosophy that the original sequential code is intact when the OpenMP compiler directives are ignored). In this parallel context, does a cancellation indicate the termination for a single thread in the parallel region (i.e. the one encountering the cancellation), or it would it indicate termination of all threads participating within the current parallel environment? Therefore, when converting sequential code to parallel code, extra directives are needed to convey the programmer's intentions. This type of directive should be flexible and easy enough to express programming logic, while still respecting the OpenMP approach of maintaining lexically sequential code.

OpenMP 4.0 standard has added some directives related to region cancella-tion [1]. According to the cancel directive, programmers are allowed to cancel the innermost parallel/for/sections/taskgroup region where the cancel directive appears. This specification provides an approach to stop execution of a par-allel region, with the combination of cancellation point directive, which allows for user-defined cancellation points. The net effect of this directive is that it results in stopping the entire parallel execution. The cancel directive lacks the ability to stop a single thread locally without interfering with the execution of other threads. This would be useful when a thread encounters an exception and cannot recover from it, so it may be desirable to only stop execution of that cur-rent thread (since it no longer needs to continue its assigned workload), without canceling the entire parallel execution. Using a break-statement goes against

OpenMP standards (since it is oblivious to OpenMP barriers). The status quo makes it difficult for programmers to specify the control flow of a parallel execution, and confines the use of exception handling when exceptions happen in a parallel execution.

*Cancellation directive.* In order to support a more flexible thread canceling mechanism, and to better support the OpenMP exception handling model, the official cancel directive is extended. This extension is achieved by adding a *thread-affiliate-clause*, which can be global, indicating the cancellation of the entire thread group (the current OpenMP definition), or local, merely indicating the cancellation for the current thread encountering the directive. The optional if clause, signaling that the cancellation is active only when the condition inside the if statement holds true, remains unchanged. Figure 2 demonstrates the extended syntax of the cancel directive. We however propose an additional optional clause, neglect_exception, for constructs parallel, for, sections and taskgroup. This is under the consideration for the simplification of parallel exception handling, which will be explained in Sect. 5.3.

---

**#pragma omp cancel** *construct-type-clause thread-affiliate-clause [if-clause] [throw-clause]*
where *construct-type-clause* is one of the following:
    **parallel, sections, for, taskgroup**
and *thread-affiliate-clause* is one of the following:
    **global, local**
and *if-clause* is:
    **if**(*scalar-expression*)

**Fig. 2.** Extended cancellation directive

The extended cancel directive expands the control over a group of threads. That is, by combining different clauses, programmers can express customized behaviors of the parallel control flow. Figure 3 visualizes the cancel directive with the combinations of different clauses. Black nodes indicate the cancellation triggering points. A thread with black node is the cancellation triggering thread. If a thread encounters a cancellation directive with the local property, it will only stop executing the innermost OpenMP construct thread-locally. Afterwards, the thread resumes when all other threads within the parallel execution reach the next statement following the canceled region. On the other hand, if the cancellation is a global cancellation, the triggering thread will set a global cancellation flag. Other threads check this cancellation flag at next cancellation checking points (indicated by white nodes). Afterwards, all threads resume from the next statement after the cancellation region.

The cancel directive can be used for two purposes. First, programmers can explicitly use this directive to express parallel control flow. Second, it works as an implicit operation when an exception happens within a parallel execution. The latter is explained in more detail in Sect. 5.3.

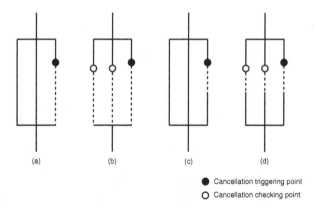

  (a)     (b)     (c)     (d)

● Cancellation triggering point
○ Cancellation checking point

**Fig. 3. Different uses of cancel directive.** (a) cancel parallel local Only single thread quits the innermost parallel region; (b) cancel parallel global Entire thread group quits current parallel region; (c) cancel for local Single thread quits current worksharing for-loop, but continues when other threads finish this for-loop iteration; (d) cancel for global All threads quit current worksharing for-loop and continue with following statement.

## 5 Exception Handling

In this section we demonstrate the exception handling model. In order to ensure the robustness and flexibility, several limitations and extensions are discussed. The discussion is categorized into two parts: Local exception handling and global exception handling.

### 5.1 Overview of Categorization

In proposing a comprehensive model for parallel exception handling, we discuss different categories of exception handling in order to set up a standard for using exception handling with OpenMP directives to prevent unexpected execution behaviors. There are two kinds of exception handling scenarios that would be useful in an OpenMP environment. One involves handling exceptions within a single thread, while the other involves exception handling across a group of threads:

**Local Exception Handling:** This means an exception is handled by the same thread that threw the exception in the parallel region. A successful local handling must ensure that the procedure of error recovery does not influence with the execution of other threads. A local exception handling *try-catch* block does not surround the entire parallel region, but is rather handled internally within the parallel region.

**Global Exception Handling:** A global exception means an exception potentially influences the entire parallel region. If an exception in a parallel region is not caught by its throwing thread, or handling this exception causes another exception to be thrown, then the exception will affect the entire parallel execution. The OpenMP standard does not categorize this behavior, since it insists it should never occur. Lexically, the *try-catch* block for handling of these types of exceptions would surround the parallel region in which the exception might happen. An uncaught global exception will make the entire parallel execution stop. If this exception is still not caught afterwards, the entire program will stop as well.

## 5.2   Local Exception Handling

Local exception handling ensures that errors are recovered inside their local threads, and the local threads continue working/progressing. In order to avoid an unexpected execution behavior (examples in Sect. 3.1), this type of handling requires two conditions to be met: (a) Any potential exception inside a *try-catch* block does not interfere with other thread's execution; (b) Any operation inside a *catch/finally* block does not affect the entire parallel region's progress.

Technically, as a legal local exception handling, the entire exception handling region requires there is no *OpenMP synchronization point* present, in either of the *try-catch* or *finally* blocks. Furthermore, it should be ensured that (a) there is no exception re-throwing or (b) if exception re-throwing happens, the re-thrown exceptions need to be handled by another legal local handling.

With regards to parallel synchronization points in the parallel region, usually represented by various OpenMP directives, this can be categorized into two groups:

**Control-flow Synchronization Point:** A control-flow synchronization point is defined as a point where a thread cannot evolve until it is synchronized with other threads in the corresponding parallel region. A typical control-flow synchronization point is the barrier directive. Other directives, may contain an implicit barrier if the nowait clause is not specified. Those directives include for, section and single. If there is a control-flow synchronization point inside the *try* block, there is a risk of not being reached by one of the threads when this thread encounters an exception.

**Thread-Context Switching Boundary:** The attribute of source code changes when encountering a thread-context switching boundary. In an OpenMP parallel region, there are mainly three types of source code regions: (a) Code regions to be executed by every thread at the same time; (b) Code regions to be executed only by one specified thread (e.g. master) or non-specified thread (e.g. single); (c) Code regions to be executed by every thread, but the executions need serialization (e.g. critical). Thread-context switching boundary works as a dividing line to change this thread-context property. Notice sometimes a control-flow synchronization point is also a thread-context switching boundary, such as for. If a *try* block contains several OpenMP code blocks which represent different thread-contexts, it is easy to cause an ambiguous exception handling semantic and unexpected runtime behavior. So avoiding thread-context switching boundaries inside a local exception handling *try-catch* block is a better programming practice.

According to this limitation, a robust compiler should be able to throw a warning to inform programmers if the OpenMP source code does not conform with local exception handling rules. This warning reminds programmers to double check the code whether the exception handling could cause any side effect.

### 5.3   Global Exception Handling

Global exception means an exception is emitted from a parallel region and it is not handled thread-locally. It indicates an unexpected behavior occurred and escaped from within the parallel execution. If this exception is not handled by its local thread, this exception will be forwarded to the parallel region. Because a thread-locally-uncaught exception could influence the correctness of parallel execution, this exception changes its property and becomes a global exception and handling this type of exception is defined as global exception handling.

**Global Exception Catch Procedure.** In a sequential program, if an exception happens, it needs to be handled by the encountering thread. If the thread cannot find a matching catch block, the program will stop with throwing an unhandled exception. However, in parallel execution, if an exception happens in a thread, it is not always necessary to stop the parallel execution. Programmers can specify the behavior when an exception happens. That is, to handle it by the encountering thread, to expose it to the parallel environment, or to stop the encountering thread only.

Figure 4 shows the flowchart for the case of an exception within an OpenMP parallel execution. When a parallel program is executing, if it encounters an exception, it first checks whether a local exception handler is defined. If yes, this exception will be handled using the thread-local approach, and then the encountering thread continues processing. Notice that it is possible to throw another exception from the handling code (i.e. *catch* or *finally* block), in which case the program continues looking for another local handler until the exception cannot be handled locally. If a thread encounters an exception and this exception is not handled locally, the default behavior will be `cancel parallel global`, which triggers the cancellation of that parallel region. In another situation a program may encounter a `cancel` directive. As discussed in Sect. 4 (Cancellation directive), `cancel` directives can also be used for deliberate control-flow stops. Therefore, execution stops due to OpenMP cancellation are not always regarded as exceptions.

**Exception Neglecting.** In some cases, it is not desirable to stop the entire parallel processing once an exception is exposed to the parallel environment. Programmers may want the remaining threads keep executing even if one or more threads fail within the thread group. This can be achieved by explicitly declaring a local cancellation at the end of local exception handling code to make the encountering thread stop locally. However, If there is no other recovery operations within the handling code, the semantic can be simplified by using

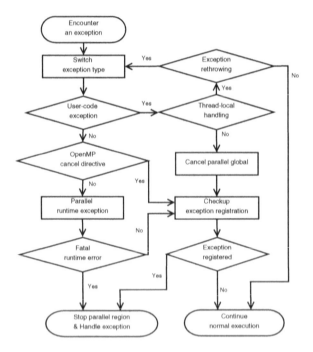

**Fig. 4.** Flowchart of exception handling within OpenMP parallel region

neglect_exception clause after the corresponding OpenMP construct. When an exception happens and it is registered by the exception neglecting mechanism, it will not trigger the parallel or worksharing execution cancellation. Instead, only the encountering thread will stop. In the meanwhile, since it is possible that some works distributed by the stopping thread is not finished, for the compensation, a dynamic work redistribution is run when the thread stopping happens.

Figure 5c shows a code example which uses the neglect_exception clause to simplify the programming logic. Inside the parallel region, an infinite loop is executed. For each loop iteration, firstly one of the thread inside thread group collects requests from the network sockets. Afterwards, a series of requested are processed by the thread group. During the worksharing process, exceptions could happen. But only some types of the exception are handled thread-locally. Other unexpected exceptions (e.g. OutOfMemoryException) could still escape from the local thread. Under this circumstance, using neglect_exception clause followed by a more general exception type (Exception) enables the parallel execution ignore the exceptions which are exposed to the parallel environment. After an automatic work redistribution (if necessary), the parallel execution keeps processing.

**Source Code Simplification.** Due to the lack of specifications for parallel exception handling, a conventional traverse-parallel-region exception handling solution would have to use predefined references (or pointers) to store the exceptions that happen in a parallel region. That is, programmers have to manually store exceptions that could possibly occur in a parallel region, and then invoke a global cancellation directive to stop the parallel execution when handling that exception. Thus, a parallel region must be followed by a series of inspections to test whether any of the specified exceptions have happened. The source code for such a manual approach is quickly tainted with multiple *try-catch* blocks, especially when programmers want to catch several potential exceptions in a parallel region.

```
ExceptionA * ea = null;
ExceptionB * eb = null;
#pragma omp parallel shared (ea, eb){
#pragma omp for
  for(int i=0; i<N; i++){
    try {
      may_cause_ExceptionA();
    }catch (ExceptionA *e){
      #pragma omp critical{
        ea = e;
      #pragma omp cancel parallel
      }
    }
  }
}
try {
  may_cause_ExceptionB();
}catch (ExceptionB *e){
  #pragma omp atomic write
    eb = e;
  #pragma omp cancel parallel
}
foo();
} //end of parallel region
if(ea){
  //handle exceptionA if happens
}
if(eb){
  //handle exceptionB if happens
}
```
(a)

```
try {
  #pragma omp parallel
  {
    #pragma omp for
      for(int i=0; i<N; i++){
        may_cause_ExceptionA();
      }
    may_cause_ExceptionB();
    foo();
  } //end of parallel region
} catch (ExceptionA *e){
  //handle exceptionA
} catch (ExceptionB *e){
  //handle exceptionB
}
```
(b)

```
#pragma omp parallel
for(;;){
  #pragma omp single
    requests = collect_requests();
  #pragma omp for
  \neglect_exception(Exception)
  for(int i=0; i<requests.size(); i++){
    try {
      data = process_request(requests[i]);
    } catch(DataNonconformityException *e){
      data = response.NONCONF;
    }
    response[i] = data;
  }
  #pragma omp single
  send_responses(responses);
}
```
(c)

**Fig. 5.** Source code complexity comparison between (a) without and (b) with exception runtime support; (c) A demo code using neglect_exception clause to simplify the recovery procedure when uncaught exception happens inside a parallel region.

The source code can be easily simplified using new exception handling semantics with OpenMP directives. *Try-catch* block can directly surround a parallel region without code re-factoring (See Fig. 5). The compiler source-to-source generation and runtime support will do all the routines in the background. This improvement makes the source code more elegant and more compliant with object-oriented design patterns.

Using exception neglecting mechanism also enables programmers to easily sustain the continuation of parallel processing when certain thread inside the thread group fails. Because remedy operations are automatically done by the underlying runtime support, programmers liberate from arduous works of converting sequential code to robust parallel code.

## 6   Implementation

This section discusses about the implementation of enhanced exception handling support. The aforementioned concepts and proposals are implemented through a source-to-source compiler and its runtime support. This section mainly explains some noticeable issues with regard to the runtime implementation.

## 6.1   Adaptable Synchronization Barrier

The extended OpenMP cancellation directive allows the cancellation of single thread without stopping the entire parallel execution. Since a stopped thread could influence the following synchronization procedure of other remaining threads, it requires an on-the-fly thread consensus number adjustment when a local thread cancellation happens.

The requirement is achieved by implementing an adaptable synchronization barrier. Different from traditional cyclic barrier, adaptable barrier has the extra interfaces `decreaseConsensus()` and `increaseConsensus()` which enables the barrier to readjust consensus number when a thread quits or joins the thread group. Every thread local cancellation invokes `decreaseConsensus()` before real thread stopping, and the synchronization consensus number decreases from $n$ to $n - 1$. The same, if a canceled thread rejoin the thread group, the interface `increaseConsensus()` is invoked and the synchronization consensus number related to this thread group increased from $n$ to $n + 1$.

## 6.2   Dynamic Work Redistribution

As mentioned before, in order to ensure all remaining worksharing chunks are processed if a thread cancels its works in an OpenMP worksharing group, work redistribution is required. We adopt the similar way as Parallel Iterator [5] does. More specifically, if a thread quits from a worksharing execution, all its remaining allocated iterations are released. If there are still other threads working, then they share these remaining iterations (after those threads complete their normal iterations) using a dynamic schedule with chunk size 1.

If multiple threads attempt to exit from a local cancellation, then all of them will succeed except the last thread. Because if there is only one thread, the worksharing construct is at risk of half finish. Under this circumstance, if the last thread cancels from the parallel execution, an extra exception is thrown out to indicate the total fail of parallel execution.

## 6.3   Exception from Synchronization Regions

There is the possibility that an exception thrown from a critical region. A legal local-exception handling could be available to catch it, as long as it does not break the rule as Sect. 5.2 discussed. Otherwise, this exception exposes to the parallel region. In order to avoid a deadlock, from the implementation level, it should release the lock resource when the exception escapes from the critical region. In the Java implementation, a finally block is sufficient to ensure this, which always makes the lock to be released when quitting the critical region. Whereas considering the implementation for C++, which does not support finally keyword, RAII [11] is the suitable technique to ensure the life cycle of lock resources to be confined inside a certain lexical scope.

## 6.4   Global Exception Throwing

Different from exception handling in sequential execution, in a parallel environment, two or more exceptions may happen at the same time. If those exceptions are not caught thread-locally, then multiple exceptions are exposed to the parallel region. Considering one global exceptions is thrown from one thread, but before other threads reach the nearest cancellation points, another global exception happens from another thread. If there is no consensus about which global exception should be handled, the entire parallel environment is in the risk of inconsistency and unexpected behavior may happen.

So in order to ensure the exception handling consistency, it is important to guarantee that when multiple global exceptions happen, all the exception exposures to the parallel region should be linear [6] and immediately visible to any other threads within the thread group. This is implemented by endowing each parallel region an exception slot, on which the data can be modified using the compare-and-set (CAS) operation. If more than one threads throw exceptions at the same time, the CAS operation ensures that only one exception is set to the exception slot. The thread which succeeds on CAS operation will trigger the cancellation flag and all other threads which fail to register their exceptions will only end in thread cancellations.

## 7   Evaluation

In this section, we evaluate the new exception handling mechanism in the new OpenMP version that we have implemented for Java.

### 7.1   Usability

According to aforesaid concepts, the compiler does the semantic check to see whether programmers made a legal local thread exception handling in a parallel region. This could prevent the unexpected bugs such as the example shown in Fig. 1b. Also, the runtime support ensures that even if an exception is not handled inside the parallel region, the execution will stop the entire parallel execution instead of causing a deadlock (example showed in Fig. 1a).

Generally, since the compiler and its runtime help to do most of the correctness checking and underground operations, programmers are able to write robust parallel code with less coding (Fig. 5) and effort.

### 7.2   Performance

With regard to performance evaluation, we mainly focus on whether the exception handling support degrades the performance even though no exception happens during the parallel execution. The possible overhead can arise from two aspects: (a) either the *try-catch* guarding on the parallel region, or (b) the explicit cancellation checking points the programmer added into the parallel region.

According to the EPCC benchmarks [2], we develop the similar benchmarks to measure the OpenMP synchronization overheads of Java version. In the benchmarks, the parallelization overhead is defined as $T_p - T_s/p$, in which $T_p$ is the parallel execution time on $p$ processors and $T_s$ indicated the sequential execution time of the same program with the same working load. The benchmark was run on a dedicated 16-core 2.4 GHz SMP machine with 64 GB memory, and Java HotSpot 64-Bit Server VM is used. In order to achieve a consistent and more accurate evaluation on the JVM, each benchmark case was run $n$ (varies between different cases) times and before each benchmark case a $n/10$ times warmup is executed. Figure 6 illustrates the absolute time of synchronization overhead of parallel, for, and barrier respectively, before introducing the support of exception handling.

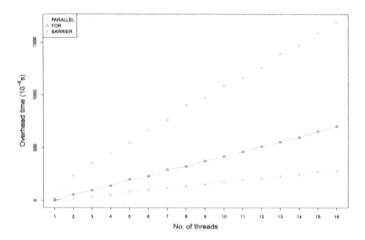

**Fig. 6.** Absolute time of synchronization overhead in a Java version of OpenMP

After the implementation of aforementioned exception handling support, two types of execution time were measured. The first is the parallel execution guarded with a *try-catch* block (TC). The second, in addition to the *try-catch* guarding, an extra cancellation checking point (CCP) is added. As a reference, the execution time without any exception handling is regarded as the baseline and the overhead differences are computed against it.

Figure 7 shows the benchmark result categorized by different types of directives. The overhead deviation of TC and TC&CCP is depicted. We notice that the overall average overhead is around 0.15 % and the worst case happens with barrier directive on TC and the overhead is 3.65 % higher than non-exception-handling one. However, in many of the cases, the overhead is negative which means the execution time of TC or TC&CCP is faster. This phenomenon may be attributed to the operating system scheduling which has a much greater impact on the execution time, so the overhead of exception-handling support does not introduce a noticeable impact on execution time.

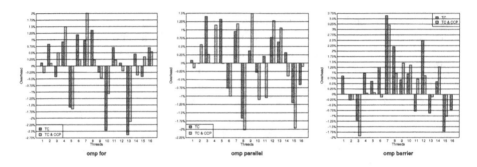

**Fig. 7.** Overhead evaluations of different OpenMP directives

# 8    Conclusion

The ability to use exception handling mechanisms in OpenMP would be a powerful feature from a software engineering point of view. The OpenMP specification lacks the integration of exception handling in object-oriented languages. In this paper, a combination of exception handling and parallel programming (based on OpenMP directives) is discussed. A proposal on the semantics, and the runtime to support this semantics, is discussed. Programmers will gain a better programming experience when writing robust high-level parallel code with OpenMP. Evaluations suggest that the new approach provides an elegant exception handling mechanism in OpenMP, without causing any performance degradation.

# References

1. OpenMP Architecture Review Board: OpenMP application program interface 4.0, July 2013
2. Bull, M.: Measuring synchronisation and scheduling overheads in OpenMP. In: Proceedings of First European Workshop on OpenMP, vol. 8, p. 49 (1999)
3. Duran, A., Ferrer, R., Costa, J.J., González, M., Martorell, X., Ayguadé, E., Labarta, J.: A proposal for error handling in OpenMP. Int. J. Parallel Program. **35**(4), 393–416 (2007)
4. Su Gatlin, K.: OpenMP 3.0 feature: error detection capability, May 2005. http://www.nic.uoregon.edu/iwomp2005/Talks/gatlin-panel.pdf
5. Giacaman, N., Sinnen, O., Akeila, L.: Object-oriented parallelisation: improved and extended parallel iterator. In: 2008 14th IEEE International Conference on Parallel and Distributed Systems, ICPADS 2008, pp. 113–120. IEEE (2008)
6. Herlihy, M.P., Wing, J.M.: Linearizability: a correctness condition for concurrent objects. ACM Trans. Program. Lang. Syst. (TOPLAS) **12**(3), 463–492 (1990)
7. Knafla, B., Leopold, C.: Parallelizing a real-time steering simulation for computer games with OpenMP. In: Parallel Computing: Architectures, Algorithms, and Applications (2008)
8. Münchhalfen, J.F., Hilbrich, T., Protze, J., Terboven, C., Müller, M.S.: Classification of common errors in OpenMP applications. In: DeRose, L., de Supinski, B.R., Olivier, S.L., Chapman, B.M., Müller, M.S. (eds.) IWOMP 2014. LNCS, vol. 8766, pp. 58–72. Springer, Heidelberg (2014)

9. Saillard, E., Carribault, P., Barthou, D.: Static validation of barriers and work-sharing constructs in OpenMP applications. In: DeRose, L., de Supinski, B.R., Olivier, S.L., Chapman, B.M., Müller, M.S. (eds.) IWOMP 2014. LNCS, vol. 8766, pp. 73–86. Springer, Heidelberg (2014)
10. Salva, S., Delamare, C., Bastoul, C.: Web service call parallelization using OpenMP. In: Chapman, B., Zheng, W., Gao, G.R., Sato, M., Ayguadé, E., Wang, D. (eds.) IWOMP 2007. LNCS, vol. 4935, pp. 185–194. Springer, Heidelberg (2008)
11. Stroustrup, B.: The Design and Evolution of C++. Pearson Education India (1994)
12. Vikas, Giacaman, N., Sinnen, O.: Pyjama: OpenMP-like implementation for Java, with GUI extensions. In: Proceedings of the 2013 International Workshop on Programming Models and Applications for Multicores and Manycores, PMAM 2013, pp. 43–52. ACM, New York (2013)
13. Vikas, Scott, T., Giacaman, N., Sinnen, O.: Using OpenMP under android. In: Rendell, A.P., Chapman, B.M., Müller, M.S. (eds.) IWOMP 2013. LNCS, vol. 8122, pp. 15–29. Springer, Heidelberg (2013)
14. Wong, M., Klemm, M., Duran, A., Mattson, T., Haab, G., de Supinski, B.R., Churbanov, A.: Towards an error model for OpenMP. In: Sato, M., Hanawa, T., Müller, M.S., Chapman, B.M., de Supinski, B.R. (eds.) IWOMP 2010. LNCS, vol. 6132, pp. 70–82. Springer, Heidelberg (2010)

# Extensions

# On the Algorithmic Aspects of Using OpenMP Synchronization Mechanisms II: User-Guided Speculative Locks

Barna L. Bihari[1], Hansang Bae[2], James Cownie[2], Michael Klemm[2], Christian Terboven[3]([✉]), and Lori Diachin[1]

[1] Lawrence Livermore National Laboratory, Livermore, USA
{bihari1,diachin2}@llnl.gov
[2] Intel Corporation, Santa Clara, USA
{hansang.bae,james.h.cownie,michael.klemm}@intel.com
[3] RWTH Aachen University, Aachen, Germany
terboven@itc.rwth-aachen.de

**Abstract.** In this paper we continue our investigations started in [8] into the effects of using different synchronization mechanisms in OpenMP-threaded iterative mesh optimization algorithms. We port our test code to the Intel® Xeon® processor (former codename "Haswell") by employing a user-guided locking API for OpenMP [4] that provides a general and unified user interface and runtime framework. Since the Intel® Transactional Synchronization Extensions (TSX) provide two different options for speculation — Hardware Lock Elision (HLE) and Restricted Transactional Memory (RTM) — we compare a total of four different run modes: (i) HLE, (ii) RTM, (iii) OpenMP `critical`, and (iv) "unsynchronized". As we did in [8], we find that either speculative execution option always outperforms the other two modes in terms of their convergence characteristics. Even with their higher overhead, the TSX options are very competitive when it comes to runtime performance measured with the "time-to-convergence" criterion introduced in [8].

## 1 Introduction

While transactional memory (TM) has been around for over two decades [13], and despite the many different implementations in both software and hardware that have been offered over the years, it has yet to become a mainstream mechanism for thread synchronization. This is partly due to the fact that any reasonable TM runtime performance strongly depends on specialized hardware, typically achieved through modifications to the L1 and/or L2 caches. So far, two major vendors, IBM* and Intel, provide hardware transactional memory (HTM); IBM on multiple machine series and Intel on Intel® Xeon® processors [14]. Despite the availability of HTM platforms, support for TM has not yet made it into the OpenMP API specification [21] (though a proposal for user-guided locks seems likely to be adopted into OpenMP 4.1). As a consequence, for those intending to write identical code for a range of systems, the elegance

© Springer International Publishing Switzerland 2015
C. Terboven et al. (Eds.): IWOMP 2015, LNCS 9342, pp. 133–148, 2015.
DOI: 10.1007/978-3-319-24595-9_10

and promised efficiency of TM is compromised by its lack of portability between different platforms.

Over three years ago IBM offered the first production-quality TM comprising BG/Q hardware and a TM runtime [12] that delivered features such as multiple rollback capability and smart heuristics in its software stack, but without burdening the user with and exposing all the details of the underlying algorithms. To use TM, the user only needed to insert directives, call runtime libraries, and tune environmental variables.

Intel platforms offer a more versatile and potentially more efficient TM capability — Intel® Transactional Synchronization Extensions (TSX) — with two options: Hardware Lock Elision (HLE) and Restricted Transactional Memory (RTM). However, the system does not come with a complete runtime library that would be readily usable with RTM: the programmer has to provide a non-transactional fall-back path which would have code to eventually acquire the lock that was elided. For most non-expert developers, some of whom maintain or modify legacy code, this is a major drawback, as each transaction (e.g., at least once in each `for` loop with race conditions) would require several lines of code to be able to use the new hardware features. A more ambitious customer may develop a home-grown library of the different transactional backup paths, but at the cost of some non-trivial time and effort.

An attractive solution to this "missing software dilemma" was introduced in [4] where a library of user-guided locks was proposed as an extension of the existing OpenMP lock API. The interfaces proposed in that paper (which are identical to those used here aside from naming details) seem likely to be adopted by the OpenMP language committee to become part of the OpenMP 4.1 API specification later in 2015, at which point the OpenMP API will provide a portable, architecture-independent interface to the hardware transactional memory features of modern processors. The purpose of this paper is not to explore the interface design issues (which were explored in [4]) but to provide another demonstration that the use of hardware transactional memory can improve application performance.

The API enables the use of HLE and RTM, and also includes other lock hints which can be used as either real alternatives to TSX, or to tune lock-synchronized code by using different lock implementations in the absence of TM. At the user level, the complete package is now comparable with IBM's system, with the added benefit that it is implemented in the open-source Intel [15] and LLVM*[3] OpenMP runtime libraries, allowing potential modifications by an expert user.

Given this background and the availability of another major vendor's HTM system (i.e., Intel TSX), we continue our experimentation with threaded mesh optimization where potential race conditions exist. Both the hardware and the software are very different from the IBM environment used in our previous work [8], thus our intent is to experimentally test and verify that the principles detailed in [8] still hold. That is, in a shared-memory environment does a threaded iterative algorithm benefit from using TM to dynamically update variables that have dependencies? We find the answer through extensive experimentation on the same code used in [8] but run in the Intel environment. The results are quite encouraging: we find similar trends to those of [8] and the same conclusions do remain true.

The rest of this paper is organized as follows. Section 2 provides background, Sect. 3 presents an overview of Intel TSX as well as the user-guided lock library as it relates to our experimentation, while Sect. 4 gives a brief review of the algorithm and the role we expect TM to play in it. We present our experimental results in Sect. 5, where we compare three different flavors of synchronizations, as well as a completely unsynchronized version of the code. We also show TM statistics and runtime performance using the new metric introduced in [8]. In Sect. 6 we conclude with a brief review of our results.

## 2   Related Work

As elaborated on in [8], to our knowledge mesh optimization codes (see e.g., [18] and the references therein) have had neither the need nor the priority to address the issue of synchronization when threading their iterative algorithms. This is partly due to the fact that these methods are quite stable and almost any reasonable ordering or threading technique will eventually converge, albeit at different convergence rates. The only distantly related work (but still within the realm of iterative schemes) that we are aware of is that of [5] where threading was systematically studied and divergence was actually observed in the context of multigrid smoothers which are more sensitive to cell-ordering than mesh smoothers. This gave us an additional hint and incentive that in some cases thread synchronization may have an effect beyond the raw efficiency of iterative methods and may actually impact the correctness of the solution itself.

Related to our work on user-guided speculative locks, there are other lock interfaces that include support for speculative locks. The POSIX thread library [10] contains support for different kinds of locks including speculative locks as part of glibc [17,20], and Threading Building Blocks (TBB) [2] provides the `speculative_spin_mutex` type which uses TSX if the hardware supports it. These interfaces also allow programmers to write a critical section that runs speculatively, but enabling it via the OpenMP API is a more convenient solution for OpenMP application writers.

IBM introduced a series of machines such as Blue Gene/Q [23], zEnterprise EC12 [16], and POWER8 [19], all of which implement transactional memory. Application writers can use their C/C++ compilers to leverage the TM feature by annotating the code and/or inserting calls to intrinsic functions [11], but this lacks cross-platform portability. Although there is a proposal for new OpenMP constructs to support transactional memory [9,24], this approach is fundamentally different from lock-based programming and complements our proposal from a different angle.

# 3    User-Guided Locking API with TSX

For completeness, we briefly review Intel TSX and show how it can be used in an OpenMP application that is compiled and linked with the Intel (or LLVM) OpenMP runtime.

## 3.1    Intel Transactional Synchronization Extensions

Intel Transactional Synchronization Extensions (TSX) are new capabilities introduced in the Intel Xeon processor series which was formerly known as "Haswell". TSX is widely supported in the current series, formerly known as "Broadwell" [1]. The extensions provide support for transactional execution while using cache-coherence protocols to detect memory access conflicts. On a transactional abort, the architectural state of the processor is restored to that at the start of the transaction (all transactional memory writes are discarded, and register state is restored). At transaction commit, all transactional writes become atomically visible to other cores.

By using Intel TSX it is possible to execute multiple dynamic instances of a critical region simultaneously, with the required mutual exclusion enforced by the hardware when conflicting memory accesses occur between these instruction streams. This allows code written with a single coarse lock to behave as if it were implemented with fine-grain reader-writer locks at cache-line granularity.

Intel TSX provides two different interfaces to speculation: Hardware Lock Elision (HLE) and Restricted Transactional Memory (RTM). In both cases, speculation is implemented in the coherence protocol of the processor caches. Since the cache protocol keeps track of the states of individual cache lines, the hardware can use this information to detect conflicting memory accesses and to abort the speculative execution in the cores executing the threads that suffered the conflicts.

HLE is a backwards binary-compatible interface that can be added to an existing lock by tagging the lock and unlock instructions with instruction prefixes that are ignored on processors without TSX support. It requests that the processor executes the protected critical region speculatively. If the speculation fails, the processor rolls back and executes the critical section non-speculatively. HLE preserves all of the semantics of existing locks, such that the lock value read inside the critical section appears to be locked, as it would be if there were no speculation.

RTM adds new instructions to put the processor into the speculative execution state, to commit the speculative state, and explicitly to abort speculation. With RTM the user has to provide a non-speculative execution path, since no lock is visible to the hardware. User code can detect speculation failure and may choose to retry speculation, but must ultimately provide a way of executing the critical region non-speculatively, since there is no architectural guarantee that speculation will make forward progress.

As some operations (inter alia any ring transition that enters the kernel) cannot be executed speculatively and will cause the speculation to abort, blindly converting all critical regions in a program to use speculative locks will likely be counterproductive. If a large amount of speculative work has been performed before the abort, discarding it becomes prohibitively expensive. Consider a lock used to serialize output, for instance, in which effort may be expended to format data before the write system call is made. If this is done within speculative execution, the formatting work will all be lost and will have to be repeated in the non-speculative backup. Therefore, it is hard for the runtime system to determine which locks should be speculated without information from the programmer (who should know what code will be executed in the critical region). This observation motivated our previous proposal for hinted locks [4].

### 3.2 Using the User-Guided Locking API

The Intel/LLVM OpenMP runtime library contains lock implementations that use HLE and RTM. Programmers can select the lock implementation either globally through an environment variable or selectively via an OpenMP extension [4].

The OpenMP extension was proposed to overcome one of the disadvantages of the OpenMP 4.0 lock API. The key feature of the new API is to give application writers the ability to choose a hint on a per-lock basis and to pass information to the runtime about the estimated degree of lock contention. As a result, users gain fine-grained control of the OpenMP runtime and can optimize their applications by adjusting the lock implementation for each lock if desired.

The proposed API is available in the latest release of Intel's open-source OpenMP runtime [15], and can be enabled at build time. Two additional lock initialization functions are provided to pass extra information to the runtime:

```
void kmp_init_lock_hinted(omp_lock_t*, kmp_lock_hint_t)
void kmp_init_nest_lock_hinted(omp_nest_lock_t*, kmp_lock_hint_t)
```

User-selectable hints (of type `kmp_lock_hint_t`) are defined as an enumeration:

```
typedef enum kmp_lock_hint_t {
  kmp_lock_hint_none,
  kmp_lock_hint_uncontended,      // Optimize for an uncontended lock
  kmp_lock_hint_contended,        // Optimize for a contended lock
  kmp_lock_hint_nonspeculative,   // Do not use hardware speculation
  kmp_lock_hint_speculative,      // Use HLE hardware speculation
  kmp_lock_hint_adaptive,         // Adaptively use RTM speculation
} kmp_lock_hint_t;
```

Programmers can use these hints together with the additional initialization routines to tag a lock with a hint. The example code in Fig. 1 shows how to use the new API to speculatively execute a critical region that is protected through the OpenMP lock API. After the lock has been initialized and the hint has been

```
void example() {
    omp_lock_t lock;
    kmp_init_lock_hinted(&lock, kmp_lock_hint_speculative);

    omp_set_lock(&lock);
    // critical section
    omp_unset_lock(&lock);
}
```

**Fig. 1.** Using user-guided locks in the Intel OpenMP runtime.

bound to the lock, the standard lock routines of OpenMP acquire and release the lock as usual. This simplifies the task of changing the code to use a specific type of lock; only the initialization of a lock needs to be located and not all the places where the lock is claimed and released. The runtime system uses the hint to choose the lock implementation for this particular lock, and, in this case, to use a speculative lock.

## 4    Applying Intel TSX to the Test Code

We will now briefly introduce the algorithm under investigation and then show how Intel TSX can be applied to its efficient thread synchronization.

### 4.1    A Brief Review of the Algorithm

In our experiments we use the same simple C++ mesh smoothing algorithm of [8] that takes the same initially distorted mesh as input and produces a final converged mesh as output. The main `for` loop accomplishing the averaging operation is symbolically represented by the equation:

$$\mathbf{x}_i^{(n+1)} = \frac{1}{N_i} \sum_{j=1}^{N_i} \mathbf{x}_j^{(m)} \tag{1}$$

where $\mathbf{x}$ is a 2- or 3-D vector, $n$ is the current (old) iteration, $n+1$ is the latest (new) iteration, $N_i$ is the number of connected vertices for grid point $i$, and $m$ can refer to either $n$ or $n+1$ depending on whether or not that point has already been updated or not. Figure 2 shows the relevant code section, as modified to run with our user-guided locking API on the Intel Xeon processor.

In order to avoid write-after-read (WAR) race conditions in Fig. 2, the code needs to protect the entire section that includes both "Step 1" and "Step 2", and not just the update operations of "Step 2". The `omp_set_lock` and `omp_unset_lock` routines delimit the entire *transaction*, which is also placed in a block for ease of reading. Note that this is essentially the same simple construct as that for the IBM BG/Q TM runtime, and, apart from the lock initialization, the code of Fig. 2 is identical to that of [8].

```
    omp_lock_t  lock;
    kmp_init_lock_hinted(&lock, kmp_lock_hint_speculative);
#pragma omp parallel for
    for(int i=0; i < numFreeVerts; i++) {
        int vertexID = freeVertexIDs[i];

// Get attached vertex ids:
        std::vector<Point2D*> &myAttachedVertices =
            attachedVertices[vertexID];
        Point2D newX={0.0,0.0};
        size_t numAttachedVertices = myAttachedVertices.size();

        omp_set_lock(&lock);        // start of critical region
        {
// Step 1: take average of neighbors
        for(int j=0;j<numAttachedVertices;j++){
            newX.x += myAttachedVertices[j]->x;
            newX.y += myAttachedVertices[j]->y;
        }  // end for (over neighbor vertices)
        newX.x = newX.x/numAttachedVertices;
        newX.y = newX.y/numAttachedVertices;
// Step 2: update current coordinates:
        x[vertexID].x = newX.x/numAttachedVertices;
        x[vertexID].y = newX.y/numAttachedVertices;
        }
        omp_unset_lock(&lock)      // end of critical region
    }            // end for (over all vertices)
```

**Fig. 2.** Simple Laplacian mesh smoothing algorithm.

The OpenMP language provides the `critical` construct for the purposes of simple coarse-grain locking, which would be the obvious choice here. However, because it does not yet support hints to change the behavior of `critical` from regular lock acquire/release to speculation, we emulate this functionality by using the API for user-guided locks. We use the lock hints to run in two additional modes, called *speculative* or *HLE*, as well as *adaptive* or *RTM* (see Sect. 3.2).

Note that if we restrict the critical region in Fig. 2 to the coordinate update in "Step 2" only, no conflicts exist since each thread only updates the points that it owns. However, the neighboring coordinates might change during "Step 1" so the result could depend significantly on whether old or new data is being used during the update. In other words, we have a write-after-read (WAR) conflict for which we cannot use `#pragma omp atomic`. Thus, we will not compare *HLE* or *RTM* with *atomic* as we did in some of our prior experiments in [9,22].

## 4.2   The Role of TSX

As seen in [8], the BG/Q TM system made a substantial difference to the quality of the solution we obtained because of the way the updates were done dynamically. With Intel's TSX system, we also expect to see a difference, especially since now we actually have two options to properly synchronize the critical code section of Fig. 2.

*HLE* When HLE is requested, the system tries to elide the lock and execute the critical region without requiring any communication through the lock. However, the TSX-enabled hardware is able to detect conflicting operations. If a conflict occurs, the system will execute the protected code section nontransactionally, that is, without elision and with an acquire/release cycle for the lock. When such a *retry* happens (often referred to as a "rollback") the code will essentially be serialized and forward progress is ensured, albeit with lower efficiency. In terms of the usual TM terminology, only one rollback is allowed with HLE. Once that happens, HLE becomes equivalent to `#pragma omp critical`.

*RTM* With RTM, the lock protecting the transactional region is also elided at first. Upon a conflict — detected by the hardware as with HLE — the transaction *aborts* and reverts to the fallback instruction address provided by the programmer. This provides a great deal of flexibility to handle the abort, as well as the implied responsibility to provide a code sequence that guarantees forward progress. In our work, we took advantage of the OpenMP extensions of [4] in order to benefit from the hardware-assisted RTM. As mentioned in Sect. 3.2, and further explained in [4], the basic system-provided RTM software interface was built into the "adaptive" option. The adaptive lock has some additional features, such as the environment variable `KMP_ADAPTIVE_LOCK_PROPS=M,N` that allows M number of maximum retries, and a "maximum badness" of N. The latter parameter is used to attempt to work out whether or not even to try RTM at all, since transactions that have previously failed may only have a slight chance of succeeding in the future and may not be worth the higher overhead of new speculative attempts, hence the name "adaptive." The adaptive lock also collects statistics related to the successes and different failure modes of the speculation. Because of all these additional features, the "adaptive" lock is naturally more expensive than its "speculative" counterpart, but it can potentially yield a higher quality result as multiple rollbacks typically mean multiple updates and, therefore, more accurate neighbor coordinates for the current mesh point.

As was the case with BG/Q [8], the way the hardware detects memory conflicts and how the software handles them will significantly affect the overall behavior of the algorithm itself. In our experiments, for example, there were many instances of multiple retries while computing one location, where RTM turned out to be quite useful, while for others HLE with its low overhead was sufficient to handle low conflict-probability cases. Indeed, the choice for handling of the critical section will have a profound influence on the algorithm and the solution quality itself. The right choice of synchronization method will likely be made by weighing quality against cost.

## 5    Experimental Results

We now present some computational experiments using the algorithm described above. As in [8], the original Cartesian mesh cells from which the currently used unstructured cells were obtained are $1 \times 1$ non-dimensional units in size. They are then disturbed by a random factor in the range of $(-0.5, 0.5)$, the largest distortion that still guarantees no initial mesh-line cross-overs. During the runs we vary the number of threads (1, 2, 4, 8, 16, 32, and 64) and use the three coarse-grain synchronization modes *HLE*, *RTM*, and *critical* as well as *unsync* which has no synchronization at all.

As this is a follow-on study of [8], we use the same single kernel described earlier for the evaluation on this new TM-enabled platform. Since both the usage of TM for mesh optimization and the concept of user-guided speculative locks are relatively new ideas, we feel it is important to study them thoroughly in simple scenarios such as 2-D meshes before moving to real application codes. Moreover, we make an explicit effort both in running the code and in presenting the results to provide a fair comparison between two very different computer architectures from two different vendors. The question of general benefits of speculative locks for scientific computing remains, as it should, an ongoing quest and the current work is but a small component of that effort.

For the evaluation, we use Intel® Parallel Studio XE for C++ (version 16.0.0.056 Beta) running on an Intel® Xeon® E5-2698v3 (2.3 GHz base frequency, 64 GB DDR3 at 2133 MHz), with Intel® Turbo Boost Technology enabled, Intel® Hyper-Threading on, as well as Intel TSX enabled. Our system runs Red Hat* Enterprise Linux* Server release 6.6 (Santiago), with kernel version 2.6.32-504.16.2. While Turbo mode being on all the time might have sped up the cores for low thread counts, we felt it was important to present the results for as realistic of a scenario as a real user would have run it in.

We now analyze the convergence, some TM characteristics, and the overall performance of the results.

## 5.1   Convergence

Convergence is measured in terms of the $l_1$ norm of the difference between the current iteration and the exact solution which is known. The *error* $e^{(n)}$ at time $n$ is defined by:

$$e^{(n)} = \frac{1}{M} \sum_{i=1}^{M} |\mathbf{x}_i^{(exact)} - \mathbf{x}_i^{(n)}| \tag{2}$$

where $(n)$ denotes the current iteration counter, $M$ is the number of interior (non-boundary) vertices, and $\mathbf{x}_i$ is the coordinate vector of point $i$. The $(exact)$ superscript denotes the solution of the mesh optimization problem, which is known a-priori for our simple problem.

We use the serial solution (which is the same as executing a single thread) as our reference in all plots. Figure 3 shows that convergence rates with 2 threads exhibit little difference between *HLE* and *critical*, which are close to each other, while *unsync* is the slowest to converge, *RTM* being in between. As explained in [8], the serial version will have the least error on all thread counts as the points will always see the most recent update possible.

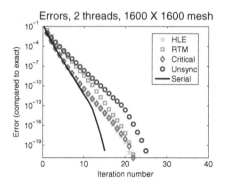

**Fig. 3.** Convergence on 2 threads.

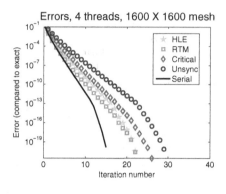

**Fig. 4.** Convergence on 4 threads.

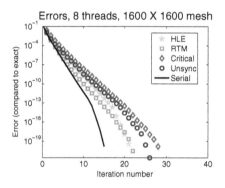

**Fig. 5.** Convergence on 8 threads.

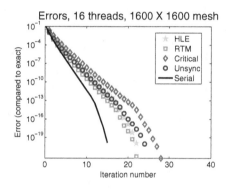

**Fig. 6.** Convergence on 16 threads.

On the other hand, Figs. 4, 5, and 6 show *RTM* overtaking the others, with *critical* performing the worst on 8 and 16 threads. On low thread counts *critical*'s relatively good performance may be due to the fact that there are fewer conflicts, but if there are any conflicts, *critical* will actually "wait" for updated neighbor information to come in, and will end up using more recent data which is not the case for higher thread counts which are closer to a Jacobi iteration. The convergence improvement of *RTM* with thread count is due to the consistent and frequent updates of the neighbors, some of which are multiple updates of the same location, as we will see in the next subsection. While *HLE* can only have a single TM-assisted update of a given mesh point, it also performs well and is expected to be faster than *RTM*.

As we increase the thread count to 32 (Fig. 7), *HLE* gets closer to *RTM*, and at 64 threads (Fig. 8) *HLE* actually performs the best. Hyperthreading may provide one explanation for this behavior since it effectively halves the available cache per thread when two threads are sharing the same L1 and L2 caches thereby

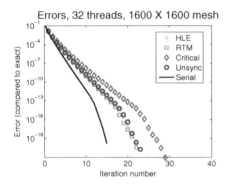

**Fig. 7.** Convergence on 32 threads.

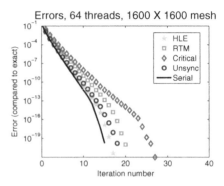

**Fig. 8.** Convergence on 64 threads.

potentially creating many false conflicts without the expected update-benefit. While both *RTM* and *HLE* catch conflicts using the same hardware mechanism, *HLE* will serialize the loop on the first failure of speculation, and, as mentioned earlier, *serial* is known to have the best possible convergence characteristics.

## 5.2   Transactional Memory Statistics

Results for threaded code with memory conflicts, with or without TM, are always timing-sensitive. Therefore, we typically repeat the same outer loop dozens or hundreds of times — as we did in e.g., [6,7,9] — and run it well past convergence. We thus obtain some statistical averages as well as the iteration-dependent variation of the TM statistics. The statistics for the *RTM* case are obtained from the `__kmp_print_speculative_stats()` utility provided by the user-guided lock runtime. At each iteration we observe the number of retries ("soft failures") that have occurred, the grand total at the end of the run, as well as several other diagnostic numbers such as "non-speculative acquires" (i.e., the number of times the code was serialized) and "hard failures"; the difference of these two numbers is the number of times speculation was not even attempted by the "adaptive" lock. For example, Fig. 9, shows the cumulative statistics for a particular iteration on 16 threads, which reveals, among other things, that many transactions had multiple retries since their number ("soft failures") was greater than the number of the transactions themselves ("total critical sections"), yet 99.7 % of these attempts eventually succeeded with very few (0.3 %) serializations. Beyond these salient indicators, even more detailed TM-related information can be obtained from snapshots like Fig. 9, however we are not using them in this study.

Plotting the number of retries in Fig. 10, we see a relatively large (one order of magnitude) spread in the number of conflicts from iteration to iteration on 64 threads, but small oscillations on low to moderate thread counts (2 to 32 threads). This may be due to the fact that the Haswell node this was run on has

```
Speculative lock statistics (all approximate!)
Lock parameters:
   max_soft_retries              :        100
   max_badness                   :          1
Non-speculative acquire attempts :     157728
Total critical sections          :   67877157
Successful speculations          :   67687327 ( 99.7%)
Non-speculative acquires         :     189830 (  0.3%)
Lemming yields                   :     357002

Speculative acquire attempts     :  154388660
Successes                        :   67687327 ( 43.8%)
Soft failures                    :   86564706 ( 56.1%)
Hard failures                    :     136627 (  0.1%)
```

**Fig. 9.** Example of the speculative lock statistics output for the *RTM* ("adaptive" lock) case run on 16 threads.

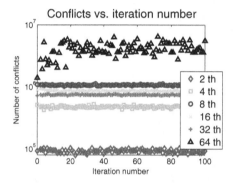

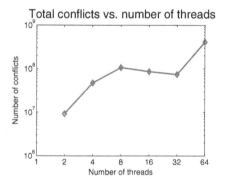

**Fig. 10.** RTM retries per iteration on 1600 × 1600 mesh on 2 through 64 threads.

**Fig. 11.** Total number of RTM retries on 1600 × 1600 mesh on 2 through 64 threads.

32 cores, and at 64 threads hyperthreading may have created some anomalies and false conflicts. For all the other thread counts, the iteration-to-iteration volatility is much smaller than that observed on the BG/Q (see [8]).

Figure 11 shows the total number of conflicts over 100 iterations for all thread counts. We observe a monotonic increase in the number of total conflicts as the number of threads increases to 8, with some drop at 16 and 32 threads, and another sharp increase at 64 threads, which will most likely contribute to some slowdown for *RTM* at that thread count affecting overall performance.

### 5.3 Performance Measurement

Finally, we use the performance measure introduced in [8] to define "run time per quality" $t_q^{(n)}$ (loosely speaking "time to convergence"), assuming $q^{(n)}$ is the inverse of the error $e^{(n)}$ defined by Eq. (2):

$$t_q^{(n)} = \frac{t^{(n)}}{q^{(n)}} = t^{(n)} e^{(n)}. \tag{3}$$

We use this measure to gauge whether one or both of the TSX options provides some benefit when their well-known overhead is balanced against their superior convergence behavior. Indeed, for an iterative scheme, the convergence rate is one of the most important indicators. That is, even though some methods may be more expensive on a per-step basis, if they converge faster they may end up being more efficient overall since fewer iterations are needed to achieve convergence, and the time to solution can actually be shorter. This reasoning can also be generalized to almost all numerical methods, an example of which is the recently renewed interest in high-order methods.

For this study, we again run the code in four different modes (*HLE*, *RTM*, *critical*, and *unsync*), and to iteration $n = 17$. The inclusion of *unsync* in the study is for information purposes only since, strictly speaking, it is an incorrect parallel program due to the data races.

We find that both *HLE* and *RTM* outperform *critical* by one or two orders of magnitude on all except 2 threads (Fig. 12). Moreover, *RTM* yields significantly better time-per-quality than *unsync* on 2, 4, and 8 threads, and is the same on 16 and 32 threads. On the other hand, *HLE* outperforms *unsync* on 2, 4, and 64 threads. At 64 threads *HLE* is significantly more efficient than even *RTM*. Indeed, at 64 threads there are an order of magnitude more retries than on all

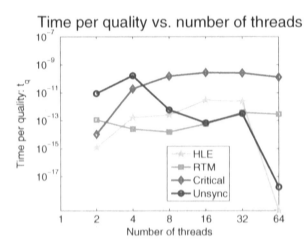

**Fig. 12.** Time per quality on a $1600 \times 1600$ mesh on up to 64 threads.

other thread counts (see Figs. 10 and 11). With *RTM* there could be multiple retries on the same variable and each retry comes with its own overhead cost, providing at least a partial explanation for the difference between *HLE* and *RTM* at 64 threads. As alluded to earlier, it is possible that the extra retires are a result of the use of hyper-threading, which is only used in this 64 thread experiment. Overall, however, we see that one of the TSX options meets or beats *unsync* at *every* thread count, with *HLE* being the overall best at 64 threads.

# 6    Conclusions and Future Work

We continued to study different OpenMP synchronization constructs using the iterative Laplacian mesh-smoothing algorithm of [8] and the user-guided locking API of [4] on the Intel® Xeon® processor. We again concentrated on evaluating the specialized TSX hardware offered by this platform as well as the open source library developed as a user interface to it. Using the new figure of merit introduced in [8], we concluded not only that both TSX options compared favorably with OpenMP `critical` — an expected result — but also that they outperformed even a completely unsynchronized version of the code when measured by the recently introduced "time-to-convergence" criterion. In all of our tests the best performance is provided by one of the two speculative execution options.

Despite these encouraging results, much more experimentation is needed to expose the limitations of speculative locks for mesh optimization. To this end, we hope to extend this study to more complicated and fully three-dimensional meshes, as well as to potentially create another addition to our user-guided speculative lock arsenal: locks that are "pure RTM" and thus have lower overhead since they would not attempt to adaptively decide whether to speculate or not.

**Acknowledgments.** The authors thank Trent E. D'Hooge of Livermore Computing for his assistance with our inquiries and in accommodating our runs on the local compute nodes.

Intel and Xeon are trademarks or registered trademarks of Intel Corporation or its subsidiaries in the United States and other countries.

\* Other names and brands are the property of their respective owners.

Software and workloads used in performance tests may have been optimized for performance only on Intel microprocessors. Performance tests, such as SYSmark and MobileMark, are measured using specific computer systems, components, software, operations and functions. Any change to any of those factors may cause the results to vary. You should consult other information and performance tests to assist you in fully evaluating your contemplated purchases, including the performance of that product when combined with other products. For more information go to http://www.intel.com/performance.

Intel's compilers may or may not optimize to the same degree for non-Intel microprocessors for optimizations that are not unique to Intel microprocessors. These optimizations include SSE2, SSE3, and SSSE3 instruction sets and other optimizations. Intel does not guarantee the availability, functionality, or effectiveness of any optimization on microprocessors not manufactured by Intel. Microprocessor-dependent optimizations in this product are intended for use with Intel microprocessors. Certain optimizations not specific to Intel microarchitecture are reserved for Intel microprocessors. Please refer to the applicable product User and Reference Guides for more information regarding the specific instruction sets covered by this notice.

# References

1. Intel ARK. http://ark.intel.com
2. Intel® Threading Building Blocks. https://www.threadingbuildingblocks.org
3. LLVM. http://www.llvm.org
4. Bae, H., Cownie, J., Klemm, M., Terboven, C.: A user-guided locking API for the OpenMP* application program interface. In: DeRose, L., de Supinski, B.R., Olivier, S.L., Chapman, B.M., Müller, M.S. (eds.) IWOMP 2014. LNCS, vol. 8766, pp. 173–186. Springer, Heidelberg (2014)
5. Baker, A.H., Falgout, R.D., Kolev, T.V., Yang, U.M.: Multigrid smoothers for ultraparallel computing. SIAM J. Sci. Comput. **33**, 2864–2887 (2011)
6. Bihari, B.L.: Applicability of transactional memory to modern codes. In: International Conference on Numerical Analysis and Applied Mathematics 2010 (ICNAAM 2010) Conference Proceedings, pp. 1764–1767. APS, Rodos (2010)
7. Bihari, B.L.: Transactional memory for unstructured mesh simulations. J. Sci. Comput. **54**, 311–332 (2012)
8. Bihari, B.L., Wong, M., de Supinski, B.R., Diachin, L.: On the algorithmic aspects of using OpenMP synchronization mechanisms: the effects of transactional memory. In: DeRose, L., de Supinski, B.R., Olivier, S.L., Chapman, B.M., Müller, M.S. (eds.) IWOMP 2014. LNCS, vol. 8766, pp. 115–129. Springer, Heidelberg (2014)
9. Bihari, B.L., Wong, M., Wang, A., de Supinski, B.R., Chen, W.: A case for including transactions in OpenMP II: hardware transactional memory. In: Chapman, B.M., Massaioli, F., Müller, M.S., Rorro, M. (eds.) IWOMP 2012. LNCS, vol. 7312, pp. 44–58. Springer, Heidelberg (2012)
10. Drepper, U., Molnar, I.: The native POSIX thread library for Linux. Technical report, Redhat (2003)
11. IBM Compiler Group: IBM XL C/C++ for Blue Gene/Q, V12.1 Compiler Reference (2012)
12. Haring, R.A., Ohmacht, M., Fox, T.W., Gschwind, M.K., Satterfield, D.L., Sugavanam, K., Coteus, P.W., Heidelberger, P., Blumrich, M.A., Wisniewski, R.W., Gara, A., Chiu, G.L.-T., Boyle, P.A., Christ, N.H., Kim, C.: The IBM blue gene/Q compute chip. IEEE Micro **32**(2), 48–60 (2013)
13. Herlihy, M., Moss, J.E.B.: Transactional memory: architectural support for lock-free data structures. SIGARCH Comput. Archit. News **51**(2), 289–300 (1993)
14. Intel Corporation: Intel® Architecture Instruction Set Extensions Programming Reference. Document number 319433-014 (2012)
15. Intel Corporation: Intel® OpenMP* Runtime Library (2015). http://www.openmprtl.org/
16. Jacobi, C., Slegel, T., Greiner, D.: Transactional memory architecture and implementation for IBM system Z. In: 2012 45th Annual IEEE/ACM International Symposium on Microarchitecture (MICRO), pp. 25–36, December 2012
17. Kleen, A.: Lock Elision in the GNU C library. LWN.net **12**(1), (2013). http://lwn.net/Articles/534758/
18. Knupp, P.: Hexahedral and tetrahedral mesh shape optimization. Intl. J. Numer. Meth. Engr. **58**, 319–332 (2003)

19. Le, H.Q., Guthrie, G.L., Williams, D.E., Michael, M.M., Frey, B.G., Starke, W.J., May, C., Odaira, R., Nakaike, T.: Transactional memory support in the IBM power8 processor. IBM J. Res. Dev. **59**(1), 8:1–8:14 (2015)
20. Miller, D.: The GNU C Library version 2.18 is now available. Announcement on the info-gnu mailing list (2013). http://lists.gnu.org/archive/html/info-gnu/2013-08/msg00003.html
21. OpenMP Architecture Review Board: OpenMP Application Program Interface, Version 4.0 (2013). http://www.openmp.org/
22. Schindewolf, M., Gyllenhaal, J., Bihari, B.L., Wang, A., Schulz, M., Karl, W.: What scientific applications can benefit from hardware transacional memory? In: International Conference for High Performance Computing, Networking, Storage and Analysis, SC 2012 (2012)
23. Wang, A., Gaudet, M., Wu, P., Ohmacht, M., Amaral, J.N., Barton, C., Silvera, R., Michael, M.: Evaluation of blue gene/Q hardware support for transactional memories. In: PACT (2012)
24. Wong, M., Bihari, B.L., de Supinski, B.R., Wu, P., Michael, M., Liu, Y., Chen, W.: A case for including transactions in OpenMP. In: Sato, M., Hanawa, T., Müller, M.S., Chapman, B.M., de Supinski, B.R. (eds.) IWOMP 2010. LNCS, vol. 6132, pp. 149–160. Springer, Heidelberg (2010)

# Using Transactional Memory to Avoid Blocking in OpenMP Synchronization Directives

## Don't Wait, Speculate!

Lars Bonnichsen[1]([✉]) and Artur Podobas[2]

[1] Technical University of Denmark, Lyngby, Denmark
lfbo@dtu.dk
[2] KTH Royal Institute of Technology, Stockholm, Sweden
podobas@kth.se

**Abstract.** OpenMP applications with abundant parallelism are often characterized by their high-performance. Unfortunately, OpenMP applications with a lot of synchronization or serialization-points perform poorly because of blocking, *i.e.* the threads have to wait for each other. In this paper, we present methods based on hardware transactional memory (HTM) for executing OpenMP `barrier`, `critical`, and `taskwait` directives without blocking. Although HTM is still relatively new in the Intel and IBM architectures, we experimentally show a 73 % performance improvement over traditional locking approaches, and 23 % better than other HTM approaches on critical sections. Speculation over barriers can decrease execution time by up-to 41 %. We expect that future systems with HTM support and more cores will have a greater benefit from our approach as they are more likely to block.

## 1 Introduction

Parallel applications use synchronization to coordinate asynchronous threads. Synchronization is not free. Depending on the structure of the parallel application, how much parallelism it exposes, and how the work is distributed among threads, the idle time spent blocked while synchronizing can be high–time that *should* be spent attempting to perform useful work.

Transactional Memory (TM) is a method for reducing the time threads are blocked. Rather than waiting for a lock to be acquired, the thread enters a *transaction* and attempts to execute the protected code without a lock. Should a data-race occur between transactions, some are aborted and re-executed. Using transactions instead of regular locking scheme can improve performance [3,19] and even power-consumption [15].

Hardware Transactional Memory (HTM) has recently been adopted by hardware manufacturers in architectures such as Intel Haswell and IBM Power8 [7,11]. Hardware implementations reduce the overhead that comes with their software counter parts, making HTM appealing to use in frameworks that support fine-grained parallelism- frameworks such as OpenMP.

© Springer International Publishing Switzerland 2015
C. Terboven et al. (Eds.): IWOMP 2015, LNCS 9342, pp. 149–161, 2015.
DOI: 10.1007/978-3-319-24595-9_11

This paper explores how HTM can be used to reduce blocking in OpenMP synchronization directives. We reveal implementation details, discuss where and why it works and quantify the performance gains that can be achieved. We speculate on critical sections and barriers, where other speculative approaches are well established, as well as speculating across taskwaits.

*We contribute* with the following:

- Methods for executing `barriers`, `critical` sections and `taskwait` speculatively, without blocking:
    - The speculative method for critical sections is more resistant to contention than prior work.
    - Unlike existing speculative methods for barriers, our methods do not require non-transactional memory accesses within transactions.
- An evaluation of aforementioned methods on a series of microbenchmarks and the Barcelona OpenMP Task-Suite, explaining why and when they work.

*The paper* has the following structure: Sect. 2 describes how to speculate critical sections, taskwaits and barriers, and Sect. 3 evaluates the performance the methods. Section 4 describes limitations of the methods, and how they relate to prior work and current extension proposals for OpenMP. Finally Sect. 5 concludes the paper.

## 2   Avoiding Blocking in OpenMP

This section describes how use HTM to minimize blocking time in locks, barriers, and taskwaits. We access HTM capabilities through three functions:

`tbegin(LABEL)` Start a transaction. If the transaction fails, it will roll back all its changes and go to the label `LABEL`.
`tend()` Commit the transaction, atomically revealing its changes to all other threads.
`tabort()` Force the transaction to fail.

The functions correspond to the subset of TM capabilities in IBM Power8 and Intel Haswell processor architectures.

### 2.1   Critical Sections

Critical sections are typically used to update shared variables in parallel code, for instance updating counters or data structures. Critical sections acts as a serialization point, where only one thread can execute the protected region at any one time. Figure 1 shows an example where three threads encounter a critical section. The threads acquire the critical section's lock before entering the critical section. $Thread_0$ acquires the lock first, which traditionally means that $Thread_1$ and $Thread_2$ will have to block until the lock is released. With *lock elision*, threads can speculatively ignore the lock acquisition, and avoid blocking.

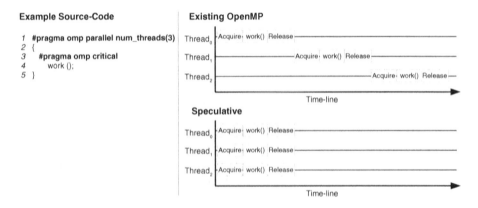

**Fig. 1.** Code and timelines for computation with 3 threads using a critical section, illustrating the difference between the existing OpenMP approach and our speculative version.

Listing 1 illustrates our lock implementation, which supports *lock elision*, and truncated exponential backoff [2]. To avoid blocking, lock elision attempts to use transactions rather than regular locks: Instead of acquiring a lock, we start a transaction (Line 4), and commit the transaction instead of releasing the lock (Line 21). If the transaction fails repeatedly, we fall back to using a test-and-set lock (Lines 8 and 23), and we do not let any transactions commit if the lock is held (Line 20). Lock elision follows normal lock semantics: successful transactions appear to execute atomically while the lock is released and failed transactions have no visible side effects.

Multiple transactions can execute a single critical section in parallel as long as the transactions succeed. Unfortunately, transactions do not always succeed. Transactions are less likely to succeed if the lock is held frequently. When transactions fail repeatedly, they fall back to using the underlying traditional lock, creating a harmful feedback loop known as the lemming effect [8]: once a few

```
 1 void acquireLock(lockVar) {        14 __thread unsigned delay;
 2    backoff();                       15 // Wait U(0;a<<delay) cycles
 3    for(int a=0; a<3; a++) {          16 void backoff();
 4 FOR:tbegin(ERR); return;            17
 5 ERR:if(tAborted()) goto FOR;        18 void releaseLock(lockVar) {
 6      if(tCannot()) break;           19    if(isInTransaction()) {
 7    }                                20       if(isLocked()) tabort();
 8    if(tryLock(&lockVar))            21       tend();
 9      return;                        22    } else {
10    delay = min(delay + 1, 0);       23       unlock(lockVar);
11    acquireLock();                   24    }
12 }                                   25    delay = max(delay - 1, b);
13                                     26 }
```

**Listing 1.** Lock with lock elision (bright orange) and exponential backoff (green).

lemmings jump off a cliff (transactions fail), the other lemmings will follow suit. If a few consecutive transactions fall back to the underlying lock, then all concurrent transactions will most likely fail, and possibly fall back to using the underlying lock.

To mitigate the lemming effect, we do not count aborted transactions (Line 5), and we use a truncated exponential backoff variant, which is highlighted green in Listing 1. We use a truncated exponential backoff with a slot size $a = 1024$ processor cycles, and a truncation of $b = 2^{8+\lfloor \log_2 t \rfloor}$, where $t$ is the number of threads. Each thread has a `delay` variable (Line 14), which indicates how contended the lock is. Before acquiring the lock, threads must backoff (wait) for a number of clock cycles sampled randomly from 0 to $2^{\texttt{delay}}$, unless `delay` is 0 (Line 2). Our lock implementation is largely based on another form of lock elision called Speculative Lock Removal (SLR) [1]. Our technique differs from SLR in how we mitigate the lemming effect.

### 2.2   Barrier/Taskwait

Barriers are typically used to orchestrate parallel computations with multiple stages, computations such as linear algebra solvers or image processing with multiple stages or filters. A thread that reaches a barrier must block until all threads arrive at the barrier. Figure 2 illustrates a computation with three threads (Thread$_{0...2}$) using a barrier. Thread$_2$ is the last thread to reach the barrier, which traditionally means that the other threads (Thread$_0$ and Thread$_1$) have to wait. With barrier elision, threads can optimistically speculate beyond the barrier to avoid blocking.

Listing 2 illustrates the barrier elision: Instead of blocking for the arrival of the remaining threads (Line 3), we start a transaction (Line 6). At the next synchronization point, we check if the other threads arrived after the barrier (Line 19); committing the transaction if all threads arrived (Line 21), and aborting otherwise (Line 20).

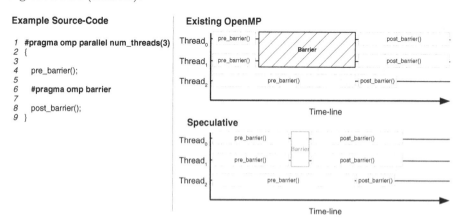

**Fig. 2.** Code and timeline illustrating the benefits of speculative execution over existing approaches for barrier synchronization.

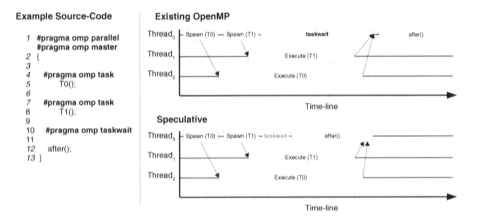

**Fig. 3.** Code and timelines illustrating the benefits of speculative execution existing approaches for taskwait synchronization.

The transaction will commit only if it was data-race free and all threads reached the barrier. This ensures that the transaction will appear to execute atomically after all threads reach the barrier.

The barrier in Listing 2 is simplified to emphasize barrier elision. The listing's barrier is usable only once and does not synchronize with tasks, whereas our implementation uses sense reversing barriers preceded by taskwait synchronization.

Taskwait synchronization cause threads to block until all children tasks finish, as illustrated by Fig. 3. We elide taskwait synchronization in the same way as barriers: Attempt to speculate beyond a taskwait if the thread cannot fetch a ready task, and either commit or abort the transaction at the next synchronization.

Our mechanism can speculate across one barrier or taskwait, theoretically halving the makespan. Ideally, the critical path before and after the synchronization can run in parallel, which would halve the makespan.

```
 1 void barrier_wait(count) {       12 __thread unsigned* spec_adr;
 2   fetch_and_add(&count, 1);       13 __thread unsigned spec_val;
 3   while(count!=num_threads) {      14
 4     while(task_schedule()) {}      15 // Called by synchronization
 5     spec_val = num_threads;        16 void handle_spec() {
 6     tbegin(RETRY);                 17   if(spec_adr == 0)
 7     spec_adr = &count;             18     return;
 8     return;                        19   if(*spec_adr != spec_val)
 9 RETRY: {}                          20     tabort();
10   }                                21   tend();
11 }                                  22 }
```

**Listing 2.** Single use barrier with speculative support (highlighted lines).

**Table 1.** Experimental machine

| Processor Name | Intel Xeon E3–1276 v3 |
|---|---|
| Processor Configuration | 4 cores, 2 hyper-threads/core, 3.6 GHz |
| Processor Caches | $4 \times 32$ kB L1D, $4 \times 256$ kB L2, 8 MB L3 |
| Compiler | GCC 5.1.0 |
| Operating System | Ubuntu Server 14.04.1 LTS |
| Kernel | 3.17.0-031700-generic |

**Table 2.** Task-parallel benchmarks and inputs. We used default cutoffs.

| Benchmark | Input-Set |
|---|---|
| Alignment | prot.100.aa |
| Fibonacci | 48 |
| Floorplan | input.20 |
| Health | large.input |
| nQueens | $13 \times 13$ chessboard |
| Sort | 134,217,728 elements |
| Strassen | $4096 \times 4096$ matrix size |
| SparseLU | $50 \times 50$ matrix, $100 \times 100$ submatrix |
| UTS | tiny.input |

# 3    Evaluation

This sections describes the evaluation methodology we used and the results achieved using our proposed implementation.

## 3.1    Experimental Setup

We implemented our speculative methods, described in Sect. 2, in the OpenMP runtime TurboBŁYSK [17]. We evaluated our implementation on the Intel Haswell-based system outlined in Table 1.

Speculative execution across `taskwaits` in task-parallel benchmarks was evaluated using BOTS [10] with tied tasks. The input sets used are given in Table 2. For all the executions we used wall clock time as a metric for performance. Speed-up was calculated by normalizing the performance to the single-thread version. All task-parallel benchmark were executed 30 times, taking the median to represent the common execution case. Cache-statistics were obtained using Linux Perf. L3 cache statistics only include transactions that were not aborted.

Evaluation of speculation across `omp critical` directives was done using a microbenchmark that randomly inserts or removes elements from a shared map. We compared the traditional `omp critical` implementations that use locks, a

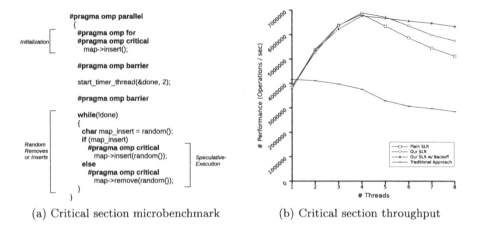

(a) Critical section microbenchmark          (b) Critical section throughput

**Fig. 4.** Source code and performance for the critical section microbenchmark.

generic software lock elision technique and our improved software-elision technique with and without backoff. The performance metric is the number of map modifications successfully completed per second.

Evaluation of speculation across `omp barrier` directives was done using a microbenchmark that randomly synchronize with all other threads. The microbenchmark is intentionally optimistic to show the performance improvements that speculation can give in barriers. The performance metric is the improvement (decrease) in execution time.

## 3.2   Results

**Critical Section Performance.** Evaluation of our proposed critical section implementation (see Sect. 2.1) was performed using a common map microbenchmark [6,9,16], illustrated in Fig. 4a. A team of threads concurrently operate on left-leaning red-black tree (GCC's STL map), which initially contains $2^{17}$ key-value pairs. Half of the operations are insert operations and the other half are remove operations, both using uniformly random keys from $[0; 2^{18} - 1]$. After the threads have operated on the tree for 2 s, we record how many operations completed in that time. The tree is protected by a critical section.

Figure 4b shows the sum of the threads throughput for different lock implementations. We evaluate the lock implementation used in GOMP, plain SLR [1], our SLR variant without backoff, and finally our SLR with backoff.

Traditional locking will suffer from a serialization bottleneck because all work in the benchmark is contained within the critical sections. Using lock elision enables the benchmark to scale, but it suffers from the previously mentioned lemming effect: When a few transactions fail, more transaction will quickly follow. Our SLR variant reduces the lemming effect somewhat by not counting failed transactions (Listing 1 line 5) and by combining it with exponential backoff the performance degrades more gracefully than the other approaches.

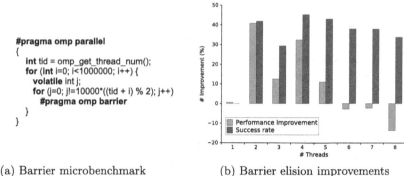

```
#pragma omp parallel
{
    int tid = omp_get_thread_num();
    for (int i=0; i<1000000; i++) {
        volatile int j;
        for (j=0; j!=10000*((tid + i) % 2); j++)
        #pragma omp barrier
    }
}
```

(a) Barrier microbenchmark                (b) Barrier elision improvements

**Fig. 5.** Source code and performance for the barrier microbenchmark.

Other variations of this microbenchmark, with different map implementations or distributions of operations, can scale significantly better than this evaluation. We chose this evaluation because it illustrates that there are both benefits (scaling) and disadvantages (the lemming effect) to lock elision.

**Barrier/Taskwait Elision.** We evaluate elision of barrier and taskwait synchronization on BOTS, as well as a microbenchmark which illustrates the best case scenario for barrier elision. The microbenchmark is illustrated in Fig. 5. A team of threads repeatedly enter a barrier. Only half of the threads will have any work to do in between the barriers, and each thread alternates between having work to do and not.

Figure 5 illustrates the performance improvement from speculating across the barriers, and the success rate of the speculations, i.e. the ratio of successful transactions to attempted transactions, The performance improvement is 41 % at 2 threads and the highest success rate is 45 % percent at 4 threads. Presumably, the speculations are less successful when using more than 4 threads, because the additional threads are hyperthreads. On Intel architectures, using hyperthreads reduces the performance of the threads' siblings, making the siblings less likely to reach the speculated barriers before the speculation finishes.

Figure 6 shows the speed-up performance with and without speculation enabled for the BOTS benchmarks. Both the speculative and non-speculative versions follow the trend of linearly scaling up to the number of cores in the system. The performance is degraded when hyper-threading is in use due to the contention for each core's resources. There are no significant differences between the two versions in terms of absolute performance. Only SparseLU gain consistently (and marginally) from speculative execution.

Figure 7a-b show memory characteristics and performance of the speculative cases normalized against the non-speculative version. Enabling speculation across taskwaits thrashes the level-1 cache significantly– all benchmarks under test experiences this to some extent. Marginal improvements in the last-level cache performance can be seen for the four-thread scenario, where the SparseLU

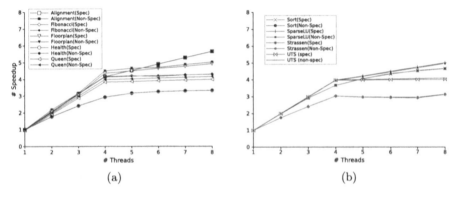

**Fig. 6.** Speed-up on the BOTS benchmarks with and without speculation.

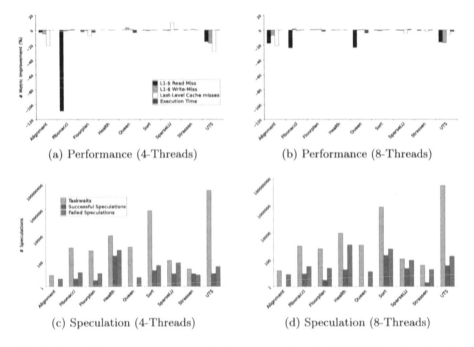

**Fig. 7.** Speculation and performance deviation statistics of the BOTS benchmark suite when enabling speculative execution with four-threads (a,c) and eight-threads (b,d).

benchmark experiences up-to 7% decrease in last-level cache misses. Overall, compute-bound benchmark that uses heavy divide-and-conquer strategies (e.g. nQueen and Fibonacci) seem to most receptive to negative memory effects when speculating – fortunately, these are benchmarks that cause few last-level cache misses.

Figure 7c-d shows the total number of taskwaits encountered and the total number of taskwait speculations that successfully committed or failed. The divide-and-conquer compute-bound benchmark rarely offers any chance for speculation.

```
1 void (*functionPtr)();
2 #pragma omp parallel
3 {
4 #pragma omp master
5   functionPtr = puts;
6 #pragma omp barrier
7   functionPtr();
8 }
```

**Listing 3.** A potentially uninitialized function pointer.

For example, even though the nQueen benchmark offers around 1200 barriers and taskwaits, most of them will fail– only 1 speculation managed to successfully retire. Strassen is the most generous application and manages successfully speculate more than it fails but with no benefits on execution time. SparseLU is also well behaved, allowing between 10 % (4 threads) to 20 % (8 threads) of speculations to succeed, yielding marginal performance improvements up to 1 %.

Our results on BOTS are quite small, in most benchmarks the impact on running time is well below 1 %. BOTS is a benchmark suite for evaluating of OpenMP run-time systems on systems with tens or hundreds of cores, whereas we our evaluation is limited to a 4 core system. As a consequence, all of the benchmarks expose plenty of parallelism, and the threads hardly ever block. Future system will likely benefit more from speculating over taskwaits and barriers, as threads will be less likely to find work.

## 4  Limitations and Related Work

Our synchronization elision techniques operate on the following principle: Continue executing speculatively when you would traditionally block for events, but check that the event occurred before committing. In other words, we defer blocking until the transactional commit.

This principle is also used for prior work on lock and barrier-elision [1,12,20], but it is not entirely correct: The principle assumes that the application code does not commit transactions started by the OpenMP runtime, or change the OpenMP runtimes data. This may seem like a small and reasonable limitation, but seemingly innocent application code, such as Listing 3, can violate the requirement.

Threads which elide synchronization risk calling uninitialized function pointers (Line 7). An uninitialized function pointer can point to anything, including the OpenMP library code, data or unmapped memory. If the function pointer points to a transactional commit instruction, then the user code will commit transactions started by the OpenMP runtime, which will violate the synchronization, and may cause the application to crash.

Similar problems can occur when executing C++ virtual methods, or JIT compiled code, or when writing to uninitialized pointers. We have been able to reproduce the problem in a controlled setting, but we have not seen it occur in the wild. The problem could be avoided by extending OpenMP with clauses which indicate whether synchronization directives can be speculated.

Recently, a lot of effort has gone into proposals for extending OpenMP with TM support. Bae et al. [3] proposed clauses which specify locking strategies, as hints: The hints include specifying that locks and locks and critical sections should use lock elision if possible. For our purposes, their hints could be extended to all OpenMP directives.

Wong et al. [21] proposed two new directives: `synchronized`, a transactional version of critical sections, and `transaction`. The `transaction` directive provides transactional execution, with defined semantics for C++ exceptions, for transaction-safe code. Transaction-safe code must follow some mild restrictions, such that it can be executed speculatively by both HTM and STM implementation.

OpenTM [4] is a programming interface that extends OpenMP with speculative capabilities. They propose (primarily) three new directives that support speculation: `omp transfor` and `omp transsection` and `omp speculation`. They also support nested speculations.

Pyla et al. [18] provides a framework for exploiting coarse-grained parallelism in OpenMP. They introduce regions where speculations take place (*speculative regions*), which can also be nested (speculation within speculation). They propose a directive (`speculate`) to simplify using them.

Miloš et al. [13,14] gives an overview *where* in OpenMP speculations can be used. They introduce a new clause, `transaction`, that can be coupled with existing directives to provide speculation. They show how to proposed directives would interact with Nebelung (a STM-based run-time system) and Mercurium [5] and evaluate their strategy on a set of synthetic benchmarks and a Gauss-Seidel application.

## 5  Conclusion

In this paper, we have shown how exploit HTM to perform speculations on some of the most frequently used directives in OpenMP. We use HTM to speculatively avoid blocking in critical sections, barriers, and taskwaits, transparently to the programmer. The speculative execution of critical sections handles contention better than Speculative Lock Removal (SLR) without sacrificing scaling. Avoiding blocking of taskwaits and barriers can improve performance by up to 41% on a microbenchmark which traditionally blocks most of the time, but it does not improve the performance of 4 core system significantly on the Barcelona OpenMP Task Suite (BOTS). We expect that future systems with more cores will benefit further from our approach, as they are more likely to block.

**Acknowledgments.** This article presents the result of a research and development work carried out in the European collaborative project PaPP (Portable and Predictable Performance on Heterogeneous Embedded Manycores) funded jointly by the ARTEMIS Joint Undertaking and national governments under the Call 2011 Project Nr. 295440.

# References

1. Afek, Y., Levy, A., Morrison, A.: Software-improved hardware lock elision. In: PODC, pp. 212–221. ACM (2014)
2. Anderson, T.E.: The performance of spin lock alternatives for shared-money multiprocessors. IEEE Trans. Parallel Distrib. Syst. $\mathbf{1}$(1), 6–16 (1990)
3. Bae, H., Cownie, J., Klemm, M., Terboven, C.: A user-guided locking API for the OpenMP* application program interface. In: DeRose, L., de Supinski, B.R., Olivier, S.L., Chapman, B.M., Müller, M.S. (eds.) IWOMP 2014. LNCS, vol. 8766, pp. 173–186. Springer, Heidelberg (2014)
4. Baek, W., Minh, C.C., Trautmann, M., Kozyrakis, C., Olukotun, K.: The opentm transactional application programming interface. In: 16th International Conference on Parallel Architecture and Compilation Techniques, PACT 2007, pp. 376–387. IEEE (2007)
5. Balart, J., Duran, A., Gonzàlez, M., Martorell, X., Ayguadé, E., Labarta, J.: Nanos mercurium: a research compiler for openmp. In: Proceedings of the European Workshop on OpenMP, vol. 8 (2004)
6. Brown, T., Ellen, F., Ruppert, E.: A general technique for non-blocking trees. In: PPoPP, pp. 329–342. ACM (2014)
7. Cain, H.W., Michael, M.M., Frey, B., May, C., Williams, D., Le, H.: Robust architectural support for transactional memory in the power architecture. In: ISCA, pp. 225–236. ACM (2013)
8. Dice, D., Lev, Y., Moir, M., Nussbaum, D., Olszewski, M.: Early experience with a commercial hardware transactional memory implementation. Sun Microsystems, Inc., Technical report (2009)
9. Drachsler, D., Vechev, M.T., Yahav, E.: Practical concurrent binary search trees via logical ordering. In: PPoPP, pp. 343–356. ACM (2014)
10. Duran, A., Teruel, X., Ferrer, R., Martorell, X., Ayguade, E.: Barcelona openmp tasks suite: A set of benchmarks targeting the exploitation of task parallelism in openmp. In: International Conference on Parallel Processing, ICPP 2009, pp. 124–131. IEEE (2009)
11. Intel: Programming with Intel Transactional Synchronization Extensions, June 2014
12. Martínez, J.F., Torrellas, J.: Speculative synchronization: applying thread-level speculation to explicitly parallel applications. In: ACM SIGOPS Operating Systems Review, vol. 36, pp. 18–29. ACM (2002)
13. Milovanović, M., Ferrer, R., Gajinov, V., Unsal, O.S., Cristal, A., Ayguadé, E., Valero, M.: Nebelung: execution environment for transactional openmp. Int. J. Parallel Prog. $\mathbf{36}$(3), 326–346 (2008)
14. Milovanović, M., Ferrer, R., Unsal, O.S., Cristal, A., Martorell, X., Ayguadé, E., Labarta, J., Valero, M.: Transactional memory and OpenMP. In: Chapman, B., Zheng, W., Gao, G.R., Sato, M., Ayguadé, E., Wang, D. (eds.) IWOMP 2007. LNCS, vol. 4935, pp. 37–53. Springer, Heidelberg (2008)
15. Moreshet, T., Bahar, R.I., Herlihy, M.: Energy reduction in multiprocessor systems using transactional memory. In: Proceedings of the 2005 International Symposium on Low Power Electronics and Design, ISLPED 2005, pp. 331–334. IEEE (2005)
16. Natarajan, A., Mittal, N.: Fast concurrent lock-free binary search trees. In: PPoPP, pp. 317–328. ACM (2014)

17. Podobas, A., Brorsson, M., Vlassov, V.: TurboBŁYSK: scheduling for improved data-driven task performance with fast dependency resolution. In: DeRose, L., de Supinski, B.R., Olivier, S.L., Chapman, B.M., Müller, M.S. (eds.) IWOMP 2014. LNCS, vol. 8766, pp. 45–57. Springer, Heidelberg (2014)

18. Pyla, H.K., Ribbens, C., Varadarajan, S.: Exploiting coarse-grain speculative parallelism. In: ACM SIGPLAN Notices, vol. 46, pp. 555–574. ACM (2011)

19. Saha, B., Adl-Tabatabai, A.R., Hudson, R.L., Minh, C.C., Hertzberg, B.: Mcrt-stm: a high performance software transactional memory system for a multi-core runtime. In: Proceedings of the Eleventh ACM SIGPLAN Symposium on Principles and Practice of Parallel Programming, pp. 187–197. ACM (2006)

20. Sato, T., Ohno, K., Nakashima, H.: A mechanism for speculative memory accesses following synchronizing operations. In: Proceedings of the 14th International Parallel and Distributed Processing Symposium, IPDPS 2000, pp. 145–154. IEEE (2000)

21. Wong, M., Ayguadé, E., Gottschlich, J., Luchangco, V., de Supinski, B.R., Bihari, B., other members of the WG21 SG5 Transactional Memory Sub-Group: Towards transactional memory for OpenMP. In: DeRose, L., de Supinski, B.R., Olivier, S.L., Chapman, B.M., Müller, M.S. (eds.) IWOMP 2014. LNCS, vol. 8766, pp. 130–145. Springer, Heidelberg (2014)

# A Case Study of OpenMP Applied to Map/Reduce-Style Computations

Mahwish Arif$^{(\boxtimes)}$ and Hans Vandierendonck

Queen's University Belfast, Belfast, UK
{m.arif,h.vandierendonck}@qub.ac.uk

**Abstract.** As data analytics are growing in importance they are also quickly becoming one of the dominant application domains that require parallel processing. This paper investigates the applicability of OpenMP, the dominant shared-memory parallel programming model in high-performance computing, to the domain of data analytics. We contrast the performance and programmability of key data analytics benchmarks against Phoenix++, a state-of-the-art shared memory map/reduce programming system. Our study shows that OpenMP outperforms the Phoenix++ system by a large margin for several benchmarks. In other cases, however, the programming model is lacking support for this application domain.

**Keywords:** OpenMP · Map/reduce · Reduction

## 1 Introduction

Data analytics (a.k.a. "Big Data") are increasing in importance as a means for business to improve their value proposition or to improve the efficiency of their operations. As a consequence of the sheer volume of data, data analytics are heavily dependent on parallel computing technology to complete data processing in a timely manner.

Numerous specialized programming models and runtime systems have been developed to support data analytics. Hadoop [2] and SPARK [22] implement the map/reduce model [6]. GraphLab [10], Giraph [1] and GraphX [20] implement the Pregel model [12]. Storm [3] supports streaming data. Each of these systems provides a parallel and distributed computing environment built up from scratch using threads and bare bones synchronization mechanisms. In contrast, the high-performance computing community designed programming models that simplify the development of systems like the ones cited above and that provide a good balance between performance and programming effort. It is fair to ask if anything important was overseen during this decades-long research that precluded the use of these parallel programming languages in the construction of these data analytics frameworks.

This paper addresses the question whether HPC-oriented parallel programming models are viable in the data analytics domain. In particular, our

© Springer International Publishing Switzerland 2015
C. Terboven et al. (Eds.): IWOMP 2015, LNCS 9342, pp. 162–174, 2015.
DOI: 10.1007/978-3-319-24595-9_12

study contrasts the performance and programmability of OpenMP [14] against Phoenix++ [17], a purpose-built shared-memory map/reduce runtime. The importance of these shared-memory programming models in the domain of data-analytics increases with the emergence of in-memory data analytics architectures such as NumaQ [7]. To program against Phoenix++, the programmer needs to specify several key functions, i.e., the map, combine and reduce functions, and also select several container types used internally by the runtime. We have found that the programmer needs to understand the internals of Phoenix++ quite well in order to select the appropriate internal containers. Moreover, we conjecture that the overall tuning and programming effort is such that the programming effort is not much reduced in comparison to using a programming model like OpenMP.

We evaluate the performance and programmability of OpenMP for data analytics by implementing a number of commonly occurring map/reduce kernels in OpenMP. Experimental performance evaluation demonstrates that OpenMP can easily outperform Phoenix++ implementations of these kernels. The highest speedup observed was around 75 % on 16 threads. We furthermore report on the complexity of writing these codes in OpenMP and the issues we have observed. One of the key programmability issues we encountered is the lack of support for user-defined reductions in current compilers. Moreover, the OpenMP standard does not support parallel execution of the reduction operation, a feature that proves useful in this domain. This drives us to design the program and its data structures around an efficient way to perform the reduction.

In the remainder of this paper we will first discuss related work (Sect. 2). Then we discuss the map/reduce programming model and the Phoenix++ implementation for shared memory systems (Sect. 3). We subsequently discuss the implementation of a number of map/reduce kernels in OpenMP (Sect. 4). Experimental evaluation demonstrates the performance benefits that OpenMP bring (Sect. 5). We conclude the paper with summary remarks and pointers for future work (Sect. 6).

## 2   Related Work

Phoenix is a shared-memory map-reduce runtime system. Since its inception [16] it has been optimized for the Sun Niagara architecture [21] and subsequently reimplemented to avoid inefficiencies of having only key-value pairs available as a data representation [17].

Several studies have improved the scalability of Phoenix. TiledMR [4] improves memory locality by applying a blocking optimizing. Mao et al. [13] stress the importance of huge page support and multi-core-aware memory allocators. Others have optimized the map/reduce for accelerators. Lu et al. [11] optimize map-reduce for the Xeon Phi and attempt to apply vectorization in the map task and the computation of hash table indices. De Kruijf et al. [9] and Rafique et al. [15] optimize the map/reduce model for the Cell B.E. architecture.

While the map-reduce model is conceptually simple, a subtly undefined aspect of map-reduce is the commutativity of reductions [19]. This aspect of the programming model is most often not documented, for instance in the Phoenix systems [16, 17, 21]. However, executing non-commutative reduction operations on a runtime system that assumes commutativity can lead to real program bugs [5] even in extensively tested programs [19]. OpenMP assumes reductions are commutative [14].

There has been effort to use OpenMP style semantics for programming data-analytics and cloud-based applications. OpenMR [18] implements OpenMP semantics on top of map-reduce runtime for cloud-based implementation. The motivation is to port OpenMP applications to the cloud as well as reduce the programming effort. Jiang *et al.* [8] introduce OpenMP annotations to a domain-specific language for data-analytics, R, to facilitate the semi-automatic parallelization of R and thus reduce the parallel programming effort.

## 3   Map-Reduce Programming Model

The map-reduce programming model is centered around the representation of data by key-value pairs. For instance, the links between internet sites may be represented by key-value pairs where the key is a source URL and the value is a list of target URLs. The data representation exposes high degrees of parallelism, as individual key-value pairs may be operated on independently.

Computations on key-value pairs consist, in essence, of a map function and a reduce function. The map function transforms a single input data item (typically a key-value pair) to a list of key-value pairs (which is possibly empty). The reduce function combines all values occurring for each key. Many computations fit this model [6], or can be adjusted to fit this model.

### 3.1   Phoenix++ Implementation

The Phoenix++ shared-memory map-reduce programming model consists of multiple steps: partition, map-and-combine, reduce, sort and merge (Fig. 1). The partition step partitions the input data in chunks such that each map task can operate on a single chunk. The input data may be a list of key-value pairs read from disk, but it may also be other data such as a set of HTML documents. The map-and-combine step further breaks the chunk of data apart and transforms it to a list of key-value pairs. The map function may apply a combine function, which performs an initial reduction step of the data. It has been observed that making an initial reduction is extremely important for performance as it reduces the intermediate data set size [17].

It is key to performance to store the intermediate key-value list in an appropriate format. A naive implementation would hold these simply as lists. However, it is much more efficient to tune these to the application [17]. For instance, in the word count application the key is a string and the value is a count. As such, one should use a hash-map indexed by the key. In the histogram application, a fixed-size histogram is computed. As such, the key is an integer lying in a fixed range. In this case, the intermediate key-value list should be stored as an array of

input range   Per-worker KV-stores

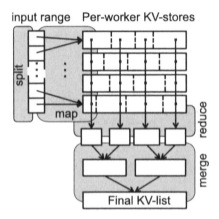

**Fig. 1.** Schematic overview of Phoenix++ runtime system

integers. For this reason, we say the map-and-combine step produces key-value data structures, rather than lists.

The output of the map-and-combine step is a set of key-value data structures, one for each worker thread. Let KV-list $j = 0, \ldots, N - 1$ represent the key-value data structure for the $j$-th worker thread. These $N$ key-value data structures are subsequently partitioned in $M$ chunks such that each chunk with index $i = 0, \ldots, M - 1$ in the intermediate key-value list $j$ holds the same range of keys. All chunks $i$ are then handed to worker thread $N$, which reduces those chunks by key. This way, the reduce step produces $M$ key-value *lists*, each with distinct keys.

Finally, the resulting key-value lists are sorted by key (an optional step) and they are subsequently merged into a single key-value list.

Phoenix++ allows the programmer to specify a map function, the intermediate key-value data structure, a combine function for that data structure, the reduce function, a sort comparison function and a flag whether sorting is required.

## 3.2   OpenMP Facilities for Map/Reduce-Style Computations

Map/reduce, viewed as parallel pattern, is fairly easy to grasp and encode in a variety of parallel programming languages. OpenMP offers multiple constructs to encode the map phase using parallel loops as illustrated in Fig. 2. A parallel for loop applies when a large data set can be partitioned by considering the iteration domain of a for loop. Alternatively, if the partitioning requires a more complex evaluation, then task spawn construct inside a for loop may be more appropriate. An example encountered in our study is word count. Although the file contents are stored in an array, the boundaries of the partitions must be aligned with word boundaries, which is most easily achieved using the task construct.

The most recent OpenMP 4.0 [14] standard introduced support for user-defined reductions (UDRs), which allows to specify reductions of variables of

```
 1     int  i ;
 2  #pragma omp parallel for
 3     for( i=0; i < N; ++i ) { map(i); }
 4
 5
 6     struct  item_t  item;
 7  #pragma omp parallel
 8  #pragma omp single
 9     while( partition ( &item ) ) {
10  #pragma omp task
11         map(&item);
12     }
```

**Fig. 2.** Generic OpenMP code structures for the map phase.

a wide range of data types with little programming effort. Unfortunately, few OpenMP compilers currently fully support user-defined reductions. This strongly limits the programmability aspect of this study, although we can expect this situation to improve with the availability of user-defined reductions. Hence the implementation and performance of the reduce phase in OpenMP depends on the data type of the reduction object. More importantly, complex OpenMP 4.0 UDRs may not be evaluated in parallel, a feature that is important for reductions on collections, which are common in data analytics workloads. For example, if each thread produces a same-sized array which must then be reduced element-wise, then UDRs allow to specify this but the execution of the reduction will be sequential. The fast way to reduce a set of arrays is, however, by assigning each section of the arrays to a thread and have all threads reduce their section in parallel. Reductions on more complex data structures such as hash tables are even harder to parallelise, even with UDR support, whereas a sequential approach results in poor performance.

## 4   OpenMP Implementations

We have ported seven map/reduce benchmarks from the Phoenix++ system to OpenMP. We describe the main characteristics of these benchmarks and the main issues encountered in porting them.

### 4.1   Histogram

The histogram benchmark processes a bitmap image to compute the frequency counts of values (in the range of 0–255) for each of its RGB components. The map phase is parallelized using the OpenMP **for** work-sharing construct. Each thread is statically assigned a subset of the pixels in the image and computes a histogram over this subset. These per-thread results are then reduced to compute the histogram of the whole image. However, due to lack of OpenMP support for user-defined reductions (UDR) in our compiler, we had to find ways to reduce the results without using locks or critical sections (which incur significant execution time overhead). We defined a shared array as large as the histogram array times the number of threads i.e. for a 24-bit image, $(256 \times 3) \times$ #threads bytes. During the map phase, each thread stores its results to the array assigned to it based on its thread id. Once the map phase is completed, the results are reduced in a second OpenMP **for** loop where each thread reduces a section of the histogram. E.g., for 16 threads, each thread reduces a slice of $16 \times 3$ values.

## 4.2  Linear Regression

Linear Regression computes the values **a** and **b** to define a line $y = \mathbf{a}x + \mathbf{b}$ that best fits an input set of coordinates. Firstly, five statistics are calculated (such as sum of squares) on the input coordinates. We have used the **parallel for** construct to distribute the work among the threads. The per-thread statistics are reduced using the **reduction** clause. Secondly, **a** and **b** are computed using the five statistics collected in the first step.

## 4.3  K-Means Clustering

This benchmark implements a clustering algorithm which groups input data points in $k$ clusters. The assignment of a data point to a cluster is made based on its minimum distance to the cluster mean. The assignment algorithm is invoked iteratively until it converges, i.e., no further changes are made to the cluster assignment. As long as the assignment algorithm has not converged, the cluster means are also recalculated iteratively.

Both the assignment and mean calculation steps have been separately parallelized with the **parallel for** construct.

## 4.4  Word Count

The word count benchmark counts the frequency of occurrence of each word in a text file. This is a stereo-typical example of a map/reduce type benchmark. For the map phase, we have used OpenMP tasks. A team of threads is first created with the OpenMP **parallel** construct. Then one of the threads is designated to iteratively calculate the input partitions and spawn the tasks for the other threads to work on. Each thread completes its word counting task for the assigned partition, and then becomes available to operate on another partition.

Here again we faced difficulty due to the absence of UDR support. We thus defined a vector of hash tables and each thread stored its results in separate hash tables. After all the threads have finished working, the results are sequentially reduced in a global hash table. Parallelizing this reduction in a similar way as histogram is challenging, due to the difficulty of isolating slices in each of the hash tables that hold corresponding ranges of keys. Although it is not impossible to solve this issue, it clearly impacts the programmability of OpenMP for workloads like these.

## 4.5  String Match

String match takes as input a set of encrypted keys and a text file. The text file is then processed to see which set of words were originally encrypted to

```
 1  int  splitter_pos  = 0;
 2  #pragma omp parallel
 3  {
 4      #pragma omp single
 5      {
 6          while( 1 ) {
 7              str_map_data_t  partition ;
 8              /* End of data reached. */
 9              if ( splitter_pos  >= keys_file_len )
10                  break;
11              /* Determine the nominal end point. */
12              int end = std::min( splitter_pos  + chunk_size,  keys_file_len );
13              /* Move end point to next word break */
14              while(end < keys_file_len && keys_file[end] != '\n')
15                  end++;
16              /* Set the start of the next data. */
17              partition .keys = keys_file + splitter_pos ;
18              partition .keys_len = end − splitter_pos ;
19              /* Skip line breaks (code skipped for brevity). */
20              splitter_pos  = end;
21
22              /* Spawn a task to do the real work */
23              #pragma omp task firstprivate( partition )
24              {
25                  /* Apply sequential algorithm on data */
26              }
27          }/* end of while(1) */
28      }
29  }
```

**Fig. 3.** OpenMP code for String Match

produce the encrypted keys. This benchmark is parallelized using OpenMP tasks (Fig. 3). A single thread, from a team of threads, partitions the input file on word boundaries. It spawns a task to handle each partition independently. A reduction phase is not required for this benchmark.

### 4.6 Matrix Multiply

It computes a matrix **C** which is a product of two input matrices **A** and **B**. We have parallelized a simple matrix multiplication algorithm with the **parallel for** construct and the **collapse** clause to increase the available parallelism. Each thread calculates a subset of elements $C(i,j)$. Moreover, we swapped the order of the two inner loops to improve the data locality.

### 4.7 Principal Component Analysis

This benchmark implements two stages of the statistical Principal Component Analysis algorithm. It takes as input a matrix which is a collection of column vectors. In the first stage, per-coordinate means are calculated along the rows and work is distributed among the threads with the loop scheduler. In the second stage, the co-variance matrix is calculated along with a total sum of co-variance. This loop nest is parallelized using the **parallel for** loop with a **reduction** clause for the scalar sum of co-variance. The second loop nest exhibits load imbalance which we mitigated by changing the granularity of static loop scheduler.

# 5    Evaluation

We evaluated the OpenMP and Phoenix++ version 1.0 programs on a dual-socket Intel Xeon E5-2650 with 8 cores per socket and hyperthreading. The operating system is CentOS 7.0 and we use the Intel C/C++ compiler v. 14.0.0. We evaluate the programs on the small, medium and large data sets supplied with Phoenix++. We pin threads to cores to ensure at most one out of each pair of hyperthreads is used.

## 5.1    Analysis

Figures 4 and 5 show the speedup curves for the OpenMP and Phoenix++ implementations of the 7 map/reduce workloads for 3 inputs with different sizes. Speedups are normalized to the execution time of a purely sequential code.

Figure 4 shows the performance of benchmarks with low computational intensity, i.e., they perform few operations per byte transferred from memory. The OpenMP implementation of histogram performs similar to Phoenix++. For string match, OpenMP is again similar to Phoenix++ except on the large

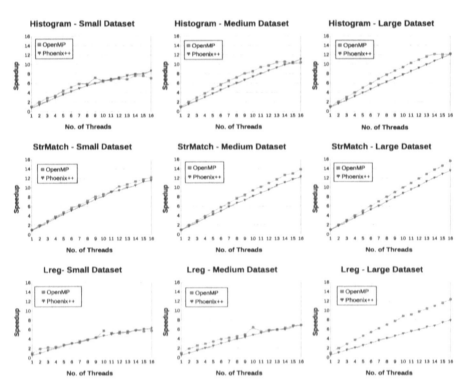

**Fig. 4.** Speedup obtained with the OpenMP implementations of the benchmarks in comparison against the Phoenix++ implementations. Benchmarks with low computational intensity.

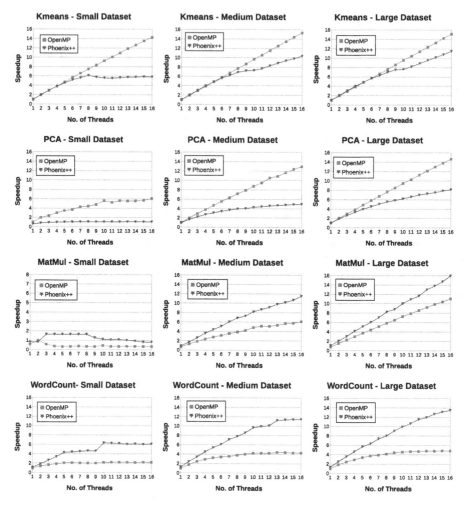

**Fig. 5.** Speedup obtained with the OpenMP implementations of the benchmarks in comparison against the Phoenix++ implementations. Benchmarks with high computational intensity.

input where the OpenMP code gains 15 % advantage. For linear regression, the Phoenix++ code scales to an 8-fold speedup at best, while the OpenMP code gains up to 12x. This is possible due to the higher efficiency of the OpenMP code, which does not use generalized data structures to mimic the emission of key-value pairs in the map task, or mimic a reduction of key-value pairs.

Two benchmarks with high computational intensity, namely kmeans and pca, perform markedly better with OpenMP than with Phoenix++ (Fig. 5). In the case of k-means this is due to a memory allocator issue in Phoenix++, which can be solved by substituting for a better multi-core-aware memory allocator. PCA has load imbalance in the iterations of its outer loop. The Phoenix++ runtime cannot deal with this by itself and also offers no controls to the programmer.

In contrast, the OpenMP API allows us to fix the load imbalance through setting the granularity of tasks for the static loop scheduler, which results in a 75 % speedup.

Phoenix++ obtains excellent scalability on matrix multiply. While we did not obtain good speedups in our implementation of matrix multiply, we assume this can be fixed with sufficient locality optimization. Note however that the Phoenix++ implementation is quite straightforward and does not exhibit any specific locality optimization.

Finally, word count shows bad scalability when implemented in OpenMP. While the map phase is trivially parallel using task parallelism, word count requires a reduction of the per-thread hash tables holding word counts. Parallelizing that reduction is hard but is key to obtaining good performance.

## 5.2   Coding Style Comparison

We present a comparison of histogram benchmark implementation in both OpenMP and Phoenix++ (Table 1) to understand the programming effort required. Phoenix++ library specifies default map, reduce and split function along with different options for containers and combiners. In most of the cases, the programmers will need to override the default map and split function to specify their own map function and distribute the work accordingly. Histogram code overrides the default map function to emit the distinct range of keys (line 6–10) for R, G and B components of the image. The selection of container depends on the cardinality of keys. The histogram implementation below uses an array container (line 2) since the number of distinct keys (or cardinality) is fixed, in this case to 768. The definition of MapReduce class also depends on whether the keys need to be sorted in a particular order or not. From different combiners provided with Phoenix++ library, histogram uses the sum combiner since the values for a particular key need to be simply added.

In case of OpenMP, the choice of container to store histogram depends on how the reduction is to be performed. Since there are fixed number of keys within a known range, a global array of the size of histogram (i.e., 768) times the number of available threads is defined. OpenMP `for` construct (line 12) parallelizes the map phase by distributing the iterations of the loop among available worker threads. Each thread then updates the respective histogram buckets based on its id (line 14–17). Due to absence of UDR support for non-scalars, programmer needs to write how the reduction is to be performed on the array. For this benchmark, a separate global array `histo` has been used to store the results of reduction performed on `histo_shared` array (line 22–25).

## 5.3   Implications to OpenMP

The implementation of most of the benchmarks was straightforward and lead to the results shown fairly easily. Obtaining excellent performance was easy especially in those cases where the reduction variable consisted of a small number of scalars. Whenever the reduction variable became more complex (e.g., an array

**Table 1.** Coding Style Comparison for histogram benchmark implementation in Phoenix++ (left) and OpenMP(right)

```
 1  /* defining a MapReduce class with a sum combiner
        and default sorting order by keys*/
 2  class  HistogramMR : public MapReduceSort<
        HistogramMR, pixel, intptr_t, uint64_t,
        array_container <intptr_t, uint64_t,
        sum_combiner,768>>
 3  {
 4  public :
 5     /* overriding  default map function*/
 6     void map(data_type const& pix, map_container&
        out) const {
 7       emit_intermediate (out,  pix.b, 1);
 8       emit_intermediate (out,  pix.g+256, 1);
 9       emit_intermediate (out,  pix.r+512, 1);
10     }
11       /* default reduce function from library to be
            used*/
12  };
13
14  /* inside main() function*/
15
16  std :: vector<HistogramMR::keyval> result;
17  HistogramMR* mapReduce = new HistogramMR();
18
19  /* calling  map−reduce on input image with image
        data bytes in bitmap[]*/
20  mapReduce−>run((pixel*)bitmap, num_pixels, result);
```

```
 1  int  num_of_threads;
 2  uint64_t * histo_shared ;
 3  #pragma omp parallel
 4  {
 5     /* map phase*/
 6  #pragma omp single
 7     {
 8        num_of_threads= omp_get_num_threads();
 9        histo_shared  = new uint64_t [768*
           num_of_threads];
10     }
11     int  id = omp_get_thread_num();
12  #pragma omp for
13     for ( long  i=0; i  < num_pixels; i++ ) {
14        pixel  *pix = (pixel *) &(bitmap[3*i]);
15        histo_shared [id*768+ (size_t)pix−>b]++;
16        histo_shared [id*768+(256+((size_t)pix−>g))
              ]++;
17        histo_shared [id*768+(512+((size_t)pix−>r))
              ]++;
18     }
19
20     /* reduce phase*/
21  #pragma omp for
22     for ( int  j=0; j< 768; j++)
23        for ( int  k=0; k<num_of_threads; k++)
24           histo [j]+=histo_shared[j+k*768];
25  }
26  delete []  histo_shared ;
```

in histogram or a hash table in word count), much of the programming effort became focused on how to efficiently perform the reduction, which required parallel execution of the combine step of the reduction. The Intel compiler we have used currently does not support user defined reductions (UDR). We expect that UDR support will simplify the programming effort substantially. However, it is unlikely that UDRs will deliver sufficient performance as the OpenMP specification does not allow parallel execution of a reduction, e.g., OpenMP pragma's within combine functions are disallowed [14]. This is a potential area of improvement for OpenMP.

The matrix multiplication problem demonstrates that OpenMP may require substantially higher effort than Phoenix++ to tune the performance of an application. Even though it is evident what parallelism is present in matrix multiply, exploiting this in OpenMP requires significant effort, while a straightforward implementation in Phoenix++ gives fairly good results.

## 6   Conclusion

This paper has evaluated the performance and programmability of OpenMP when applied to data analytics, an increasingly important computing domain. Our experience with applying OpenMP to map/reduce workloads shows that the programming effort can be quite high, especially in relation to making the evaluation of the reduction step efficient. For most benchmarks, however, OpenMP outperforms Phoenix++, a state-of-the-art shared-memory map/reduce runtime.

To simplify the programming of these workloads, OpenMP will need to support much more powerful reduction types and support parallel execution of the reduction. User-defined reductions, currently unavailable to us, promise ease of programming but parallel execution of reductions is not supported.

**Acknowledgment.** This work is supported by the European Community's Seventh Framework Programme (FP7/2007–2013) under the ASAP project, grant agreement no. 619706, and by the United Kingdom EPSRC under grant agreement EP/L027402/1.

# References

1. Apache Giraph. http://giraph.apache.org/
2. Apache Hadoop. http://hadoop.apache.org/
3. Apache Storm. http://storm.apache.org/
4. Chen, R., Chen, H.: Tiled-mapreduce: efficient and flexible MapReduce processing on multicore with tiling. ACM Trans. Archit. Code Optim. **10**(1), 3:1–3:30 (2013). http://doi.acm.org/10.1145/2445572.2445575
5. Csallner, C., Fegaras, L., Li, C.: New ideas track: testing Mapreduce-style programs. In: Proceedings of the 19th ACM SIGSOFT Symposium and the 13th European Conference on Foundations of Software Engineering, ESEC/FSE 2011, pp. 504–507. ACM, New York (2011). http://doi.acm.org/10.1145/2025113.2025204
6. Dean, J., Ghemawat, S.: Mapreduce: simplified data processing on large clusters. In: Proceedings of the 6th Conference on Symposium on Opearting Systems Design & Implementation, OSDI 2004, vol. 6, p. 10. USENIX Association, Berkeley (2004). http://dl.acm.org/citation.cfm?id=1251254.1251264
7. Eadline, D.: Redefining scalable OpenMP and MPI price-to-performance with Numascale's NumaConnect (2014)
8. Jiang, L., Patel, P.B., Ostrouchov, G., Jamitzky, F.: OpenMP-style parallelism in data-centered multicore computing with R. SIGPLAN Not. **47**(8), 335–336 (2012). http://doi.acm.org/10.1145/2370036.2145882
9. de Kruijf, M., Sankaralingam, K.: MapReduce for the Cell broadband engine architecture. IBM J. Res. Dev. **53**(5), 10:1–10:12 (2009)
10. Low, Y., Bickson, D., Gonzalez, J., Guestrin, C., Kyrola, A., Hellerstein, J.M.: Distributed GraphLab: a framework for machine learning and data mining in the cloud. Proc. VLDB Endow. **5**(8), 716–727 (2012). http://dx.doi.org/10.14778/2212351.2212354
11. Lu, M., Zhang, L., Huynh, H.P., Ong, Z., Liang, Y., He, B., Goh, R., Huynh, R.: Optimizing the MapReduce framework on Intel Xeon Phi coprocessor. In: 2013 IEEE International Conference on Big Data, pp. 125–130, October 2013
12. Malewicz, G., Austern, M.H., Bik, A.J., Dehnert, J.C., Horn, I., Leiser, N., Czajkowski, G.: Pregel: a system for large-scale graph processing. In: Proceedings of the 2010 ACM SIGMOD International Conference on Management of Data, SIGMOD 2010, pp. 135–146. ACM, New York (2010). http://doi.acm.org/10.1145/1807167.1807184

13. Mao, Y., Morris, R., Kaashoek, F.: Optimizing MapReduce for multicore architectures. Technical report. MIT-CSAIL-TR-2010-020, MIT Computer Science and Artificial Intelligence Laboratory (2010)
14. The OpenMP Application Program Interface, version 4.0 edn., July 2013
15. Rafique, M., Rose, B., Butt, A., Nikolopoulos, D.: CellMR: a framework for supporting MapReduce on asymmetric Cell-based clusters. In: IEEE International Symposium on Parallel Distributed Processing, IPDPS 2009, pp. 1–12, May 2009
16. Ranger, C., Raghuraman, R., Penmetsa, A., Bradski, G., Kozyrakis, C.: Evaluating MapReduce for multi-core and multiprocessor systems. In: Proceedings of the 2007 IEEE 13th International Symposium on High Performance Computer Architecture, HPCA 2007, pp. 13–24. IEEE Computer Society, Washington, DC (2007). http://dx.doi.org/10.1109/HPCA.2007.346181
17. Talbot, J., Yoo, R.M., Kozyrakis, C.: Phoenix++: modular MapReduce for shared-memory systems. In: Proceedings of the Second International Workshop on MapReduce and Its Applications, MapReduce 2011, pp. 9–16. ACM, New York (2011). http://doi.acm.org/10.1145/1996092.1996095
18. Wottrich, R., Azevedo, R., Araujo, G.: Cloud-based OpenMP parallelization using a MapReduce runtime. In: 2014 IEEE 26th International Symposium on Computer Architecture and High Performance Computing (SBAC-PAD), pp. 334–341, October 2014
19. Xiao, T., Zhang, J., Zhou, H., Guo, Z., McDirmid, S., Lin, W., Chen, W., Zhou, L.: Nondeterminism in MapReduce considered harmful? An empirical study on non-commutative aggregators in MapReduce programs. In: Companion Proceedings of the 36th International Conference on Software Engineering, ICSE Companion 2014, pp. 44–53. ACM, New York (2014). http://doi.acm.org/10.1145/2591062.2591177
20. Xin, R.S., Gonzalez, J.E., Franklin, M.J., Stoica, I.: GraphX: a resilient distributed graph system on spark. In: First International Workshop on Graph Data Management Experiences and Systems, GRADES 2013, pp. 2:1–2:6. ACM, New York (2013). http://doi.acm.org/10.1145/2484425.2484427
21. Yoo, R.M., Romano, A., Kozyrakis, C.: Phoenix rebirth: scalable MapReduce on a large-scale shared-memory system. In: Proceedings of the 2009 IEEE International Symposium on Workload Characterization (IISWC), IISWC 2009, pp. 198–207. IEEE Computer Society, Washington, DC (2009). http://dx.doi.org/10.1109/IISWC.2009.5306783
22. Zaharia, M., Chowdhury, M., Franklin, M.J., Shenker, S., Stoica, I.: Spark: cluster computing with working sets. In: Proceedings of the 2Nd USENIX Conference on Hot Topics in Cloud Computing, HotCloud 2010, p. 10. USENIX Association, Berkeley (2010). http://dl.acm.org/citation.cfm?id=1863103.1863113

# Compiler and Runtime

# Enabling Region Merging Optimizations in OpenMP

Thomas R.W. Scogland[✉], John Gyllenhaal, Jeff Keasler, Rich Hornung, and Bronis R. de Supinski

Lawrence Livermore National Laboratory, Livermore, CA 94551, USA
scogland1@llnl.gov

**Abstract.** Maximizing the scope of a parallel region, which avoids the costs of barriers and of launching additional parallel regions, is among the first recommendations in any optimization guide for OpenMP. While clearly beneficial and easily accomplished for code where regions are visibly contiguous, regions often become contiguous only after compiler optimization or resolution of abstraction layers. This paper explores changes to the OpenMP specification that would allow implementations to merge adjacent parallel regions automatically, including the removal of issues that make the transformation non-conforming and the addition of hints that facilitate the optimization. Beyond simple merging, we explore hints to fuse workshared loops that occur in syntactically distinct parallel regions or to apply `nowait` to such loops. Our evaluation shows these changes can provide an overall speedup of 2–8× for a microbenchmark, or 6 % for a representative physics application.

## 1 Introduction

That OpenMP programs should minimize the number of synchronization points and parallel regions is well known optimization guidance. The region's team of threads must be initialized when it begins and joined when it ends, each entailing costly synchronizations, especially when a team spans multiple sockets. Reducing these costs can significantly improve performance, especially for programs composed of many short parallel regions. Traditional OpenMP benchmarks contain only tens of regions, but as target directives and performance portable abstraction layers become the norm, parallelism is becoming finer grained as a necessity. As the number of regions grows from tens to hundreds or thousands, the overhead of constructing and tearing down parallel regions is becoming increasingly important. In the common case, manually merging contiguous parallel regions with no intervening serial code is trivial. However, many cases where this optimization would be worthwhile are not evident to the programmer because the

This material is based upon work supported by the U.S. Department of Energy (LLNL-CONF-670944).

The rights of this work are transferred to the extent transferable according to title 17 §105 U.S.C.

regions are obscured behind function calls or library abstractions. Further, the OpenMP specification implicitly forbids the merging of parallel regions.

While the OpenMP specification does not explicitly allow region merging, a few simple changes would allow it while preserving the semantics of parallel regions. Even with those adjustments however, some cases for which merging is desired would not be facilitated without hints on the parallel constructs that they can be merged safely. This paper proposes the necessary changes to allow region merging, and extensions to the parallel construct to control merging and to generate more efficient code. Specifically, we make the following contributions:

– Specification changes to allow merging of adjacent parallel regions;
– Syntax to guide region merging and synchronization of merged regions;
– Evaluation of region merging benefit with several OpenMP runtimes.

The remainder of the paper is composed as follows. Section 2 describes the proposed optimizations along with the proposed clauses to support them. Section 3 presents our evaluation. Section 4 presents related work.

## 2    Region Merging and Control

The overhead of starting a thread team has been considered a key performance issue for nearly as long as OpenMP has existed. Recently, however, users have begun to interact with OpenMP and other threading models from higher levels of abstraction. These abstraction levels support portable parallel frameworks across multiple threading models or target devices, including C++ frameworks like RAJA [6] and Kokkos [1], where there may be thousands of unseen parallel regions. When using these frameworks, programmers may not even be aware that an OpenMP parallel region exists in their code.

For example, in Fig. 1, the `parallel for` is conditionally applied in a library header. While the user could simply fuse the loops of this trivial example, more complex cases can make the source level fusion undesirable or hard to detect by eye. Even if the loops cannot be fused, however, the parallel regions could be if they were accessible. After the template instantiation and inlining passes of the compiler, the function is transformed to the one that Fig. 2 shows. Since no user ever sees this code, a compiler optimization pass is the only option to merge the regions short of contorting the abstraction to fit OpenMP's fork/join model. While code using C++ lambdas, or Apple's C blocks, in this way is not yet common, the benefits of such abstractions are numerous so we expect the use of lambdas will soon be common in a wide range of applications.

Even without a higher-level abstraction, cases for which source code merging is difficult or impossible can arise from functions or libraries that contain OpenMP regions, such as the example that Fig. 3 shows. The two calls into `mutate_all` do not visibly create OpenMP parallel regions at the call-site but, after an inlining pass, as in Fig. 4, region merging is clearly desirable.

The rest of this section first discusses the validity of region merging under the current OpenMP specification. We then detail the additional clauses that we

```
1   // parallel_forall.hpp
2   template<typename FunT, typename It>
3   void parallel_forall(It begin, It end, FunT fun){
4   #if defined(USE_OMP)
5   #pragma omp parallel for
6   #endif
7     for(It i = begin; i < end; ++i){
8       fun(i);
9     }
10  }
11  // user_code.cc
12  #include <parallel_forall.hpp>
13  void foo(double* a, double* b, size_t N){
14    std::vector<double> c(N);
15    parallel_forall(0, N, [&](int i){
16        c[i] = a[i] * b[i];
17      }
18    );
19    parallel_forall(0, N, [&](int i){
20        a[i] = sqrt(c[i]);
21      }
22    );
23  }
```

**Fig. 1.** A C++ lambda abstraction over OpenMP

```
1   void foo(double* a, double* b, size_t N){
2     std::vector<double> c(N);
3   #pragma omp parallel for
4     for(int i=0; i < N; i++){
5       c[i] = a[i] * b[i];
6     }
7   #pragma omp parallel for
8     for(int i=0; i < N; i++){
9       a[i] = sqrt(c[i]);
10    }
11  }
```

**Fig. 2.** Lambda code after the templates are inlined

propose to assist compilers in making appropriate and efficient decisions when considering regions for merging.

## 2.1  Region Merging Validity in OpenMP

Continuing the example in Fig. 3, we define the effect of merging the two regions to produce the version of the code in Fig. 5. Since the loop construct ends with an implicit barrier, the memory access ordering and synchronization semantics of the merged version remain identical to the original. However, the specification of parallel regions creates a few key differences. First, the number of threads

```
1    //Library function
2    void mutate_all(double* a, size_t N){
3    #pragma omp parallel  //Launch thread team
4    #pragma omp for //Schedule loop onto threads
5      for(int i=0; i < N; i++){
6        mutate(a[i]);
7      }// Implicit barrier followed by join, threads idle or block
8    }
9    void foo(double* a, double* b, size_t N){
10     mutate_all(a, N);
11     mutate_all(b, N);
12   }
```

**Fig. 3.** Function call indirection

```
1    void foo(double* a, double* b, size_t N){
2    #pragma omp parallel  //Launch thread team
3    #pragma omp for //Schedule loop onto threads
4      for(int i=0; i < N; i++){
5        mutate(a[i]);
6      }// Implicit barrier followed by join, threads idle or block
7    #pragma omp parallel //Re-activate thread team
8    #pragma omp for //Schedule loop onto threads
9      for(int i=0; i < N; i++){
10       mutate(b[i]);
11     }// Implicit barrier followed by join, threads idle or block
12   }
```

**Fig. 4.** Regions after inlining

in a parallel region must be computed according to a specific algorithm in the specification. The algorithm is sufficiently flexible that merged regions could provide no more apparent threads than specified in a num_threads clause on the construct. Compilers could fail to merge regions with different sizes in the general case, but even regions with different numbers of threads could be merged by using techniques that effectively idle threads for part of the merged region or by using the fewest number of threads requested. In cases with complex nested parallelism, a program could observe the difference in behavior, but the worst result would be over- or under-subscription if the program conforms to the specification. We also recommend that the data environment, be only minimally constructed and destructed, honoring privatization but only constructing and destructing outer scope variables at the outermost boundaries of the region. Scopes inside the region would honor their construct/destruct pattern as normal.

In addition to the algorithm to calculate the number of threads, the specification explicitly states that tasks are joined and executed and only the master thread continues execution of the enclosing task region after the join operation. For a case such as Fig. 4, one could reasonably argue that eliminating the join, as in Fig. 5, does not create an observable difference despite not temporarily returning to master-only execution. Fundamentally, neither this rule nor the selection

```
1    void foo(double* a, double* b, size_t N){
2    #pragma omp parallel //Launch thread team
3      {
4        { // Create data environment
5    #pragma omp for //Schedule loop onto threads
6            for(int i=0; i < N; i++){
7              mutate(a[i]);
8            }// Implicit barrier, threads idle or block
9        } // Destroy data environment
10        { // Create data environment
11   #pragma omp for //Schedule loop onto threads
12            for(int i=0; i < N; i++){
13              mutate(b[i]);
14            }// Implicit barrier followed by join, threads idle or block
15        } // Destroy data environment
16      }
17   }
```

**Fig. 5.** Regions after merging

of the number of threads make region merging necessarily non-conforming, but they do obscure whether the transformation is conforming. Thus, the specification arguably already allows it. However, we suggest that the OpenMP specification explicitly state that region-merging and similar transformations that result in well-defined semantically consistent behavior are conforming. Additionally we recommend providing defined semantics for tasks, specifically a taskwait at the merging point would be reasonable.

## 2.2  Syntax Extensions to Support Merging

For regions that are lexically back-to-back, possibly after simple transformations such as inlining as in Fig. 3, the compiler can easily determine that the merging transformation is both possible and desirable. However, slightly more complicated scenarios, with serial code between the regions, can still benefit from a slightly more advanced transformation, although the extent to which it should be applied is less clear. For this reason, we propose additional clauses for the parallel construct to guide optimization.

First, we propose a new **mergeable** clause. While we could apply this clause to other constructs, we first limit the proposal to the **parallel** construct and the combined or composite constructs for which it is logically the outermost construct. This clause indicates that the compiler should fuse, or merge, the current region with the next construct in the translation unit, and as with the clause of the same name on the task construct also asserts that the region may not create a data environment as a parallel region normally would. It is a descriptive clause (i.e., it is a hint); merging is not required for conformance. However, if another parallel region can be reached then ideally the compiler will merge the two constructs into a single parallel region, even across serial code. This merge transformation would result in code such as that shown in Fig. 6.

```
1    void foo(double* a, double* b, size_t N){
2    #pragma omp parallel  //Launch thread team
3      {
4    #pragma omp for //Schedule loop onto threads
5        for(int i=0; i < N; i++){
6          mutate(a[i]);
7        }// Implicit barrier, threads idle or block
8    #pragma omp master
9        {
10         orthogonal_serial_work();//serial
11       }
12   #pragma omp barrier

13   #pragma omp for //Schedule loop onto threads
14       for(int i=0; i < N; i++){
15         mutate(b[i]);
16       }// Implicit barrier followed by join, threads idle or block
17     }
18   }
```

**Fig. 6.** A merged pair of regions with an embedded serial section

This transformation encapsulates the serial region in a `master` region, which ensures that it only runs on a single thread. While a single region might be more efficient, the master region ensures that the same thread executes the code as in the untransformed case, preserving correctness in the presence of thread local state. This transformation does have some drawbacks. We must insert barriers after the first loop region and after the master region in order to preserve the original semantics. However, in our example, the serial region has no dependence on the results of the first loop, so we could theoretically omit the first barrier. In order to support this potentially common use case, we propose that the `parallel` and `parallel loop` constructs accept the `nowait` clause. If we include this clause on the first construct in the source code that corresponds to our example, the compiler should apply the `nowait` clause to the first loop construct of the transformed code. The nowait clause is a contract to the compiler that nothing between that loop and the end of the next OpenMP construct that does not have a `nowait` clause depends on results of the loop. Further exploration into the safety and ergonomics of this construct are advised, it may be worthwhile for example to require a receiving construct on a subsequent region for the nowait to take effect for example.

Our proposal still requires an explicit barrier after the master region, which our example also does not require. We cannot apply a clause to the first construct to remove this barrier because its semantic meaning would involve dependencies of the *second* parallel loop construct in the original code. We have considered support for a third clause that addresses dependence on the code *preceding* a region, however, it would need to identify data dependences within the region explicitly or otherwise limit its scope. We leave this issue for future proposals due to its complexity and potentially limited applicability.

**Table 1.** Evaluated systems. Note: Power8 tests were conducted in little-endian mode

| Name | Processor | OMP runtimes | Cores | Threads/Core |
|------|-----------|--------------|-------|--------------|
| BlueGene/Q | IBM PowerPC A2 | default, LOMP1/2 | 16 | 4 |
| RZMerl | Intel Xeon E5-2670x2 | Intel, GNU | 8 | 2 |
| RZAlastor | Intel Xeon E5-2680x2 | Intel | 10 | 2 |
| RZMist | IBM Power8x2 | GNU | 12 | 8 |
| Mic | Intel Xeon Phi 7120P | Intel | 61 | 4 |

# 3    Results and Evaluation

This section presents results for manually merged parallel regions of representative OpenMP applications in the context of four hardware platforms and five OpenMP runtime libraries. We base our microbenchmark on CLOMP [2], which we modify into two new variants that specifically target the overhead of OpenMP region setup and synchronization. The first variant, referred to as *CLOMPK*, has its inner-loop composed of ten back-to-back parallel loop regions that use a function call to update independent values. The second, *CLOMPKS*, interposes dependent serial work between each of the parallel loop regions. To provide a representative application for testing, we also investigate a version of the LULESH [7] benchmark that has been parallelized with the RAJA [6] template library. All results are presented in terms of speedup over an OpenMP execution of the code with no (manual) merging or annotation applied on the same number of cores unless otherwise noted. Table 1 lists the test environment that we use for our evaluation. Notably, we test two versions of a custom low-overhead lightweight OpenMP runtime designed for minimum region startup latency called LOMP [5]. Version 1, or LOMP1 as we refer to it elsewhere, has been in production use for a number of years, but does not offer full support for all OpenMP constructs. LOMP2 is an updated version with full support for OpenMP 3 constructs, but is still under evaluation and development.

## 3.1    Back to Back Regions

Figure 7 shows results for CLOMPK, which is the best case that does not include any serial code between the ten parallel loop regions. In order to explore the space, we tested four different levels of merging in addition to the un-merged baseline. The merging factor in the figure refers to the number of merged regions at a given level, so two refers to running five parallel regions each containing two workshared loops. Since ten does not divide evenly by three, the three case is actually distributed as $3 \times 3 \times 4$. In nearly all cases, basic parallel region merging improves performance, often substantially. Merging pairs of regions gains 2–5 % in most cases, although notably it loses approximately 2 % with BlueGene/Q's default OpenMP runtime. When merging into groups of three or more, basic parallel merging always improves performance, from a 15 % speedup for some cases on BG/Q to over 2× with the GNU OpenMP runtime on Power8.

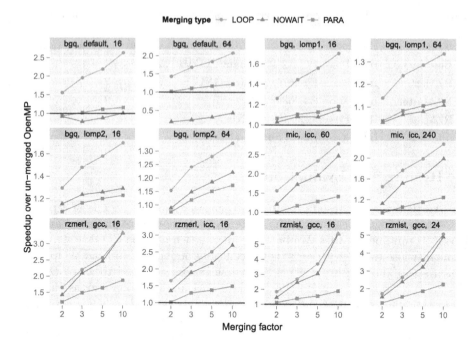

**Fig. 7.** Performance of back-to-back microbenchmark (CLOMPK): parallel region merging (PARA); loop barrier elimination (NOWAIT); and loop fusion (LOOP).

In principle, the `nowait` option only removes the implicit barrier between parallel loop regions, so it should always improve performance. On all of the Linux-based platforms, including the Intel Xeon Phi accelerator, adding `nowait` provides the expected benefit, producing as much as a 5× speedup over the baseline on Power8. However, the BG/Q default and LOMP1 results suggest that adding the nowait clause can result in more complicated side-effects. With the BG/Q default runtime, it results in a slowdown of as much as 75 %. With LOMP1, it remains faster than the baseline, but is a slowdown compared to parallel region merging. With LOMP2, however, the `nowait` option provides benefits on BG/Q similarly to the Linux-based platforms. The overall runtimes also track this trend, with LOMP1 outperforming default, and LOMP2 outperforming LOMP1 in overall runtimes with nowait.

Since each iteration of each of the loops is dependent only on the value produced by the same iteration in the previous loop, we can fuse the loop regions into one loop region. While we do not expect most compilers to implement this optimization, it is valid for back-to-back loop regions that use the static schedule and no cross-iteration dependences. This optimization provides significant performance benefit on BG/Q, achieving as much as a 2× more speedup in one case, but only slightly outperforms the `nowait` option on the Linux-based platforms.

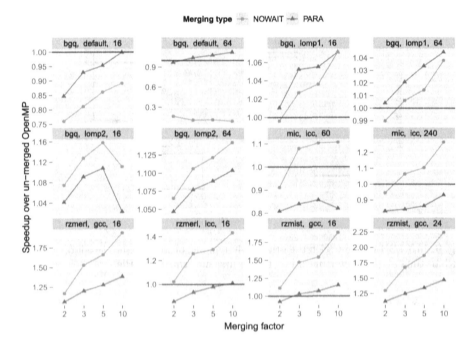

**Fig. 8.** Performance of intervening serial code microbenchmark (CLOMPKS): parallel region merging (PARA); and loop barrier elimination (NOWAIT).

## 3.2 Parallel Regions with Intervening Serial Regions

Using the merge directive discussed in Sect. 2.2, users can request that compiler merge consecutive parallel regions even with intervening serial code. As previously discussed, parallel region merging is performed with the serial code encapsulated in a master region followed by an additional barrier directive. Figure 8 shows results with this optimization, using the untransformed code, including the intervening serial region as the baseline. The serial regions essentially prevent the loop fusion optimization so we omit the LOOP variant. As expected in a case with additional serial overhead, as well as the barriers required to protect the master region, the speedups are not as large as with the back-to-back tests. Notably, both the default BG/Q OpenMP runtime and the Intel MIC OpenMP runtime lose performance in some cases. Specifically the BG/Q results for 16 threads slow down by as much as 25 %, and on 64 threads by as much as 80 % for the use of nowait. This pathological weakness of the default BG/Q OpenMP runtime is not shared by the LOMP runtimes on the same platform. In fact, even with the default runtime as much as a 10 % speedup is achieved in the 64 thread case with basic parallel region merging. Other runtimes behave approximately as they do for the back-to-back case. The largest benefits are a speedup of 2.25× for the GOMP runtime on rzmist, the IBM Power8 system.

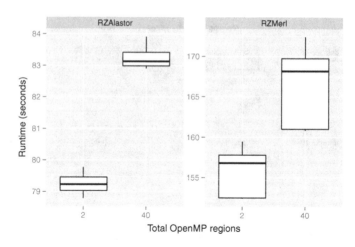

**Fig. 9.** LULESH runtime with the original 40 regions, or merged into two large regions. Median time at the center lines, box to the first and third quartile.

### 3.3   Lulesh

Lulesh is a representative application for shock hydrodynamics that serves as a widely available and comparable algorithm for programming model evaluation. It is also composed of a significant number of parallel loop regions, many of which can be fused into larger parallel regions. Figure 9 shows results of four runs each of the original code, which has forty distinct parallel regions with a version in which we manually merged the forty regions into two larger regions. As each of the forty regions performed a large amount of work, the overall application speedup is not as large as for the microbenchmarks, but the median speedup remains slightly above 5 % on RZAlastor and over 6 % on RZMerl. Given that these results apply the optimization to a realistic and reasonably optimized code, 5 % is a significant improvement.

## 4   Related Work

The synchronization, thread launching and scheduling overheads inherent in multi-threaded programming models have been topics of research and discussion since the concept of threading came into being. OpenMP is no exception; the EPCC benchmark suite [3] was published in 1999. At the time, launching a parallel region was approximately as costly as executing a barrier across all threads inside the region. Later work by Müller [8] found that parallel region launch was still as expensive, and recommended merging regions to be as comprehensive as possible. This work also asserts that both the SGI native compilers and the PGI compiler of the time merge contiguous parallel regions based on their performance results. Our tests, discussed in Sect. 3, show that this optimization does not take place in several current compilers.

Attempts have been made to construct OpenMP compiler and runtime environments that reduce the overhead of launching a parallel region. Eichenberger [5] proposed a lightweight OpenMP runtime, called LOMP, designed to cut the overhead to as much as possible on BG/Q while following the OpenMP specification. Some of the optimizations applied included caching thread contexts, distributing region setup to the thread team, the use of low-overhead sleep and wake primitives and creating fast-paths for parallel launches using default parameters. Overall, this work decreased the cost of launching a team of threads across the system, and especially re-entering the region later, but region launch still takes thousands of cycles, and barriers remain a bottleneck. We further evaluate the original LOMP runtime, as well as an updated version, LOMP2, in Sect. 3.

One compiler that does support region merging is craycc from the Cray Compiling Environment [4]. It offers the -h threadn flag, which when set to a value of two or higher instructs the compiler to attempt to merge, to expand, or otherwise to transform parallel regions. The option documentation implies that these optimizations break strict conformance with the OpenMP specification, which may be why other compilers do not perform parallel region merging.

## 5   Conclusion

In this paper we re-affirm the common wisdom that merging nearby, and especially contiguous, OpenMP regions improves performance. Further, we identify situations in which regions become contiguous as a result of compiler optimization or evaluation of code at compile time, making the optimization require compiler support. OpenMP as a rule does not require a compiler to perform analysis of the correctness of transformations, and our recommended specification changes maintain that property by ensuring that proper synchronization remains wherever it may be expected. The extended clauses, mergeable and nowait, for parallel regions make this possible while giving the user greater control over the interpretation of a parallel region and the following serial code, if any. Our evaluation shows that for a realistic representative application, region merging can achieve a 5 % speedup over the original, and as much as 5× in microbenchmarks. In summary, parallel region merging is an effective optimization with a significant benefit to include in OpenMP compilers.

## References

1. Kokkos. http://trilinos.org/packages/kokkos/
2. Bronevetsky, G., Gyllenhaal, J., de Supinski, B.R.: CLOMP: accurately characterizing OpenMP application overheads. In: Eigenmann, R., de Supinski, B.R. (eds.) IWOMP 2008. LNCS, vol. 5004, pp. 13–25. Springer, Heidelberg (2008)
3. Bull, J.M.: Measuring synchronisation and scheduling overheads in OpenMP. In: Proceedings of First European Workshop on OpenMP, vol. 8, p. 49 (1999)

4. Cray. craycc manual page. http://docs.cray.com/cgi-bin/craydoc.cgi?mode=View; id=sw_releases-j4spa4zu-1396361754;idx=man_search;this_sort=title;q=; type=man;title=Cray%20Compiling%20Environment%20%28CCE%29%208. 3%3a%20C/C%2b%2b/Fortran%20Compiler%20Man%20Pages
5. Eichenberger, A.E., O'Brien, K.: Experimenting with low-overhead OpenMP runtime on IBM Blue Gene/Q. IBM J. Res. Dev. **57**(1/2), 8:1–8:8 (2013)
6. Hornung, R., Keasler, J.: The RAJA portability layer: overview and status. Technical report, Lawrence Livermore National Laboratory (LLNL), Livermore, CA (2014)
7. Karlin, I., Bhatele, A., Keasler, J., Chamberlain, B.L., Cohen, J., Devito, Z., Haque, R., Laney, D., Luke, E., Wang, F., Richards, D., Schulz, M., Still, C.H.: Exploring traditional and emerging parallel programming models using a proxy application. In: International Parallel and Distributed Processing Symposium, pp. 919–932 (2013)
8. Müller, M.: Some simple OpenMP optimization techniques. In: Eigenmann, R., Voss, M.J. (eds.) WOMPAT 2001. LNCS, vol. 2104, pp. 31–39. Springer, Heidelberg (2001)

# Towards Task-Parallel Reductions in OpenMP

Jan Ciesko[1], Sergi Mateo[1,2]([✉]), Xavier Teruel[1], Xavier Martorell[1,2],
Eduard Ayguadé[1,2], Jesús Labarta[1,2], Alex Duran[3], Bronis R. de Supinski[4],
Stephen Olivier[5], Kelvin Li[6], and Alexandre E. Eichenberger[6]

[1] Barcelona Supercomputing Center, Barcelona, Spain
{jan.ciesko,sergi.mateo,xavier.teruel,xavier.martorell,
eduard.ayguade,jesus.labarta}@bsc.es
[2] Universitat Politècnica de Catalunya, Barcelona, Spain
[3] Intel Iberia Corporation, Madrid, Spain
alejandro.duran@intel.com
[4] Lawrence Livermore National Laboratories, Livermore, USA
bronis@llnl.gov
[5] Sandia National Laboratories, Livermore, USA
slolivi@sandia.gov
[6] IBM Corporation, New York, USA
kli@ca.ibm.com, alexe@us.ibm.com

**Abstract.** Reductions represent a common algorithmic pattern in many scientific applications. OpenMP* has always supported them on parallel and worksharing constructs. OpenMP 3.0's tasking constructs enable new parallelization opportunities through the annotation of irregular algorithms. Unfortunately the tasking model does not easily allow the expression of concurrent reductions, which limits the general applicability of the programming model to such algorithms. In this work, we present an extension to OpenMP that supports task-parallel reductions on task and taskgroup constructs to improve productivity and programmability. We present specification of the feature and explore issues for programmers and software vendors regarding programming transparency as well as the impact on the current standard with respect to nesting, untied task support and task data dependencies. Our performance evaluation demonstrates comparable results to hand coded task reductions.

**Keywords:** OpenMP · Task · Reduction · Recursion

## 1 Introduction

Migrating applications to multi-core and many-core architectures is a challenging but necessary step to achieve scalable performance on modern systems. Thus, parallel programming models such as *OpenMP* [7] have gained popularity through concepts and tools to introduce portable concurrency in a broad range of algorithms with relatively little programming effort. This work proposes a task redutcion extension to OpenMP that supports a yet wider class of algorithms.

© Springer International Publishing Switzerland 2015
C. Terboven et al. (Eds.): IWOMP 2015, LNCS 9342, pp. 189–201, 2015.
DOI: 10.1007/978-3-319-24595-9_14

A reduction is an iterative update of a variable *var*, defined as:

$$iter: \ var = op(var, expression),$$

where *op* is an associative function and *var* does not occur in *expression*. Typically, a *for-loop* (bounded loop) or *while-loop* (unbounded loop) iteratively or recursively defines the iteration space.

For-loops have a constant iteration space. OpenMP supports their concurrent execution through worksharing constructs. The iterations space of while-loops and recursions is dynamic, which prohibits efficient use of worksharing constructs. OpenMP 3.0 added support for these irregular algorithms through the `task` directive. In this formulation, loop iterations and recursive calls create task instances of the enclosed code, typically the loop body.

While for-loops and while-loops can be efficiently parallelized through worksharing constructs or tasks, reductions within them require special attention. A closer look reveals that the reduction operation represents a read-modify-write sequence that is not atomic so that its parallel execution introduces data races.

Figure 1 shows while-loop reductions over a linked list that avoid data races by introducing locks or by applying techniques like thread-privatization. Programming model support would eliminate the required boilerplate code. Even though manual implementations are viable solutions, they are error prone and require the programmer to select a specific implementation, which may be inefficient on a given architecture or incur unnecessary memory overheads.

OpenMP needs a solution that supports task reductions and minimizes the effect on unrelated constructs. It should comprehensively define the scope of the reduction and a data context for the private reduction variable.

## 2   Related Work

OpenMP supports reductions on parallel and worksharing constructs through the reduction clause. It implies data privatization of the reduction variable that removes race conditions by replacing accesses to the original variable with accesses to per-thread private copies. Each copy is initialized with the operation's identity and is reduced to the original variable at the end of the construct.

While the specification does not yet support task reductions, prior work has explored them for OpenMP [3] and OmpSs [1]. These papers discussed different scenarios in which to use task reductions and compared the results with manual transformations that use atomics. This general approach could specify the task reduction scope through the *taskgroup*, *taskwait* or *barrier* constructs or task dependences on the reduction variable. This paper extends that work.

Intel[R] Cilk[TM] [5] coordinates the view of a variable of a task and its descendants through *hyperobjects* [4]. A reduction operation can combine these views when a descendant task finishes execution. This mechanism targets a multilevel task hierarchy. We target the task hierarchy within a taskgroup region.

```
 1 //Compute reduction by traversing nodes
 2 float var = 0;
 3
 4    ...
 5
 6    while ( node ) {
 7       var += node->value;
 8       node = node->next;
 9    }
10
11    ...
12
13
14 ...
```

(a) Original code (serial version)

```
 1 //Compute reduction by traversing nodes
 2 float var = 0;
 3 #pragma omp parallel
 4 {
 5    #pragma omp single
 6    while ( node ) {
 7       #pragma omp task firstprivate(node)
 8       {
 9          #pragma omp atomic
10          var += node->value;
11       }
12       node = node->next;
13    }
14 }
```

(b) Parallel with atomics

```
 1 //Compute reduction by traversing nodes
 2 float var = 0;
 3 float part[nthreads] = { 0 };
 4
 5 #pragma omp parallel reduction(+:var)
 6 {
 7    #pragma omp single
 8    {
 9       while ( node ) {
10          #pragma omp task \
11                     firstprivate(node)
12          {
13             part[thread_id] +=
14                           node->value;
15          }
16          node = node->next;
17       }
18    }
19    var += part[thread_id];
20 }
```

(c) Parallel with manual privatization

```
 1 //Compute reduction by traversing nodes
 2 float var = 0;
 3 float part = 0;
 4 #pragma omp threadprivate(part)
 5
 6 #pragma omp parallel reduction(+:var)
 7 {
 8    #pragma omp single
 9    {
10       while ( node ) {
11          #pragma omp task \
12                     firstprivate(node)
13          {
14             part += node->value;
15          }
16          node = node->next;
17       }
18    }
19    var += part;
20 }
```

(d) Parallel with thread-privatization

**Fig. 1.** Different versions of a while-loop reduction over a linked list

The X10 [2] programming model supports task reductions through phaser-accumulators [8,9]. Focused on the Partitioned Global Address Space environment, X10's *phaser-accumulators* can send and receive results from different activities and combine them in a point-to-point pattern.

## 3   Discussion

We propose to extend the *taskgroup* and *task* constructs to support task reductions. Prior work identified *taskgroup* construct as a possible scope of the reduction [3]. We prefer this choice since it does not affect other OpenMP mechanisms (e.g., barriers) and the taskgroup structured block defines a clear reduction scope.

We extend the *taskgroup* and *task* construct with the clauses *reduction* and *in_reduction* respectively. The *in_reduction* clause declares a task as a participant in the computation of *var* that was previously declared in an enclosing taskgroup *reduction* clause with the same *reduction-identifier*. We deliberately use the *in_reduction* clause instead of reusing the *reduction* clause in order to stress the differences in behavior to the programmer. The *reduction* clause in the *taskgroup* construct follows its current specification for other constructs. Alternatively, the *in_reduction* clause on a task construct defines an access pattern (an update operation) to one of those copies. Figure 2(a) illustrates our proposal for the previous example.

```
 1 //Compute reduction by traversing nodes        1 //Compute reduction by traversing nodes
 2 float var = 0;                                   2 float var = 0;
 3                                                   3
 4 #pragma omp parallel                             4 #pragma omp parallel
 5 {                                                 5 {
 6    #pragma omp single                            6    #pragma omp single
 7    #pragma omp taskgroup \                        7    {
 8              reduction(+:var)                     8       #pragma omp task
 9    while ( node ) {                               9       var++;
10       #pragma omp task \                         10
11                firstprivate(node) \              11       #pragma omp taskgroup \
12                in_reduction(+:var)               12                reduction(+:var)
13       {                                          13       while ( node ) {
14          var += node->value;                     14          #pragma omp task \
15       }                                          15                   firstprivate(node) \
16       node = node->next;                         16                   in_reduction(+:var)
17    }                                             17          {
18 }                                                18             var += node->value;
19                                                  19          }
20                                                  20          node = node->next;
21                                                  21       }
22                                                  22    }
23 ...                                              23 }
```

(a) While-loop reduction (tentative)    (b) While-loop reduction (race condition)

**Fig. 2.** Examples of our proposal

### 3.1 Updates of a Reduction Variable Outside a Reduction Context

Programmers must consider that an update of the original reduction variable occurs just after the *taskgroup* region and that accesses to that outside of the taskgroup may create a race condition. Figure 2(b) shows code that updates the reduction variable both inside and outside a taskgroup reduction. The task created in line 8 can be executed concurrently with the taskgroup reduction update occurring at the end of the taskgroup created in lines 11–12. This situation may also occur when multiple taskgroup reductions are working with the same variable simultaneously. The programmer must provide proper synchronization to avoid this situation. This requirement is analogous to existing restrictions on reductions:

> To avoid race conditions, concurrent reads or updates of the original list item must be synchronized with the update of the original list item that occurs as a result of the reduction computation (line 20, p. 170 [7]).

### 3.2 Over-Specifying the Reduction Identifier

The declaration of the reduction identifier in the *in_reduction* clause could be inferred from the *taskgroup* context and thus could be omitted to minimize the potential for programming errors. However, vendor feedback indicates that omitting the identifier could limit compiler optimizations, or at least introduce some additional overhead (i.e., registering the reduction inside the runtime) to perform these optimizations. OpenMP vendors may use the identifier to combine a local-copy of a reduction variable with the original/thread-copy (depending on the implementation approach), which specification of the identifier in the *in_reduction* clause would facilitate. Thus, we choose to require it.

### 3.3   Supporting Untied Tasks

Untied tasks can be suspended at a task scheduling point and later resumed on
a different thread. Without proper handling, a task might resume execution on
a different thread but still continue using the thread-private copy of the thread
that started its execution, which could create a race condition. Tied tasks do not
encounter this issue since they execute entirely on one thread even if they are
suspended at some point. Thus, they can safely use that thread's copy as they
will not be suspended while accessing it.

Several solutions could support untied reduction tasks. First, an implementation could not migrate any task (e.g., treat it as tied) if it is involved in a
reduction even though it is declared as *untied*. This approach is simple but eliminates the potential benefit of untied task migration.

Alternatively, an implementation could introduce an additional local variable
for each untied reduction task. This task-local variable must be initialized to
the identity. A reference to the local variable would replace all references to
the reduction variable inside the untied task. Finally, at the end of the task,
the partial result stored in the task-local variable would be combined with the
thread-private copy of the thread that finalizes the task. This approach supports
tasks that migrate among threads at the cost of an additional task-local copy
that must be initialized and an additional partial reduction per untied task.

Finally, the compiler could generate a request for the thread-private copy
after each possible task scheduling point, thus supporting the use of the thread-
private copy. The reduction task would then always access the thread-private
copy of the thread that is executing it. This approach supports tasks that migrate
among threads at the cost of repeatedly obtaining the thread-private location.

We recommend that the following be implementation defined:

– Whether untied tasks involved in reductions can migrate;
– The number of private copies that are created for a task reduction.

The number of private copies could be defined as the number of tasks that
participate in the reduction. Our recommendation thus allows an implementation
to choose any of the above solutions (or a hybrid of them). Untied tasks could
migrate and the number of private copies could be anything between the number
of threads to the number of tasks.

**Evaluating Support for Untied Tasks:** We use two benchmarks to evaluate
the choice of supporting untied tasks by not migrating them or by introducing
a new local copy per task. The first performs a reduction over a scalar. The
performance of both versions is equivalent since the extra overhead introduced
in the task-local approach is small in scalar reductions and the benchmark is
well-tuned to obtain good performance using tasks so the extra overhead of the
task-local version is insignificant compared to the task granularity.

Our second benchmark, Array Sum UDR (since it has a *User Defined Reduction*) reduces an array of structs to a unique struct. This struct has a static array

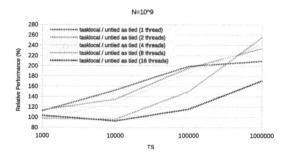

**Fig. 3.** Array Sum UDR benchmark results

of $TS$ integers. The UDR's initializer sets every element of the struct to zero and its combiner adds the values of the two arrays. We choose this benchmark since it increases the cost to allocate and to initialize the extra copy and to perform its associated reduction.

Figure 3 shows the relative performance of the task-local version compared against the untied-as-tied version, with different number of threads and fixing the total number of integers to $N = 10^9$. The relative performance is computed dividing the execution time of an approach by the execution time of another.

The overhead of the task-local version increases with $TS$, the size of the static array. The differences among the different relative perfomances require further analysis and it's deferred to future work. Thus, the task-local approach is reasonable for scalar reductions but may incur excessive overhead for array reductions or UDRs; implementations could define values based on the type of the reduction.

### 3.4   Supporting Nested Taskgroups

Nested taskgroup reductions can be defined either over different list items or the same ones, as Fig. 4 shows. If the nested taskgroup defines a reduction over a different list item (Fig. 4(a)), the runtime registers a new reduction that is independent of the ongoing outermost taskgroup reduction. Thus, the runtime creates a new set of thread-private copies to compute the reduction.

```
 1 int  a = 0;
 2 #pragma  omp  taskgroup  reduction(+:a)
 3 {
 4     ...
 5     int b = 0;
 6     #pragma  omp  taskgroup  reduction(+:b)
 7     {
 8         ...
 9     }
10     ...
11     a += b;
12 }
```

```
 1 int  a = 0;
 2 #pragma  omp  taskgroup  reduction(+:a)
 3 {
 4     ...
 5
 6     #pragma  omp  taskgroup  reduction(+:a)
 7     {
 8         ...
 9     }
10     ...
11
12 }
```

(a) Nesting over two different variables        (b) Nesting over the same variable

**Fig. 4.** Nested taskgroup reduction scenarios

Two alternatives exist if the nested taskgroup reduction is over the same list item (Fig. 4(b)). The first uses the same approach as when the list item is different: register a new reduction. The second alternative reuses the same set of private copies for both reductions. With this approach, we cannot reduce the private copies at the end of the nested taskgroups reductions: the final reduction must be computed at the end of the outer *taskgroup* region, counter to current reductions semantics that compute the reduction at the end of the construct that has the reduction clause.

### 3.5  Cancellation, Dependencies and Merged Tasks

Cancellation implies the value of the reduction variable is unspecified since we cannot guarantee how far the computation of the reduction has progressed. The programmer must anticipate this behavior.

The specification of a dependency (using the task *depend* clause) over a reduction variable might introduce a conceptually misleading situation. The programmer might intend a dependency over the original variable or the private copy in the data context of the taskgroup reduction. We could explicitly restrict the use of the *in_reduction* clause and depend clause over the same variable. However the current OpenMP specification does not restrict similar cases. A dependency over a private variable produces a similar situation where the OpenMP specification does not provide clarification about the interaction between data-sharing attributes and dependencies.

A merged task that participates in a reduction does not have a data environment. Thus, it must use the parent's data environment that includes the private copy of the reduction variable. Since the parent environment for a reduction task can only be either a taskgroup reduction or another reduction task environment, the use of the corresponding private copy[1] in the parent region is always guaranteed. Thus, this case also does not require additional specification.

## 4  Syntax Additions

This section describes the syntax of our proposal. We update the syntax of the taskgroup construct to:

```
#pragma omp taskgroup [clause[[,]clause]...] new-line
     structured-block
```

where clause is:

   **reduction**(*reduction-identifier: list*)

We also modify the *reduction* clause description to cover taskgroup regions. Once the scope of a reduction is defined, we must identify tasks within the taskgroup

---

[1] This case may involve multiple private copies due to support for untied tasks.

that participate in the computation. Thus, we extend the clauses allowed on a task construct to include:

in_reduction(*reduction-identifier* : *list*)

We add a section for the *in_reduction* clause and modify the description of the *reduction* clause to specify the semantics of references to the list items that we discussed in the previous section. The section on the *in_reduction* clause includes this restriction:

– The task to which the *in_reduction* clause is applied on a list-item must be closely nested in a *taskgroup* region to which a *reduction* clause is applied on the same list-item.

## 5    Evaluation

This section compares the performance of our prototype implementation of our proposed taskgroup reduction with manual implementations that Fig. 1 shows.

### 5.1    System Environment

We obtained our results on MareNostrum III and the Knight system located at the Barcelona Supercomputing Center. Each Marenostrum III node contains two 8-core Intel Xeon E5-2670 CPUs running at 2.6 GHz with 20 MB L3 cache and 32 GB of main memory organized as two NUMA nodes. Each Knight node includes an Intel Xeon Phi coprocessor with C0 silicon and board version C0PRQ-7120 (61 cores at 1238095 Khz, 16 GB of GDDR Memory at 5.5 GT/sec, 300W TDP), driver v3.4-1, MPSS v3.4 and flash v2.1.02.0390).

Applications on Marenostrum and Knight were compiled using the Mercurium source-to-source compiler v1.99.8[2] (using GCC v4.7.2 and Intel[R] C Compiler 15.0.2 as the back-end/native compiler respectively). In both cases the compiler optimization level was -O3, and the parallel runtime used in all experiments was based on the Nanos++ RTL v0.9a[3].

### 5.2    Benchmark Descriptions

Array Sum: This algorithm takes a single array of $N$ integers as an operand and computes the sum of its elements. We create a task for each $TS$ elements.

Dot Product: The dot product algorithm is a simple operation on two vector operands of $N$ elements. The result is the sum of the products of their components. We create a task for each $TS$ elements.

---

[2] mcxx 1.99.8 (git 538d492).
[3] nanox 0.9a (git master 10f6134).

`NQueens`: This application computes the number of placements of $N$ chess queens on a $NxN$ chessboard such that none of them can attack any other. This implementation uses a Branch and Bound algorithm following a recursive pattern, taskified and using the final clause to control task granularity.

`Unbalanced Tree Search (UTS)`: This benchmark computes the number of nodes in an implicitly defined unbalanced tree [6]. The program begins with a single tree node and an initial seed that is used to generate a sequence of pseudo-random numbers. For each node, the next value in the sequence is used to sample a parameterized probablity distribution to determine the number of children for a given node. This algorithm creates an unpredictably unbalanced workload that makes the use of a cut-off value in the final clause difficult.

## 5.3   Performance Results on Intel Xeon Processors

In this section we evaluate the performance of our proposal against the performance of manual versions of the benchmarks on Intel Xeon processors.

Figure 5 shows the performance results of the Array Sum and Dot Product benchmarks. Both benchmarks exhibit similar behavior in which performance drops levels off with higher thread counts. In this case, scalability is limited by memory bandwidth. In Array Sum, bandwidth saturation starts with 12 threads (with a 10x speed-up), while for Dot Product this effect becomes visible with 6 threads (reaching a speedup of 5x). These two different phases (scale and saturate) have a counterpart in the relative performance (the green dashed line in the figure). For all thread counts with Array Sum, the performance reaches at least 94 % of the performance of the manual version. For larger thread counts, the differences between the implementations become smaller because task execution time shifts towards the computation as the algorithm saturates the memory bandwidth and reduces the importance of reduction performance. For the Dot Product benchmark, the relative speedup is between 95 % and 100 %. For both benchmarks, gains in maintainability and portability easily compensate for the slight differences in relative performance.

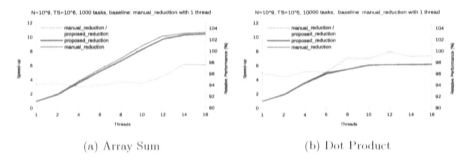

(a) Array Sum                           (b) Dot Product

**Fig. 5.** Array Sum and Dot Product benchmarks results

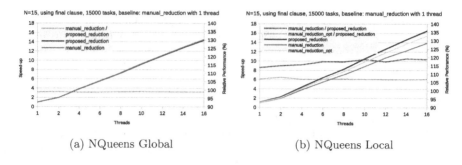

(a) NQueens Global                    (b) NQueens Local

**Fig. 6.** NQueens benchmark results

Figure 6 shows the results for the NQueens benchmark. For this application we have implemented two versions: one that reduces over a global variable (sub-figure a) and another that reduces over a local variable (subfigure b). We explore these two versions primarily because the global version only registers one reduction in the whole program while the local version registers a new reduction at each recursive level. When reducing over a global variable, speedup is essentially linear and relative performance is close to 100 %. When the reduction is performed over a local variable, we compare our proposal against two different manual versions. The first one is the regular transformation presented previously whereas the second version optimizes the code when in a final task. The problem with the regular transformation is that we are still allocating, intializing and reducing an array of NUM_THREADS elements even if we are going to use just one element. Thus, the optimized versions makes use of the *omp_in_final()* runtime service to avoid this extra overhead. Despite comparing our proposal against the manual optimized version, the scalability and the relative performance of our version is still better.

Figure 7 shows the results of executing the UTS benchmark with configurations that vary the number of created tasks from 50 k to 1 M tasks. All configurations achieve essentially linear speedup (subfigure a), and relative performance is between 96 % and 99 % for programmability issues again more than compensate.

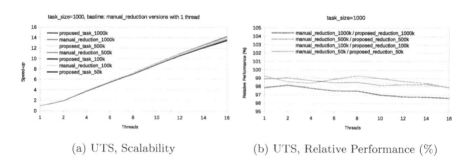

(a) UTS, Scalability              (b) UTS, Relative Performance (%)

**Fig. 7.** Unbalance Tree Search benchmark results

## 5.4    Performance Results on Intel Xeon Phi Coprocessors

In this section we evaluate the performance of our proposal against the performance of manual versions on a Intel Xeon Phi coprocessor.

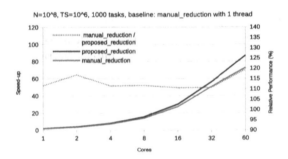

**Fig. 8.** Array Sum benchmark results on Xeon Phi

Figure 8 shows that our approach scales slightly better than the manual version of Array Sum. The relative performance line shows that the performance of our proposal is at least 10 % better than the performance of the manual version in almost all cases. While not shown in the figure, the exceptions is when we use all 60 cores and more than 2 threads per core, in which case our approach underperforms and does not scale well due to cache problems and more contention when we increase the number of threads.

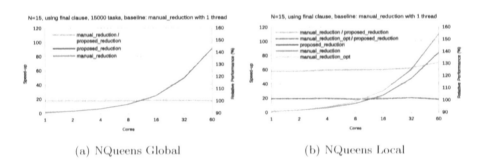

(a) NQueens Global                          (b) NQueens Local

**Fig. 9.** NQueens benchmark results on Xeon Phi

Figure 9 shows the results of the NQueens benchmark on the Xeon Phi. For the global version of the NQueens, the scalability and the relative performance between our approach and the manual version are identical. For the local version, the scalability and the relative performance of our proposal is equivalent to the manual optimized version and far better than the nonoptimized one.

# 6    Conclusions and Future Work

In this paper we have presented a proposal to support task-parallel reductions in OpenMP that extends the *taskgroup* and *task* constructs with *reduction* and *in_reduction* clauses. We find that the *taskgroup* construct provides a convenient data environment for reductions and the scope of the reduction is clearly defined by the deep synchronization at the end of the *taskgroup* region. The *in_reduction* clause for the task construct associates tasks with a reduction declared in a *taskgroup* construct. This approach does not impact barriers or other task synchronization constructs. We explored implementation options to support nested taskgroups and untied tasks, which demonstrate that implementors can explore a range of implementations and optimizations. Our performance results demonstrate that the approach incurs little overhead compared to manual versions currently required and it may provide small performance benefits in some specific cases like recursive benchmarks. Most importantly, it significantly reduces boilerplate code that programmers must currently use to implement reductions manually.

In the future, we continue our work in this area by conducting more analysis and evaluation. Apart from that, we plan to provide a draft of the OpenMP specification to the OpenMP committee.

**Acknowledgments.** This work has been developed with the support of the grant SEV-2011-00067 of Severo Ochoa Program, awarded by the Spanish Government and by the Spanish Ministry of Science and Innovation (contracts TIN2012-34557, and CAC2007-00052) by the Generalitat de Catalunya (contract 2014-SGR-1051) and the Intel-BSC Exascale Lab collaboration project.

Sandia National Laboratories is a multi-program laboratory managed and operated by Sandia Corporation, a wholly owned subsidiary of Lockheed Martin Corporation, for the U.S. Department of Energy's National Nuclear Security Administration under contract DE-AC04-94AL85000.

Also the authors would like to thank the OpenMP community for their substantial contribution to this work.

Intel, Xeon, Xeon Phi and Many Integrated Core are trademarks or registered trademarks of Intel Corporation or its subsidiaries in the United States and other countries.

*Other brands and names are the property of their respective owners.

# References

1. Barcelona Supercomputing Center.: OmpSs Specification, 25 April 2014. http://pm.bsc.es/ompss-docs/specs
2. Charles, P., Grothoff, C., Saraswat, V., Donawa, C., Kielstra, A., Ebcioglu, K., von Praun, C., Sarkar, V.: X10: an object-oriented approach to non-uniform cluster computing. In: SIGPLAN Notices, vol. 40(10), pp. 519–538 (2005)
3. Ciesko, J., Mateo, S., Teruel, X., Beltran, V., Martorell, X., Badia, R.M., Ayguadé, E., Labarta, J.: Task-parallel reductions in OpenMP and OmpSs. In: DeRose, L., de Supinski, B.R., Olivier, S.L., Chapman, B.M., Müller, M.S. (eds.) IWOMP 2014. LNCS, vol. 8766, pp. 1–15. Springer, Heidelberg (2014)

4. Frigo, M., Halpern, P., Leiserson, C.E., Lewin-Berlin, S.: Reducers and other Cilk++ hyperobjects. In: Proceedings of the Twenty-First Annual Symposium on Parallelism in Algorithms and Architectures, SPAA 2009, pp. 79–90. ACM, New York (2009)
5. Leiserson, C.E.: The Cilk++ concurrency platform. In: Proceedings of the 46th Annual Design Automation Conference, DAC 2009, pp. 522–527. ACM, New York (2009)
6. Olivier, S., Huan, J., Liu, J., Prins, J.F., Dinan, J., Sadayappan, P., Tseng, C.-W.: UTS: an unbalanced tree search benchmark. In: Almási, G.S., Caşcaval, C., Wu, P. (eds.) KSEM 2006. LNCS, vol. 4382, pp. 235–250. Springer, Heidelberg (2007)
7. OpenMP Architecture Review Board.: OpenMP Application ProgramInterface Version 4.0, July 2013
8. Shirako, J., Peixotto, D.M., Sarkar, V., Scherer, W.N.: Phasers: a unified deadlock-free construct for collective and point-to-point synchronization. In: ICS 2008: Proceedings of the 22nd Annual International Conference on Supercomputing, pp. 277–288. ACM, New York (2008)
9. Shirako, J., Peixotto, D.M., Sarkar, V., Scherer, W.N.: Phaser accumulators: a new reduction construct for dynamic parallelism. In: IEEE International Symposium on Parallel and Distributed Processing, IPDPS 2009, pp. 1–12. IEEE, Rome, May 2009

# OpenMP 4.0 Device Support
# in the OMPi Compiler

Alexandros Papadogiannakis, Spiros N. Agathos,
and Vassilios V. Dimakopoulos[⊠]

Department of Computer Science and Engineering, University of Ioannina,
P.O. Box 1186, 45110 Ioannina, Greece
{apapadog,sagathos,dimako}@cse.uoi.gr

**Abstract.** OpenMP 4.0 represents a major upgrade in the language specifications of the standard. Important constructs for the exploitation of SIMD parallelism, the support for dependencies among tasks and the ability to cancel the operations of a team of threads have been added. What is arguably the most important addition, however, is the introduction of the *device* model. A variety of computational units, such as GPUs, DSPs and general or special purpose accelerators are viewed as attached devices, where portion of a unified application code can be offloaded for execution. In this work we present the infrastructure for device support in the OMPi research compiler, one of the few compilers that currently implement the new device directives. We discuss the necessary compiler transformations and the general runtime organization. For the first time, special emphasis is placed on the important problem of data environment handling. In addition, we present a prototype implementation on the popular Parallella board which exploits the dual-core ARM host processor and the 16-core Epiphany accelerator of the system.

## 1 Introduction

OpenMP, the de facto standard for shared-memory programming, has been recently augmented with new directives that target arbitrary accelerator devices [18]. In the spirit of OpenACC [17], OpenMP 4.0 provides a higher level directive-based approach; it allows the offloading of portions of the application code onto the processing elements of an attached accelerator while the main part executes on the general-purpose host processor. In contrast, programming models such as OpenCL [13] and CUDA [14] provide efficient but rather primitive mechanisms for an application to exploit the hardware capabilities of GPGPUs and other devices. Such models project the heterogeneity of hardware directly onto software, forcing different programming styles and multiple code modules to accommodate each of the devices that is to be utilized.

Modern architectures present a mix of different processor organizations and memory hierarchies within the same system. Systems as small as a personal

---

S.N. Agathos is supported by the Greek State Scholarships Foundation (IKY).

C. Terboven et al. (Eds.): IWOMP 2015, LNCS 9342, pp. 202–216, 2015.
DOI: 10.1007/978-3-319-24595-9_15

workstation may pack many compute cores in a socket, and/or combine general purpose multicore CPUs with accelerator devices such as GPGPUs, DSPs and specialized, application-specific FPGAs. Given the multiplicity of devices and the diversity of their architectures, the real challenge is to provide programming models that allow the programmer to extract satisfactory performance while also keeping his/her productivity at high levels. OpenMP 4.0 strives to play a major role in this direction, letting the programmer blend the host and the device code portions in a unified and seamless way.

Although support for the OpenMP 4.0 device model has been slow to be adopted by both compiler and device vendors, it is gaining momentum. Currently, the Intel ICC compiler [12,16] and GNU C Compiler, GCC (as of the latest version [11]) support offloading directives, with both of them only targeting Intel Xeon Phi as a device. GCC offers a general infrastructure to be tailored and supplemented by device manufacturers. Preliminary support for the OpenMP **target** construct is also available in the ROSE compiler. Chunhua et al. [8] discuss their experiences on implementing a prototype called HOMP on top of the ROSE compiler, which generates code for CUDA devices. A discussion about an implementation of OpenMP 4.0 for the LLVM compiler is given by Bertolli et al. [5] who also propose an efficient method to coordinate threads within an NVIDIA GPU. Finally, in [15] the authors present an implementation on the TI Keystone II, where the DSP cores are used as devices to offload code to.

In this work we present an infrastructure for device support in the context of the OMPi OpenMP compiler [9], currently one of the few compilers that implement the OpenMP 4.0 directives for offloading code onto a device. We discuss the necessary compiler transformations and the general runtime organization, emphasizing the important problem of data environment handling. To the best of our knowledge, this is the first time this problem is given detailed consideration in the open literature; we present novel runtime structures to address it efficiently. While we deal mostly with the device-agnostic parts of the infrastructure, we also discuss our experiences with a concrete implementation on the highly popular Parallella board [2]. It is the first OpenMP implementation for this particular system, and supports the concurrent execution of multiple independent kernels. In addition, it allows OpenMP directives in each offloaded kernel, supporting dynamic parallelism within the system coprocessor.

The paper is organized as follows. In Sect. 2 we give the necessary background material. We present the compiler transformations in Sect. 3, while the corresponding runtime issues are discussed in Sect. 4. We then describe our prototype implementation for the Parallella board in Sect. 5. Finally, Sect. 6 concludes this work.

## 2   Background

One of the goals of version 4.0 of the OpenMP API [18] was to provide a state of the art, platform-agnostic model for heterogeneous parallel programming by extending its widely accepted shared-memory paradigm. The extensions introduced are designed to support multiple *devices* (accelerators, coprocessors, GPGPUs, etc.) without the need to create separate code bases for each device. Portions of the unified source code are simply marked by the programmer for offloading to a particular device; the details of data and code allocations, mappings and movements are orchestrated by the compiler. The execution model is a host-centric one: execution starts at the host processor, which is also considered a device, until one of the new constructs is met; this may cause the creation of a data environment and the execution of a specified portion of code on a given device.

The `target` directive is used to transfer control flow to a device. The code in the associated structured block (*kernel*) is offloaded and executed directly on the device, while the host task waits until the kernel finishes its execution. Each `target` directive may contain its own data environment which is initialized when the kernel starts and freed when the kernel ends its execution. In order to avoid repetitive creation and deletion of data environments, the `target data` directive allows the definition of a data environment which persists among successive kernel executions. Furthermore, the programmer may use the `target update` directive between successive kernel offloads to explicitly update the values of variables shared between the host and the device.

The execution of an OpenMP program has a set of initial device data environments (that is, a set of variables associated with a given code region), one for each available device. The data environment can be manipulated through `map` clauses within `target data` and `target` directives. These clauses determine how the specified variables are handled within the data environment. Finally, the variables declared within `declare target` directives are also allocated in the global scope of the target device, and their lifetime equals the program execution time.

The original and the corresponding variables, have common name, type and size but the task that executes in the context of a device data environment, refers to the corresponding variable instead of the original one. Data environments can be nested and a corresponding variable of a device data environment is inherited by all enclosed data environments. This means that a variable can not be remapped during the definition of nested data environments.

## 3    Compiler Transformations

The OMPi compiler [9] is a lightweight OpenMP C infrastructure, composed of a source-to-source compiler and a flexible, modular runtime system. The input of the compiler is C code annotated with OpenMP `pragmas` and the output is an intermediate multithreaded code augmented with calls to the runtime system. A native compiler is used to generate the final executable. OMPi is an open source project and targets general-purpose SMPs and multicore platforms. It adheres to V3.1 of the OpenMP specifications, but support for V4.0 is under way. In addition to the device constructs presented here, initial implementations exist for the cancellation constructs, the `taskgroup` construct and task dependencies.

The main transformation step of OMPi for `parallel`, `task` and `target` directives is *outlining*. A new function is created, containing the transformed body, and the construct is replaced by a runtime call with the new function and a struct as parameters. The struct contains any variables declared before the construct but used in the body of the construct, and is initialized according to the data-sharing attribute clauses. In the following sections, we will use the code in Fig. 1 as an example in order to illustrate the transformation details.

When outlining a `target` region, we store a copy of the outlined function along with any other outlined functions that may occur during the transformation of its body (e.g. when having a `parallel` region inside the `target`), in a global list. After the main transformation phase of the code, we use the information stored in that list to produce kernel files, one for each `target` construct.

## 3.1  Target Data

According to the specifications, if a variable that appears in a `map` clause, already exists in the device data environment, no new space should be allocated and no assignments should occur. Since the `device` clause is an arbitrary expression and there is no restriction on the `device` clause of nested `target data` directives, the compiler is unaware of the devices that a variable has already been mapped on. For example, there could be a `target data` that adds variable $a$ in device 1 and then another `target data` with the same variable that does not contain a `device` clause, and therefore will use the default device which, however, can be changed during execution.

To overcome this subtle problem we inject calls to the runtime for creating, initializing and finalizing environments with variables that appear in `map` clauses, regardless of whether they have appeared or not in an enclosing `target data` directive, and let the runtime handle it, as described in Sect. 4.1. In Fig. 1, this occurs for variables x and y in lines 12 and 13.

When transforming the `target data` directive, a `start` and an `end` call are injected before and after the body of the directive. If the directive is nested in another `target data` directive, the latter data environment is passed in the `start` call (Fig. 1, line 10). For each variable, depending on the map type, an `alloc` (for alloc/from maps) or an `init` (for to/from maps) call is inserted at the start of the body (Fig. 1, lines 12–13). If the variable is from/tofrom a `finalize` call is inserted at the end of the body (Fig. 1, lines 28–29).[1]

## 3.2  Target

Each `target` directive is outlined similarly to `parallel` and `task` directives, albeit with different handlers for the variables. We create a new data environment, as if the construct was a `target data` one (lines 8–13 in Fig. 1). All variables that have already appeared in any enclosing data environment are inserted in the new one. Pointers to these variables are then placed in the *devdata*-struct, which will be passed to the outlined function. The pointers are initialized using runtime calls to get the address of the variables on the device space (lines 20–21).

---

[1] Similar calls are used when transforming `target update` directives.

*Original code:*

```
#pragma omp target data map(x,y)
    #pragma omp target map(from: x) device(2)
        x=y=z=1;
```

*Transformed code:*

```
 1 {                              // start target data
 2      _devid = -1;              // default device
 3      _ddenv = _start_ddenv(NULL, _devid, ..);
 4      _initvar(&x, sizeof(x), _ddenv, _devid);
 5      _initvar(&y, ..);
 6
 7      {                         // start target
 8          _devid = 2;           // requested device
 9          _ddenv_prev = _ddenv;
10          _ddenv = _start_ddenv(_ddenv_prev, _devid, ..);
11
12          _allocvar(&x, ..);    // ignored if default device is 2
13          _initvar(&y, ..);     // ditto
14
15          struct __dd__ {
16              int (* x);
17              int (* y);
18              int z;
19          } * _devdata = _devdata_alloc(_devid, sizeof(struct __dd__));
20          _devdata->x = get_vaddress(&x, ..); // request address @device
21          _devdata->y = get_vaddress(&y, ..);
22          _devdata->z = z;      // optimized
23
24          ort_offload_kernel(_kernelFunc0_, _devdata, ..); // kernel code
25
26          z = _devdata->z;
27
28          _finvar(&x, _ddenv);
29          _finvar(&y, _ddenv);
30
31          _end_ddenv(_ddenv);
32      }                         // end target
33
34      _finvar(&x, _ddenv);
35      _finvar(&y, _ddenv);
36      _end_ddenv(_ddenv);
37 }                              // end target data
```

**Fig. 1.** Compiler transformation example.

As an optimization, if a variable does not appear in any enclosing **target data** directive, space for the variable is created directly within the *devdata*-struct, instead of using a pointer (line 22).

In our example, the kernel body (x=y=z=1;) has been moved to an outlined function _kernelFunc0_(); the actual execution of the kernel occurs in line 24, where the runtime call is given the function name and the *devdata*-struct.

## 3.3   Declare Target

When the compiler encounters a **declare target** region, it stores any contained functions, function prototypes and variables in appropriate lists, and marks them in the symbol table. The body of the directive is left as is during the main transformation phase of the code. Any declared variables within the `declare target` region are ignored during the transformation of the `target` directive.

**Host Code.** The transformation for the `declare target` constructs occurs after the normal transformation phase ends, where all the declared variables have already been marked. A new static function is created in every source file for registering the declared variables with the runtime. For each initialized variable, a separate static variable is also created, using the same initializer. This is needed by the runtime when the initialization of the declared variable takes place on the available devices.

The above function is called whenever a `target update` or a `target` directive is met, which uses one of the `declared` variables. This guarantees that the runtime registers all these variables before they are actually used. In addition, precautions are taken so that the operation is completed only once and is not subject to concurrent invocations. Finally, the `declared` variables, which are used in a `target` region, are placed in a separate struct and are given to the runtime at offload time; in the example of Fig. 1, this struct would be an additional argument to the offloading call in line 24.

**Kernel Code.** For each `target` directive we produce a separate kernel file. The code of a kernel starts with the `declared` function prototypes. All variables declared in `declare target` regions are converted to pointers. Then, we transform the declared functions and the outlined function of the `target` directive, replacing any occurrences of the declared variables by pointers.

Moreover, a wrapper function is created, which is the first function called by the runtime library of the device. The wrapper serves two purposes; first it initializes the pointers for the declared variables from the struct passed in the offload function, and second, it calls the actual outlined kernel function.

## 4    Runtime Support

The runtime system of OMPi has been extended to support part of the new features of OpenMP 4.0. Except for the new runtime functions and environmental variables, the existing worksharing infrastructure was updated to support the cancellation directives. In addition, the tasking infrastructure adds preliminary support for the `taskgroup` functionality, as well as for task dependencies.

Regarding the new device model, OMPi is organized as a collection of modules which implement support for accelerators. The core module which coordinates OpenMP execution on the host is a largely unmodified version of the V3.1 runtime of OMPi; it is only augmented with functionality needed for the coordination of devices, and with a device interface that acts as glue between the host and the other device modules. On the other hand, new device modules are created, with each of them responsible for the manipulation of a particular device. Each module is divided into two parts; the first part is executed on the host and the second is executed on the device, accompanying the offloaded kernels.

## 4.1    Data Environment Handling

The host device needs a bookkeeping mechanism in order to store and retrieve information regarding the variables that constitute the data environments. This information is used when the host accesses these variables for reading or writing, for example during the mapping of a variable, before/after the execution of a kernel, and when the **target update** directive is used. This information is also used during the initialization phase of a kernel. Because of the arbitrary nesting of data environments, and the possibility of multiple devices, the bookkeeping cannot be statically handled at compile time. In what follows, we present our runtime solution to this non-trivial problem.

To allow the host to have fast access to information regarding the variables involved in a data environment, we utilize a special mechanism based on typical separately-chained hash tables (HT). It works approximately as a functional-style compiler symbol table [4], albeit operated by the runtime. A sequence of nested data environments in the source program produces a dynamic sequence of HTs with entries for the mapped variables. The information stored on each entry includes the id of the device which the mapping refers to, and a pointer to the actual storage space of the variable. The hash function takes as input the original variable address combined with the device number and returns the corresponding bucket. Collisions are handled through separate chaining.

```
1    int a, b;
2
3    #pragma omp target data map(a)            // DE1
4       #pragma omp parallel num_threads(2)
5       {
6          int c;
7          #pragma omp target data map(b)      // DE2^(1), DE2^(2)
8             #pragma omp target map(a, c)     // DE3^(1), DE3^(2)
9             ....
10      }
```

**Fig. 2.** Nested device data environments created by a team of threads.

We present our mechanism through two illustrative examples; detailed analysis follows right after. In Fig. 2 we show a code snippet where in line 3 a data environment (DE1) is created with the mapping of variable $a$. Then a team of two threads is created on the host device and each thread defines a separate data environment ($DE2^{(1)}$ and $DE2^{(2)}$) which includes the variables $a$ and $b$. Finally, each thread offloads a code block, while at the same time creates a new data

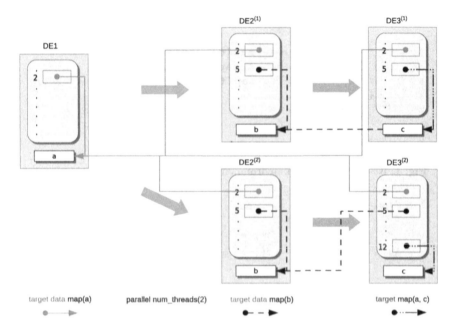

**Fig. 3.** Hash table sequence for code in Fig. 2. Solid yellow, dashed blue and mixed black arrows denote allocations and definitions made at lines 3, 7 and 8, respectively (Color figure online).

environment ($\text{DE}3^{(1)}$ and $\text{DE}3^{(2)}$) which includes the variables $a$ and $c$. All the mappings in the example refer to the default device.

The sequence of HTs for the above example is given in Fig. 3. The result of line 3 is the creation of DE1 which stores only one entry, that for variable $a$. The creation of the thread team does not affect the bookkeeping mechanism, and both threads can access the data of DE1 without the need of locks. Line 7 defines $\text{DE}2^{(1)}$ and $\text{DE}2^{(2)}$ (one for each thread); this causes the creation of new HTs, both of which are created as copies of the previous HT. As a result, each thread retains access to the enclosing data environment. The mapping of variable $b$ adds a new entry for $\text{DE}2^{(1)}$ and $\text{DE}2^{(2)}$ and the addition of a pointer from the HT to this entry. Similarly, in line 8 we have the creation of new HTs that handle $\text{DE}3^{(1)}$ and $\text{DE}3^{(2)}$, respectively, as copies of the previous two HTs. In the case of the second thread, variable $c$ is hashed onto bucket 12, which is a free bucket. In contrast, variable $c$ of the first thread caused a collision (hashed onto bucket 5), resulting in a chain between the variables $c$ and $b$.

An additional complication arises by the possible presence of multiple devices, where a data environment may be nested within another environment that refers to a different device, as can be seen in the code of Fig. 4. In this example, in line 3, a data environment is defined for device 1 (DE4), with variable $d$. Then, DE5 is created in line 4 for device 2 that includes variables $d$ and $e$. Finally, DE6 is created in line 5 for device 1 and a block of code is offloaded for execution.

```
1    int d, e, f;
2
3    #pragma omp target data map(d) device(1)          // DE4
4      #pragma omp target data map(d, e) device(2)     // DE5
5        #pragma omp target map(f) device(1)           // DE6
6        {
7          e = d++; // implicit mapping of variable e
8          ...           // in device 1
9        }
```

**Fig. 4.** Nested device data environments created for two different devices.

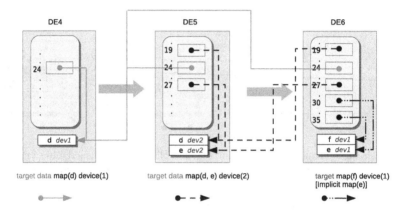

**Fig. 5.** Hash table sequence for code in Fig. 4. Solid yellow, dashed blue and mixed black arrows denote allocations and definitions made at lines 3, 4 and 5, respectively (Color figure online).

Notice that $d$ is already mapped through DE4 while there is an implicit mapping for variable $e$ on device 1. The corresponding sequence of HTs is shown in Fig. 5. In DE4 there is only one entry for $d$ on device 1. The HT for DE5 starts with a copy of DE4; entries for variables $d$ and $e$ are then added in buckets 19 and 27, correspondingly. Notice that because $d$ now refers to device 2, the hash function results to a different bucket than the one used for device 1. Finally, DE6 starts as a copy of DE5 and has two entries added for variables $f$ and $e$. Since $d$ is already present in the data environment of device 1, no further actions are required.

**Details of the Mechanism.** The data handling mechanism is operated by the host, resides in the host address space, and is independent from any attached devices. The HTs allow for efficient variable insertion and look-up operations. Each time a nested data environment is created, a new HT is initialized as a copy of the HT used by the enclosing data environment, as in functional-style symbol tables; destruction of the data environment requires a single memory deallocation for the corresponding HT. If a team of threads is created within a target data region, separate HTs are created, when needed, for each thread; this completely eliminates mutual exclusion problems.

In addition, we employ a further optimization. When initializing a new data environment for a particular device, the compiler informs the runtime about the *maximum possible number of variables added* to the environment. This is calculated statically during the analysis of the program; an exact number is not possible to derive because the devices the environments refer to are given by full expressions and can only be calculated at runtime, in the general case. In practice, only variables not already mapped on this device are actually inserted in the HT. Because of this information, the runtime is able to acquire memory for the HT *and* the entries in a single allocation request (this explains why in Figs. 3 and 5 the HTs and the corresponding entries lie within the same rectangle). This also has the desirable side-effect of increased data locality, as the hash table and the entry information reside on the same memory block.

The space requirements of the presented mechanism have an upper bound of $O(L \cdot K + n)$, where $L$ stands for the maximum number of alive data environments, $K$ is the size of a hash table (derived from the static compiler information discussed above) and $n$ is the total number of variables that are mapped in all data environment definitions. In a program that defines a total of $E$ data environments, exactly $\Theta(E)$ of memory allocations and deallocations are made, which include the memory required for the HT and the memory used for the entries. With a load factor at most equal to 1, the average time for an insertion or a lookup is $\Theta(1)$.

## 5   The Epiphany Accelerator as a Device

The Parallella-16 board [2] is a popular 18-core credit card-sized computer and comes with standard peripheral ports such as USB, Ethernet, HDMI, GPIO, etc. The computational power of the board comes from its two processing modules. The main (host) processor is a dual-core ARM Cortex A9 with 512 KiB shared L2 cache, built within a Zynq 7010 or 7020 SoC. The other is an Epiphany 16-core chip which is used as a co-processor. The board has 1 GiB of DDR3 RAM, addressable by both the ARM CPU and the Epiphany. The former runs Linux OS and uses virtual addresses, whereas the latter does not have an OS and uses a flat, unprotected memory map.

Two versions of the Epiphany co-processor are actually available: the Epiphany-16 (with 16 cores and a $4 \times 4$ mesh NoC) and the Epiphany-64 (with 64 cores and an $8 \times 8$ mesh). Although our discussion here holds for both versions, we refer mostly to the first one since it is the one widely available. Each Epiphany core (eCORE) is a 32-bit superscalar RISC CPU, clocked at 600 MHz, capable of performing single-precision floating point operations, and equipped with 32 KiB local scratchpad memory and two DMA engines. The ARM and the Epiphany use a 32 MiB portion of the system RAM as *shared memory* which is physically addressable by both of them. All common programming tools are available for the ARM host processor. For the Epiphany, a Software Development Kit (eSDK [1]) is available, which includes a C compiler and runtime libraries for both the host (eHAL) and the Epiphany (eLIB). Furthermore, OpenCL is provided by the COPRTHR SDK [6]. The latter also provides a threading API similar to POSIX.

## 5.1  Runtime Organization

In this section we will briefly describe the key features of the runtime module that implements the support of the Epiphany accelerator as an OpenMP 4.0 device, based on the eSDK. More details are available in [3]. The module consists of two parts; one executed by the host CPU and one executed by the eCOREs.

**The Host Part.** The communication between the Zynq and the eCOREs occurs through the shared memory portion of the system RAM. The shared memory is logically divided in two sections: The first section has a fixed size of 4 KiB, and is used transparently by OMPi for kernel coordination and manipulation of parallel teams created within the Epiphany. The second part is used for storing the kernel data environments and part of the tasking infrastructure of the Epiphany OpenMP library.

In order to be able to control the eCOREs independently through eHAL calls, the initialization phase creates 16 workgroups, one for each of the available Epiphany cores and puts them to the idle state for energy and thermal efficiency. For offloading a kernel, the first idle core is chosen and the precompiled kernel object file is loaded to it for immediate execution. Due to the high overheads of the eSDK when offloading kernels to different workgroups, we developed an optimized low-level offload routine to assist the creation of OpenMP teams. We support multiple, independent kernels, executing concurrently within the Epiphany. Because the current version of eHAL does not provide a way for an eCORE to notify directly the host for kernel completion, a special region of the shared memory is designated for synchronization with the eCOREs.

For the `target teams` directive special care is taken regarding the choice of the eCOREs which will execute the associated kernel. In order to keep intra-team NoC traffic localized, the team masters are placed as if a `spread` thread affinity policy was in effect for them. For example, if all eCOREs are idle and the creation of 4 teams is requested, then the eCOREs with ids 0, 3, 12 and 15 (the ones in the four corners on the $4 \times 4$ grid) will be activated.

**OpenMP Within the Epiphany.** Supporting OpenMP within the device side presents many challenges due to the lack of dynamic parallelism and the limited local memory of each eCORE. Regarding the former, when a kernel is offloaded to a specific eCORE, the core executes its sequential part until a `parallel` region is encountered. Because only the host can activate other eCOREs, the master core contacts the host, requesting the activation of a number of cores. A copy of the same kernel is then offloaded to the newly activated cores. During the parallel code execution all synchronization between the cores occurs through their fast local memories. When the region completes, the cores return to the idle, power saving state, while the master core informs the host thread about the termination of the parallel team.

The small scratchpad memory makes it impossible to fit sophisticated OpenMP runtime structures alongside the application data. To support the worksharing constructs of the OpenMP, the infrastructure originally designed for the host was trimmed down so as to minimize its memory footprint; this is linked and offloaded with each kernel. The coordination among the participating eCORES utilizes structures stored in the local memory of the team master. The eSDK provides mechanisms for locks and barriers between the eCORES but they assume that the synchronized cores belong to same workgroup. Since in our runtime each eCORE constitutes a different workgroup, we were forced to modify all these mechanisms. Finally, our tasking infrastructure is based on a blocking shared queue stored in the local memory of the master eCORE, while the corresponding task data environments are stored in the shared memory.

## 5.2   Experiments

We have conducted a number of tests in order to measure the efficiency of our offloading mechanisms alongside the space and timing performance of the OpenMP runtime within the Epiphany accelerator. Our board is the Parallella-16 SKUA101020 and we use eSDK 5.13.9.10. To examine the memory overhead of our Epiphany-resident runtime, we created a set of simple OpenMP programs to compare with the size of the kernels produced when the native eLIB is used. In the case of an empty kernel, containing only a single assignment OMPi incurs a 4.5 KiB overhead as compared to the kernel created by the native eLIB. In other scenarios which involved a team of 16 cores and complex OpenMP functionality, up to 10 KiB more than a similar eLIB-based kernel were needed. We are currently optimizing the runtime memory footprint even more.

In order to measure the OpenMP construct overheads within the Epiphany, we created a modified version of the EPCC microbenchmark suite [7] where their basic routines are offloaded through `target` directives. In Fig. 6 we plot a sample of the synchronization benchmark results. While most results are quite satisfactory, our initial prototype employs a non-optimized barrier, which also has a direct impact on the overheads of the `for` construct. We are currently optimizing its behavior. Sample results for the tasking benchmark are given in Fig. 7. The noticeable cases are those of the Taskwait and Master task tests. The contention on our simple lock-based shared task queue is quite high in these tests and shows up vividly in the case of 16 threads. Our implementation can be further improved, but at this point we strive mostly for functional correctness.

Finally, we include performance results for a few simple OpenMP applications. In Fig. 8 we plot timing results for a typical iterative computation of $\pi = 3.14159$, based on the trapezoid rule with 2,000,000 intervals, and using a kernel which spawns a parallel team of 1 to 16 threads. While the scalability is almost ideal, the serial execution is quite slow; the reason is that the Epiphany does not support double-precision numbers natively and the eCORE floating point

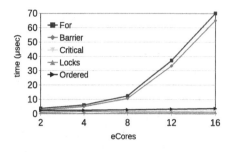

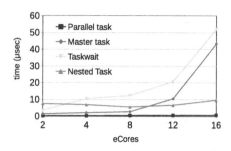

**Fig. 6.** EPCC synchronization results      **Fig. 7.** EPCC tasking results

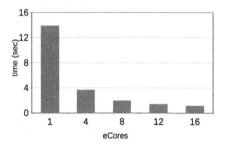

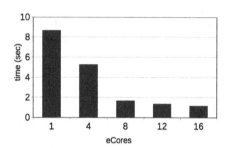

**Fig. 8.** Pi computation                    **Fig. 9.** Nqueens(12)

unit does not implement division. In Fig. 9 we present the performance of a modified version of the Nqueens task benchmark, taken from the Barcelona OpenMP Tasks Suite (BOTS) [10]. This application computes all solutions of the $n$-queens placement problem on an $n \times n$ chessboard, so that none of the queens threatens any other. Due to the severe memory limitations of the Epiphany, we considered the manual cut-off version of the benchmark, where the nested production of tasks stops at a given depth. The figure shows the timing results for 12 queens, and a cut-off value of 2 (144 tasks produced). As it can be seen, with the addition of eCORES we obtain an almost linear speedup.

## 6    Discussion and Current Status

We presented the infrastructure of the OMPi compiler related to the new OpenMP 4.0 device model. We put an emphasis on the efficient handling of data environments both from the compiler and the runtime sides, because the specifications allow considerable freedom in the way data environments can be nested. Our infrastructure is used to support OpenMP within the popular Parallella board, where we treat the Epiphany-16 as an accelerator device, attached to a dual-core ARM host processor, allowing the dynamic creation of parallel teams within the device itself. We are currently focused on optimizing our system, and supporting additional OpenMP 4.0 functionality.

From our experimentation with the Parallella board, it became clear that offloaded kernels should not make use of sophisticated OpenMP features, in devices with limited resources. We also observed that a major overhead is the time needed to offload a kernel. If the computation is structured in a way where kernels are repeatedly offloaded, to operate on different data each time, then it is questionable whether the application will experience significant performance gains. For such scenarios, we believe that support of resident kernels may bring considerable improvements. A kernel would be offloaded only once, while at specific points the host would communicate new data (through **target updates**) for the kernel to operate on. Of course, this would also require new synchronization mechanisms between the kernel and the host task, which could be part of future OpenMP extensions.

**Acknowledgment.** The authors would like to thank Adapteva for providing them with a Parallella-16 board through the Parallella University Program.

# References

1. Adapteva: Epiphany SDK reference Manual, September 2013
2. Adapteva: Parallella Reference Manual, September 2014
3. Agathos, S.N., Papadogiannakis, A., Dimakopoulos, V.V.: Targeting the parallella. In: Träff, J.L., Hunold, S., Versaci, F. (eds.) Euro-Par 2015. LNCS, vol. 9233, pp. 662–674. Springer, Heidelberg (2015)
4. Appel, A.W.: Modern Compiler Implementation in C. Cambridge University Press, Cambridge (1999)
5. Bertolli, C., Antao, S.F., Eichenberger, A.E., O'Brien, K., Sura, Z., Jacob, A.C., Chen, T., Sallenave, O.: Coordinating GPU threads for OpenMP 4.0 in LLVM. In: Proceedings of LLVM-HPC 2014, New Orleans, Louisiana, pp. 12–21, November 2014
6. Brown Deer Technology, LLC: COPRTHR API Reference (2014)
7. Bull, J.M.: Measuring synchronisation and scheduling overheads in OpenMP. In: Proceedings of 1st EWOMP, Lund, Sweden, pp. 99–105, September 1999
8. Liao, C., Yan, Y., de Supinski, B.R., Quinlan, D.J., Chapman, B.: Early experiences with the OpenMP accelerator model. In: Rendell, A.P., Chapman, B.M., Müller, M.S. (eds.) IWOMP 2013. LNCS, vol. 8122, pp. 84–98. Springer, Heidelberg (2013)
9. Dimakopoulos, V.V., Leontiadis, E., Tzoumas, G.: A portable C compiler for OpenMP V. 2.0. In: Proceedings of EWOMP 2003, Aachen, Germany, pp. 5–11, September 2003
10. Duran, A., Teruel, X., Ferrer, R., Martorell, X., Ayguadé, E.: Barcelona OpenMP tasks suite: a set of benchmarks targeting the exploitation of task parallelism in OpenMP. In: Proceedings of ICPP 2009, Vienna, Austria, pp. 124–131, September 2009
11. GNU: GCC 5 Release Series. https://gcc.gnu.org/gcc-5/changes.html
12. Intel Corporation: User and Reference Guide for the Intel C++ Compiler 15.0, OpenMP* Support. https://software.intel.com/en-us/node/522679
13. Khronos OpenCL Working Group: The OpenCL Specification Version: 1.2, November 2012

14. Kirk, D.B., Hwu, W.M.W.: Programming Massively Parallel Processors: A Hands-on Approach, 2nd edn. Morgan Kaufmann, San Francisco (2012)
15. Mitra, G., Stotzer, E., Jayaraj, A., Rendell, A.P.: Implementation and optimization of the OpenMP accelerator model for the TI keystone II architecture. In: DeRose, L., de Supinski, B.R., Olivier, S.L., Chapman, B.M., Müller, M.S. (eds.) IWOMP 2014. LNCS, vol. 8766, pp. 202–214. Springer, Heidelberg (2014)
16. Newburn, C., Deodhar, R., Dmitriev, S., Murty, R., Narayanaswamy, R., Wiegert, J., Chinchilla, F., McGuire, R.: Offload Compiler Runtime for the Intel Xeon Phi$^{TM}$ Coprocessor. In: Proceedings of ISC 2013, Leipzig, Germany, pp. 239–254, June 2013
17. OpenACC: The OpenACC Application Programming Interface, V. 2.0, June 2013
18. OpenMP ARB: OpenMP Application Program Interface V4.0, July 2013

# Energy

# Application-Level Energy Awareness
# for OpenMP

Ferdinando Alessi[1], Peter Thoman[1(✉)], Giorgis Georgakoudis[2],
Thomas Fahringer[1], and Dimitrios S. Nikolopoulos[2]

[1] University of Innsbruck, Innsbruck, Austria
{petert,tf}@dps.uibk.ac.at
[2] Queen's University of Belfast, Belfast, UK
{g.georgakoudis,d.nikolopoulos}@qub.ac.uk

**Abstract.** Power, and consequently energy, has recently attained first-class system resource status, on par with conventional metrics such as CPU time. To reduce energy consumption, many hardware- and OS-level solutions have been investigated. However, application-level information - which can provide the system with valuable insights unattainable otherwise - was only considered in a handful of cases. We introduce OpenMPE, an extension to OpenMP designed for power management. OpenMP is the de-facto standard for programming parallel shared memory systems, but does not yet provide any support for power control. Our extension exposes (i) per-region multi-objective optimization hints and (ii) application-level adaptation parameters, in order to create energy-saving opportunities for the whole system stack. We have implemented OpenMPE support in a compiler and runtime system, and empirically evaluated its performance on two architectures, mobile and desktop. Our results demonstrate the effectiveness of OpenMPE with geometric mean energy savings across 9 use cases of 15 % while maintaining full quality of service.

## 1  Introduction

Mobile computing devices such as laptops, tablets and smartphones are becoming more widespread. The performance that these devices offer is increasing at a steady pace, with octa-core processors powering contemporary smartphones. Mobile systems are even being considered as low-cost energy-efficient candidates for HPC [19]. However, mobility comes at a price: energy is a scarce resource on these devices, especially with power-hungry media consumption constituting a major use case. Furthermore, mobile computing is not the sole field where energy is increasingly relevant - the tremendous increase in power consumption by performance-oriented servers has made power budgeting unavoidable in HPC as well.

Several solutions have been proposed to address the energy problem on different levels. On the hardware level, energy-driven circuit design and features such as multiple available dynamic voltage and frequency scaling (DVFS) levels are widely employed. Proposed energy-aware OSes exploit these operating

© Springer International Publishing Switzerland 2015
C. Terboven et al. (Eds.): IWOMP 2015, LNCS 9342, pp. 219–232, 2015.
DOI: 10.1007/978-3-319-24595-9_16

modes according to actual and predicted device load, in some cases with additional knowledge provided by the application itself [22]. On the user level, frameworks have been introduced to implement content adaptation policies based on resource availability [2] and more generally to define a power management strategy steering multi-mode operating devices [14]. While system-level approaches have been explored to a certain extent, we believe there still exists a lot of room for improvement on the application level since no power management interface that can be considered complete, generic and easy to use has been proposed so far.

To fill this gap we propose a dedicated API for application-level energy awareness – and, more generally, multi-objective optimization. Rather than designing a completely new interface, we opt for extending OpenMP API [16], the de-facto standard for parallel shared-memory computing. Our choice is driven by the inherent parallelism of modern architectures, which exposes opportunities to save energy requiring close interaction with the parallel runtime system.

This paper explores application-level energy saving opportunities through the specification, implementation and evaluation of OpenMPE – an OpenMP extension for Energy. OpenMPE adds new directives and clauses to enable per-region customization of multiple optimization objectives and tunable parameters. We provide three major contributions:

- A novel API for application-level energy-aware programming, allowing programmers to expose energy saving opportunities through (i) characterizing application behavior by providing a semantic region structure, (ii) setting per-code region multi-objective goals and constraints, and (iii) exposing application-level tunable parameters.
- A compilation and runtime system supporting OpenMPE. The runtime system exploits opportunities exposed by programmers through several techniques such as dynamic voltage and frequency scaling, dynamic concurrency throttling (DCT), and application-level content adaptation.
- An empirical evaluation of the effectiveness of OpenMPE. A video codec reference implementation is enriched with OpenMPE and benchmarked on a desktop and mobile platform.

The rest of this paper is organized as follows: Sect. 2 motivates the proposed research work. Section 3 introduces OpenMPE, and Sect. 4 presents a compiler and runtime prototype implementation. To demonstrate the validity of our extension, experimental results are shown in Sect. 5. Related work and our conclusions are presented in Sects. 6 and 7, respectively.

## 2    Motivation

In this section we illustrate the three main considerations that motivate our proposed OpenMPE extensions.

Firstly, single-objective optimization is no longer sufficient. While execution time was the main and only concern in the past, with the advent of mobile platforms and the currently unsustainable energy consumption of supercomputers, new objectives must be considered as well. With OpenMPE, energy and power are also raised to first-class resources, forming a total of four, potentially conflicting, goals with the inclusion of quality of service. Furthermore, our generic design is extendable for any additional objectives which might become relevant in the future.

A second observation concerns phase detection, which is still generally hard without application-level support. Different program regions have different requirements and applying the same optimization strategies without distinction can deteriorate optimization goals such as execution time and energy use. Consequently, correctly identifying program phases is a main concern for dynamically adaptable systems. Many solutions have been proposed so far to detect and predict program behavior automatically, both online and offline, yet current techniques still suffer from overhead and misclassification [4]. Therefore, we believe that allowing developers to easily expose program phases directly at the application level is the most practical approach.

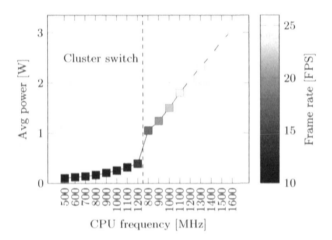

**Fig. 1.** Average power consumption of a video decoder at various DVFS levels

Thirdly and most crucially, *application semantics are not derivable by underlying layers*. Functional constraints and goals are only known by the application programmer. For example, in soft real-time use cases, the time constraints are unknown to underlying layers unless explicitly communicated. As such, developers have access to important information that is unattainable by runtime and operating systems: in this paper we demonstrate how beneficial it can be to forward such application-level knowledge to underlying layers.

As a concrete example of this issue, Fig. 1 illustrates the average power consumption of a video decoder executed at multiple CPU frequencies. This data was collected on a mobile development board (detailed in Sect. 5) where two heterogeneous CPU clusters coexist. Points to the left of the "Cluster switch" line depict the results when using all 4 low power cores, while the ones to the right use the high power cores. As the frequency is lowered, the average power decreases but the same occurs for the frame rate achieved by the application: only the performance-oriented cluster can maintain an optimal frame rate (of 24 FPS for the given video), down to a minimum of 1100 MHz. Clearly, this frame rate threshold should be taken into account by DVFS algorithms, but the desired framerate is semantic information only known at the application level.

As a side rationale, ease of use cannot be disregarded while designing an application-level interface. Our choice for a minimal directive-based API extension is intended to address this point.

# 3    OpenMPE

OpenMPE is based on OpenMP 4 and extends it for multi-objective optimization. Preserving the execution and memory models, directives and API functions defined in the base OpenMP language, OpenMPE adds one new construct and two clauses as listed in Table 1. Both clauses may annotate the **parallel**, **for**, **task** and **region** constructs.

*Explicit regions* Since OpenMP addresses parallel computing, it allows marking code regions for parallelization, worksharing and synchronization. While adding clauses to existing constructs would be sufficient to achieve our goals for such regions, for completeness we also offer the possibility to delineate code regions independently of parallelization purposes, by introducing the **region** construct. The **region** construct defines a region encompassing the subsequent single-entry-single-exit language block. This construct supports both OpenMPE clauses, and its syntax is specified in Table 1.

*Multi-objective optimization goals* By means of this clause, programmers can instruct the system about multi-objective optimization goals in terms of execution time, power, energy and quality of service for a specific code region: the

**Table 1.** OpenMPE constructs and clauses

| **Constructs** |
| --- |
| // *Definition of an explicit region* |
| **#pragma omp region** [**objective**(...)] [**param**(...)] |
|     *structured-block* |
| **Clauses** |
| // *Specification of a multi−objective optimization goal* |
| **objective**(*weights* : *constraints*) |
| // *Specification of a tunable parameter* |
| **param**(*var*, [**range**(*value-range:quality-range*) \| **enum**(*values, size:quality-range*)]) |

compiler and runtime system are guided by the `objective` clause in their transformation and resource allocation policies.

Objectives can be expressed through a set of weights or constraints with the
following syntax:

$$weights = f_1 * P_1 + f_2 * P_2 + \cdots + f_N * P_N$$
$$constraints = \{P_i < c_i; constraints\} \mid \emptyset$$

where $c_i \in \mathbb{R}$, $f_i \in \mathbb{R}$ and $\sum_{i=1}^{i<=N} f_i = 1.0$. $P_i$ can be any of the non-functional
parameters associated with the given region of execution: $T$ (execution time),
$P$ (power consumption), $E$ (energy consumption) or $Q$ (quality of service). The
unit for $c_i$ is, respectively, seconds, watts, joules, or a pure integer value. While
estimating performance in terms of execution time, power and energy consumption is straight-forward, quality of service requires a specific definition. We define
the quality of service delivered by a code region indirectly by its degradation, as
an integer value between 0 and $\infty$ where 0 is the best achievable.

Some usage examples of the `objective` clause are:

```
1   #pragma omp ... objective(E)
2   #pragma omp ... objective(0.8*E+0.2*T)
3   #pragma omp ... objective(T : P<p)
```

On line 1 the programmer instructs the OpenMPE system to attempt minimizing
the energy consumption for executing the binding region. Instructed with line
2, the system performs a weighted optimization between energy and time, with
0.8 as the weighting factor for energy and 0.2 for time. Processing line 3, the
system tries to achieve the minimum run time possible while staying below a
given power consumption $p$ (specified in watts in double precision floating point
– $p$ can be a dynamically evaluated expression).

*Tunable application parameters* The `param` clause specifies tunable parameters
affecting the behavior of the program which are not introduced by the compiler
or hardware platform but are inherent in user code. Its syntax specifies a base
language variable storing the tunable parameter and either (i) `range` specified as
a lower bound expression, upper bound expression and step, all three expressions
of the same type as the variable, (ii) `enum` specified as a base language array
storing elements of the same type as the variable and the size of the array,
or (iii) if the variable type is boolean, no `range` or `enum` expressions need to
be specified. Each of these specifications can optionally be enriched with an
expression defining the mapping between possible values for the variable and
quality-of-service ratings, evaluated by the system to achieve $Q$ objectives.

Some usage examples of the `param` clause are:

```
1   #pragma omp ... param(rate, range(24, 74, 10))
2   #pragma omp ... param(rate, range(24, 74, 10: 5, 0, −1))
3   #pragma omp ... param(name, enum(names_array, names_len)
```

The example on line 1 specifies that the base language variable `rate` can assume for the binding code region any value $val$ which satisfies $val = 24 + i * 10; val <= 74$ where $i \in N$. Line 2 enriches the semantics of line 1 with a mapping to quality weights: a `rate` of 24 has an associated quality metric of 5, 34 maps to quality 4 and so on up to value 74 with quality 0 (the best possible). With line 3, the value of the variable `name` for the binding code region is picked by the OpenMPE runtime system among the first `names_len` elements of the array `names_array`.

## 4   Compilation and Runtime System

This section outlines a reference implementation of OpenMPE, built upon the *Insieme* project [12]. It comprises two central components, the *Insieme Compiler* and the *Insieme Runtime System* (Insieme RS). To implement OpenMPE, these were modified by extending (1) the compiler frontend to process OpenMPE clauses and directives, (2) both the Insieme internal representation and encoding of meta-information statically collected by the compiler to reflect OpenMPE semantics, (3) the compiler backend to forward OpenMPE meta-information to the runtime system, (4) the runtime system framework to acquire OpenMPE information and achieve defined multi-objective goals through an optimization algorithm, and (5) the runtime system instrumentation facilities according to the requirements of the optimization algorithm.

*Source-to-source compilation* The Insieme compiler is a source-to-source compiler for C/C++ which supports OpenMP. Source code is translated into an internal representation (IR), optimizations are performed, and it is converted back to C. Figure 2 depicts the compilation process.

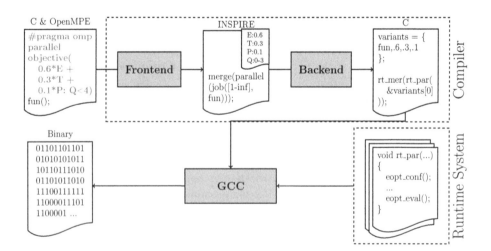

**Fig. 2.** OpenMPE compilation workflow

To integrate OpenMPE directives into Insieme, we directly translate `region` and `param` directives into IR constructs, while the `objective` clause is handled as meta-information annotating IR nodes. The compiler backend was extended to convert this representation into suitable Insieme RS calls and meta-information into appropriate C data structures.

*Runtime system* Insieme RS is an execution framework complementing the Insieme Compiler. Its application model is based on low-overhead user-level task processing and scheduling enriched by the availability of a large set of meta-information. It features a powerful instrumentation infrastructure capable of collecting per-region performance data from a variety of architectures and APIs, including PAPI, Intel RAPL – taking care of potential overflow issues – and an interface specifically designed for the mobile system described in Sect. 5.

Within the scope of OpenMPE, the runtime system is also responsible for achieving per-region multi-objective goals specified by programmers. An additional module, the *e-optimizer*, was introduced for this purpose. Its task is the (re)configuration of available optimization knobs based on collected performance data to fulfill defined per-region objectives. In this implementation, we consider as optimization knobs system-level features such as DVFS and DCT as well as OpenMPE tunable parameters exposed via the `param` clause.

| | |
|---|---|
| `iteration` | iteration counter |
| `done` | true if a definitive configuration has been identified |
| `best_conf` | best configuration found so far |
| `best_perf_data` | performance data for the best configuration |
| `curr_conf` | current configuration |
| THRESHOLD | iterations before hill climbing |

```
1   if !done then
2     if iteration++ < THRESHOLD then
3       curr_conf = random_selection()
4     else
5       (curr_conf, done) = hill_climbing()
6     end if
7   else
8     curr_conf = best_conf
9   end if
10  annotated_task()
11  if !done and get_curr_perf_data() > best_perf_data
        and constraints_are_satisfied(get_curr_perf_data()) then
12    best_perf_data = get_curr_perf_data()
13    best_conf = curr_conf
14  end if
```

Fig. 3. The *e-optimizer* algorithm

The *e-optimizer*, outlined in Fig. 3, is an online optimizer, exploiting the fact that `objective` enriched code regions are typically executed several times. For one, the `objective` clause augments constructs such as `for` which semantically require multiple executions. Moreover, many applications iterate over those constructs, as is the case for the benchmark described in Sect. 5. This structure provides an opportunity to evaluate different configurations for the same task in a single program execution. To this end, *e-optimizer* configuration and evaluation function calls are inserted at the beginning and end of each code region representing a task annotated with multi-objective goals. During the configuration phase, a *configuration* of optimization knobs is selected, including a specific CPU frequency, number of threads to employ and a set of values for the possible `param` variables. During the evaluation phase, performance data is collected and stored for the previous configuration and region. After a given task has been executed a threshold number of times, the *e-optimizer* picks the best configuration fulfilling the defined goals among the ones evaluated. This configuration is subsequently refined by a multi-dimensional hill climbing over all optimization knobs until a definitive solution is found. Configurations are initially selected randomly for two main reasons: (a) it is not trivial to determine how different values for a specific knob will affect energy consumption (reducing core frequency will reduce power consumption but execution time will increase) and (b) to mitigate the issue of local optima which might occur in a pure hill-climbing approach.

## 5    Evaluation

To demonstrate the effectiveness of OpenMPE, we have annotated an existing real-world application with our proposed API. We subsequently employed our reference OpenMPE compiler and runtime system, and analyzed the energy consumption of the resulting program on two distinct hardware architectures. The results obtained with our implementation are compared to the same application parallelized with plain OpenMP and compiled by GCC.

*Hardware setup* For our experiments we use systems representative of two device classes, mobile and desktop. The mobile system is an ODROID XU+E developer board based on a Samsung Exynos 5 Octa (5420) SoC, implementing the ARM big.LITTLE architecture comprising a Cortex-A15 quad-core and a Cortex-A7 quad-core. Either one of the clusters can be active at a time and both offer DVFS, with 9 frequencies available for the Cortex-A15 and 8 for the Cortex-A7. The board is equipped with current and voltage sensors to individually measure power consumptions of both core clusters, memory and gpu.

The desktop system is an Intel i7-3770k Ivy Bridge quad-core offering 16 frequency settings. For this system, energy estimations are collected from the Intel RAPL interface. In terms of software infrastructure, the Exynos board runs Linux kernel version 3.4.75, while the Ivy Bridge system uses 3.11.0. GCC 4.8.3 was employed as the backend compiler and for comparison purposes on both systems.

*Benchmark application* To evaluate our proposal we choose an application from the benchmark suite MediaBench II [8]. Among the available options we selected *tmndec*, a video decoder based on the ITU H.263 standard. Although more recent codecs are available in the suite, their far greater complexity would add major engineering and parallelization effort to our study while not providing significant new insight. We optionally enable vertical and horizontal deposterization filters in order test our proposal on additional load scenarios.

```
1    #pragma omp parallel for schedule(dynamic)
2    for (int y=0; y<rows; y+=2)
3        for (int x=0; x<cols_2; x++) { ... }
```

**Listing 1.1.** *tmndec* main loop parallelized using a dynamic schedule

```
1    #pragma omp parallel for schedule(dynamic)
         objective(E : T<1/f_rate; Q<3) param(scaling, range(1:8:1))
2    for (int y=0; y<rows; y+=2*scaling)
3        for (int x=0; x<cols_2; x+=scaling) {
4            ...
5            if(scaling > 1) { ... }
6        }
```

**Listing 1.2.** *tmndec* with multi-objective goals and tunable parameter

Since *tmndec* is a purely sequential implementation, as a first step we parallelize it via OpenMP. The application features a central two-level nested loop which accounts for video frame decoding: thus, it was a prime target for optimization (Listing 1.1).

Semantically, this code region needs to be executed sufficiently fast such that the application can still achieve its target frame rate. A constraint of this type is easily expressible through OpenMPE as shown in Listing 1.2. The *weights* expression of the objective hints at a minimization of energy consumption without regard for power or time, while the *constraints* expression guarantees that a specific frame rate *f_rate* is maintained.

Finally, we introduce content-adaptation by the OpenMPE param clause and a constraint on the quality of service. With the addition of the subsampling factor *scaling* it is possible to adjust the resolution – and thus quality – of the decoded video. As shown in Listing 1.2, the param clause indicates that the variable *scaling* can assume any integral value in range [1,8] at runtime. Subsampling is enabled accordingly on line 5. The addition of the quality constraint (Q<3) prevents the optimizer from choosing scaling factors which significantly degrade quality – a user-adjustable variable could be employed in real-world scenarios.

*Experimental results* We performed experiments using two resolutions, 704×576 (4CIF) and 1408×1152 (16CIF), and for each of them we used three load variants: (i) full (horizontal and vertical) deposterization, (ii) a single vertical deposterization pass, and (iii) no filter at all. On the *mobile* system only the 4CIF resolution was tested, while both were explored on the *desktop* system for a total of 6 configurations. For comparison purposes, the **ondemand** *cpufreq* governor

[17], default for most Linux systems, was also evaluated for each configuration. It sets the CPU frequency based on OS-level CPU usage tracking, without access to application-level information.

The *e-optimizer* search phase is generally very short (around 20 frames, less than a second) and will not significantly impact performance in production scenarios. However, for our testing, the insufficient temporal resolution of the energy measurement hardware provided by our *mobile* system required us to evaluate the otherwise single execution of each OpenMPE code region in groups, with a resulting expansion of the *e-optimizer* search time. A longer, realistic video playback scenario would still mitigate this initial loss of performance but would also dramatically increase the experiment duration. For this reason, the data collected from our experiments and shown in Fig. 4 is limited to the final 3000 frames of a 12000 frames video.

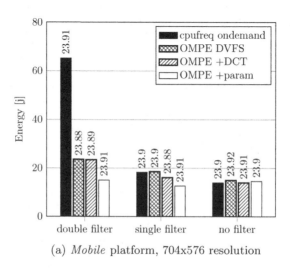

(a) *Mobile* platform, 704x576 resolution

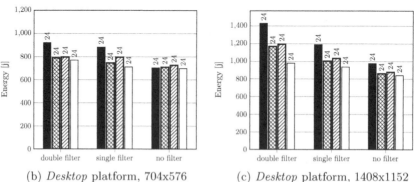

(b) *Desktop* platform, 704x576          (c) *Desktop* platform, 1408x1152

**Fig. 4.** Energy consumption of *tmndec* with different optimization knobs and filtering applied; frame rate achieved noted on top of each bar

When discussing the results presented in Fig. 4, we would first like to note that despite the energy savings it achieves, our system maintains a quality of service (FPS, as indicated by the numbers on each bar in the chart) on par with the reference governor in all scenarios. Some observations can be made across both platforms and are related to the features of this particular benchmark application: (1) allowing the *e-optimizer* to use DCT capabilities (+DCT) does not add to energy gains for this testing scenario. This is due to the fact that both systems provide an ample variety of DVFS frequencies, and that the algorithm features nearly linear parallel scaling. (2) the addition of content-adaptation (+param) is not effective when no filters are applied, as in such cases the overall computational load is very small. (3) the geometric mean of the energy savings achieved by our system using all of its capabilities compared to the baseline, across all 9 scenarios, is 15 %.

On the *mobile* system we observe a large range of findings from an energy point of view, with our system performing significantly better than the **ondemand** governor for the full filter configuration, saving up to 77 % energy, while managing about 20 % energy savings in the single filter case and performing on par with no filtering. This range of effectiveness is related to the relative CPU load incurred in the various scenarios: in the very low-load no-filtering scenario, the default governor is able to determine that the lowest CPU frequency is sufficient because of the long sleep periods of the application, bringing its performance up to par with our approach.

On the *desktop* system achieving an optimal frame rate is not an issue and our implementation generally performs better than the *cpufreq* governor with energy savings up to 31 %. Once again, the only exception is the 704×576 resolution scenario with no filtering: due to the comparatively light computational load of this configuration, both approaches detect that the lowest possible frequency setting is sufficient. It is interesting to note that even though the range of available frequencies is larger on the *desktop* system, they offer a smaller gain in terms of energy savings compared to the *mobile* system. This is evident from Fig. 4c: the *desktop* system is capable of maintaining an optimal frame rate with each of the available frequencies, but the energy savings with DVFS, while significant, are comparatively minor remaining between 12 % and 18 %.

## 6   Related Work

Proposed solutions for energy and power management range from the lowest to the upper levels of the system stack involved: hardware-, system software- and application-based approaches have been investigated over the last decade.

At the hardware level, energy savings can be achieved through low-power circuit design [1] or providing different operational modes for a particular component [9].

At the system software level, studies range from energy-oriented operating systems [5, 15, 18], over compilers [11, 21] to runtime systems [10, 20]. Interactions between OpenMP and energy consumption have also been investigated. A pure

OpenMP runtime that applies DVFS and DCT according to predicted performance of application phases has been proposed [3], and this concept was also generalized to hybrid MPI/OpenMP programming [13]. However, none of these works consider application-level knowledge for power management.

At the application level, Odyssey [6,7] is one of the first projects to demonstrate the benefits of content adaptation for a reduced energy profile. In this work, the user provides a goal for battery duration to the operating system that, assessing the system status, informs the application about a target quality for the output. A multimedia oriented operating system is proposed with Grace OS [22]. With starting time and duration of tasks provided by applications, Grace OS determines a system-wide CPU voltage and frequency. A more generic approach is evaluated within *Anole* [2]. This proposed framework updates the application about the current energy status of the device and the application can then adapt its behavior in an arbitrary manner. Notifications about energy availability are forwarded to the operating system as well: hardware and service adaptation can then be offered through ad-hoc modules. A different triggering strategy characterizes the *Chameleon* interface [14]. A compliant application does not react to energy events, rather it can monitor processor load and set a desired speed.

Even though some of these studies pro pose power management interfaces with application-level involvement, they differ substantially from our work. Previous work focuses on dynamic objectives and overall system load, while we opt for highlighting per-application-region static energy saving opportunities to the underlying levels of the system. The OpenMPE API, compared to prior work, is:

- less intrusive and easier to integrate, since we provide a minimal directive-based interface,
- more expressive, since it is possible to directly specify energy constraints (power budgeting) and arbitrary tunable parameters (content adaptation),
- more generic, as user-defined multi-objective goal functions and constraints across an existing, easily extensible set of four metrics are supported,
- more flexible, since the OpenMPE specification does not prescribe or restrict the optimization techniques applied by the runtime system, and
- up-to-date, since we inherently deal with parallel codes in the parallel architecture era by basing our approach on OpenMP.

# 7    Conclusion and Future Work

This paper describes an extension to OpenMP, OpenMPE, which provides two novel features: *multi-objective goals and constraints* and *application adaptation*. These features allow our interface to address the issue of energy consumption and power budgeting, fundamental on modern mobile and HPC systems. Application programmers know the non-functional requirements and adaptation opportunities of each code region, and with OpenMPE they can conveniently provide this knowledge to all underlying layers. We have developed a compiler and associated runtime system for OpenMPE which are able to perform system- and program-level adjustments to achieve specified multi-objective goals while respecting given constraints. Experimental results demonstrate energy savings up to 77 % are feasible with this prototype implementation.

In the future, more extensive evaluation of the OpenMPE API would be desirable, targeting several applications. Furthermore, analysis and refinement of the system's interaction with external load is an important goal.

**Acknowledgments.** This research has been partially funded by the FWF Austrian Science Fund under contract I01079 (GEMSCLAIM).

# References

1. Chandrakasan, A.P., et al.: Low-power CMOS digital design. IEEE J. Solid State Circuits **27**(4), 473–484 (1992)
2. Chen, H., et al.: Anole: a case for energy-aware mobile application design. In: 2012 41st International Conference on Parallel Processing Workshops (ICPPW), pp. 232–238 (2012)
3. Curtis-Maury, M., et al.: Prediction models for multi-dimensional power-performance optimization on many cores. In: Proceedings of the 17th International Conference on Parallel Architectures and Compilation Techniques (PACT 2008), pp. 250–259. ACM, Toronto, Ontario, Canada (2008)
4. Dhodapkar, A.S., Smith, J.E.: Comparing program phase detection techniques. In: Proceedings of the 36th IEEE/ACM International Symposium on Microarchitecture (MICRO 36). IEEE Computer Society, Washington, DC, USA (2003)
5. Flautner, K., et al.: Automatic performance setting for dynamic voltage scaling. Wirel. Netw. **8**(5), 507–520 (2002)
6. Flinn, J., Satyanarayanan, M.: Energy-aware adaptation for mobile applications. In: Proceedings of the Seventeenth ACM Symposium on Operating Systems Principles (SOSP 1999), pp. 48–63. ACM, Charleston, South Carolina, USA (1999)
7. Flinn, J., Satyanarayanan, M.: Managing battery lifetime with energy-aware adaptation. ACM Trans. Comput. Syst. **22**(2), 137–179 (2004)
8. Fritts, J.E., et al.: MediaBench II video: expediting the next generation of video systems research. Microprocess. Microsyst. **33**(4), 301–318 (2009)
9. Hewlett-Packard Corp., Intel Corp., Microsoft Corp., Phoenix Technologies Ltd., Toshiba Corp., Advanced Configuration and Power Interface Specification (ACPI). Specification Revision 5.0. (2013)
10. Hsu, C.-H., Feng, W.-C.: A power-aware run-time system for high-performance computing. In: Proceedings of the 2005 ACM/IEEE Conference on Supercomputing (SC 2005), pp. 1. IEEE Computer Society, Washington, DC, USA (2005)
11. Hsu, C.-H., Kremer, U.: The design, implementation, and evaluation of a compiler algorithm for CPU energy reduction. In: Proceedings of the ACM SIGPLAN 2003 Conference on Programming Language Design and Implementation (PLDI 2003), pp. 38–48. ACM, San Diego, California, USA (2003)
12. Jordan, H., et al.: A multi-objective auto-tuning framework for parallel codes. In: Proceedings of the International Conference on High Performance Computing, Networking, Storage and Analysis (SC 2012), pp. 10:1–10:12. IEEE Computer Society Press, Salt Lake City, Utah (2012)
13. Li, D., et al.: Hybrid MPI/OpenMP power-aware computing. In: 2010 IEEE International Symposium on Parallel Distributed Processing (IPDPS), pp. 1–12 (2010)

14. Liu, X., et al.: Chameleon: application-level power management. IEEE Trans. Mob. Comput. **7**(8), 995–1010 (2008)
15. Lorch, J.R., Smith, A.J.: Operating system modifications for task-based speed and voltage. In: Proceedings of the 1st International Conference on Mobile Systems, Applications and Services (MobiSys 2003), pp. 215–229. ACM, San Francisco, California (2003)
16. OpenMP Architecture Review Board. OpenMP Application Program Interface. Specification Version 4.0. (2013)
17. Pallipadi, V., Starikovskiy, A.: The ondemand governor. In: Proceedings of the Linux Symposium, vol. 2, pp. 215–230 (2006)
18. Pettis, N., et al.: Automatic run-time selection of power policies for operating systems. In: Proceedings of the Design, Automation and Test in Europe (DATE 2006), vol. 1, pp. 1–6 (2006)
19. Rajovic, N., et al.: Supercomputing with commodity CPUs: are mobile SoCs ready for HPC? In: Proceedings of the International Conference on High Performance Computing, Networking, Storage and Analysis (SC 2013), pp. 40:1–40:12. ACM, Denver, Colorado (2013)
20. Rountree, B., et al.: Adagio: making DVS practical for complex HPC applications. In: Proceedings of the 23rd International Conference on Supercomputing (ICS 2009), pp. 460–469. ACM, Yorktown Heights, NY, USA (2009)
21. Qiang, W., et al.: Dynamic-compiler-driven control for microprocessor energy and performance. IEEE Micro **26**(1), 119–129 (2006)
22. Yuan, W., Nahrstedt, K.: Practical voltage scaling for mobile multimedia devices. In: Proceedings of the 12th ACM International Conference on Multimedia (MULTIMEDIA 2004), pp. 924–931. ACM, New York, NY, USA (2004)

# Evaluating the Energy Consumption of OpenMP Applications on Haswell Processors

Bo Wang[1,2,3]($\boxtimes$), Dirk Schmidl[1,2,3], and Matthias S. Müller[1,2,3]

[1] IT Center, RWTH Aachen University, 52074 Aachen, Germany
{wang,schmidl,mueller}@itc.rwth-aachen.de
[2] Chair for High Performance Computing, RWTH Aachen University,
52074 Aachen, Germany
[3] JARA - High-Performance Computing, Schinkelstraße 2, 52062 Aachen, Germany

**Abstract.** Modern processors contain a lot of features to reduce the energy consumption of the chip. The gain of these features highly depends on the workload which is executed. In this work, we investigate the energy consumption of OpenMP applications on the new Intel processor generation, called Haswell. We start with the basic chip characteristics of the chip before we look at automatic energy optimization features. Then, we investigate the energy consumed by load unbalanced applications and present a library to lower the energy consumption for iteratively recurring imbalance patterns. Here, we show that energy savings of up to 20 % are possible without any loss of performance.

## 1 Introduction

Energy consumption has become an essential factor in high-performance computing (HPC) systems. For computing centers the power consumption is one of the major factors in the running costs of HPC systems and the processor chip (host processor or accelerator) is the main consumer of power. Therefore, many energy-saving opportunities are integrated in modern chips, such as automatic power gating, clock gating, and dynamic voltage and frequency scaling(DVFS). The latest Intel Xeon architecture, codenamed Haswell, extends some of those features and contains more advanced features in this direction.

The impact of all these features depends on the workload. For applications like the Linpack benchmark, where caches and compute units of the processor are fully utilized, nearly no processor energy saving is possible without any loss of performance is possible. For many application codes, when the CPU cannot be used as efficiently, e.g. because the memory bandwidth is the bottleneck or when the amount of parallelism is not sufficient to constantly utilize all cores, modern chips can reduce their power consumption.

OpenMP applications can have imbalanced load, which causes some threads in a certain period of time to have no work to do. In this case, using different runtime configurations of `OMP_WAIT_POLICY`, i.e. passive waiting and active waiting, leads to varying varied energy consumption. This variation indicates an opportunity to save energy.

© Springer International Publishing Switzerland 2015
C. Terboven et al. (Eds.): IWOMP 2015, LNCS 9342, pp. 233–246, 2015.
DOI: 10.1007/978-3-319-24595-9_17

DVFS is a well-explored technology for energy saving that has already been automated and is employed by Linux through so-called governors. However, this kind of engagement is not specialized for OpenMP applications. The energy consumption can be further lowered by a customized use of DVFS.

In this work, we investigate the power consumption of the Haswell processor while running OpenMP programs. Thereby, we analyze the efficiency of the automatic features provided by the hardware, the operating system and by the OpenMP runtime. Furthermore, we investigate whether more energy savings could be achieved by the user controlling the clock frequency directly. We use several kernel benchmarks, which are compute- or memory-bound and have a good or bad load balance, to identify application characteristics, which influence the efficiency of the energy saving features. Finally, we present and evaluate our ENAW library, which can be used to reduce the energy consumption of an imbalanced OpenMP application with iterative imbalance patterns.

The rest of this work is structured as follows: In Sect. 2 we give an overview of related works. Then we present the new energy-saving features of the Haswell processor and analyze the energy consumption with automatic control of those features in Sect. 3. In Sect. 4, we explore the opportunities for the user to further optimize the energy savings. Finally, we conclude our work in Sect. 5.

## 2  Related Works

After the Intel Haswell processor has been released in 2014, the performance features of the new processor have been investigated in works like [4] and [14]. In contrast to these papers, we focus on the energy efficiency in combination with the performance features for OpenMP applications.

Previously, other studies have been done that optimize the energy consumption of processors. Those studies concentrate on different applications or problems: [15] and [13] optimize the energy efficiency with an acceptable performance loss, whereas [5] investigates the energy consumption problems of HPC applications theoretically. We investigate the energy consumption of OpenMP applications and implement a library that improves the energy efficiency of an OpenMP application without any performance loss.

Works of [8] and [9] concentrate on similar problems to ours. They explored how to adjust the CPU for a light loaded thread waiting in a barrier that is executed repeatedly. [8] can be completely replaced by using OMP_WAIT_POLICY. [9] investigated primarily different predictors for the waiting time of a thread in a barrier. We study different kinds of applications using the last-value predictor. Moreover, the experiments in [8] and [9] were performed on older processors with energy efficiency features widely different from those of the Haswell processors.

Dynamic concurrency throttling (DCT) [12] is another relevant method beside DVFS that can be used to optimize the energy consumption. However, this work does not employ this approach.

DCT and DVFS can also be used with MPI applications [2] and with hybrid applications [7] where OpenMP and MPI are utilized simultaneously.

# 3   Basic Characteristics

## 3.1   Energy-Saving Features of Haswell

The new Intel processor, codenamed Haswell, is equipped with lots of features
for lowering the used power. It allows p-states on a per core basis, separate
frequency scaling for AVX units and uncore frequency scaling, which allows to
scale the clock frequency of the uncore part of a chip independently from the
frequencies of the cores.

The most important feature should be the fully integrated voltage regula-
tor (FIVR) [2]. This feature consists of multiple VRs that are split up into two
stages. A single first stage VR located on the motherboard converts the PSU
or battery voltage to the input voltage of the processor die. Within the second
stage, each processor domain, such as cores, uncore, and graphics unit, has its
independent VR with individual voltages. Together with the Power Control Unit
(PCU) [3], FIVR enables:

- independent voltage and frequency for each domain as needed;
- a deeper sleep state in which a standby domain consumes less energy;
- turbo boost a domain that is heavily loaded with a higher priority by throttling
  other domains. At the same time, the overall power and thermal are also kept
  within limits.

Another improvement is the energy-efficient turbo, which prevents turbo
boosts that do not significantly increase the performance. That is especially
useful for memory-bound applications whose performance depends mainly on
bandwidth of the main memory rather than on the CPU speed.

## 3.2   Load-Dependent Behavior

First, we determined the margin in which the power consumption of the processor can reside. We measured the power consumption of the processor in (a) idle
mode, (b) for a memory-bound application (the Stream benchmark) and (c) for a
compute-bound benchmark, which calculates multiple times the sine and cosine
of register variables. The benchmarks produce a uniform load within a given
time interval and run multi-threaded on all cores of the system. The energy consumption is measured by reading model specific registers (MSRs) for the RAPL
(running average power limiting) counters that are part of the Haswell processor. The average power consumption in watts was calculated as $energy/runtime$.
Figure 1 shows the resulting average power consumption during the benchmark
runs on both Haswell chips in our two-socket test system with 36 cores.

In idle mode (Fig. 1a), the processors consume between 35 and 41 watts. The
power consumption is independent of the clock frequency of the cores. This is
because the processor can shut down the cores by putting them into C1 or deeper
C-states. When the cores are not operating, the clock frequency is irrelevant. But
we learn that the system will never use less than 35 watts running the Haswell
chips.

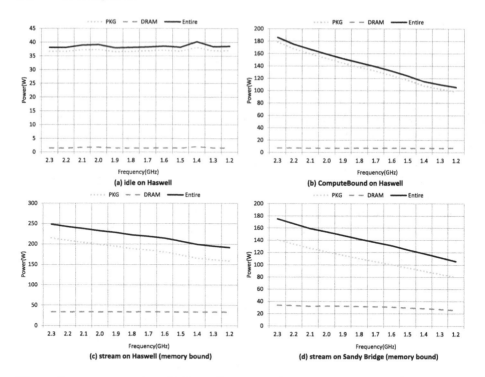

**Fig. 1.** Power consumption of a Haswell processor (Intel Xeon E5-2699 V3) for different workloads (idle/memory-bound/compute-bound)

With the compute-bound benchmark running, it can be observed (Fig. 1b), that the frequency influences the power consumption. In total about 190 watts are consumed when running at 2.3 GHz, about 10 watts for the memory and 180 watts for the CPU cores. At lower clock frequencies the cores coume less energy, down to 110 watts for frequency of 1.2 GHz. The memory consumes constantly about 10 watts, independent of the core frequency.

With the memory-bound Stream benchmark the behavior is similar (Fig. 1c). The memory consumes a roughly constant amount of energy whereas the energy consumption of the cores shrinks drastically with the core frequencies. However, the energy consumption of the memory is much higher than it is for the compute-bound benchmark because of its activities.

In comparison to the Haswell processor, the previous models (Sandy Bridge processor, shown in Fig. 1d) have variable memory energy consumption. Here, the energy consumption of the memory shrinks by about 30 % when the clock frequency is reduced.

This information gives us only an upper and a lower bound of the system's power consumption for different types of applications. More interesting of course is the energy consumption per task. Therefore, the runtime of benchmarks Stream and a compute-bound benchmark were measured and Fig. 2 shows

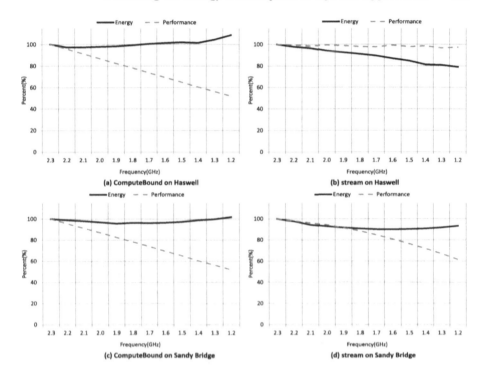

**Fig. 2.** Energy consumption and performance with frequency scaling.

the relative performance as the inverse of the runtime and energy consumption compared to the test at the highest frequency without Turbo Boost enabled.

It can be observed, that the improvements in the Haswell design work fine, especially for memory-bound applications. For the stream benchmark on Haswell the runtime is not influenced by the core frequency, since the uncore part has an independent frequency, as described in Sect. 3.1. Having a constant performance and a lower power consumption for lower frequency, leads to a relative energy consumption of about 80 % when the cores run at 1.2 GHz instead of 2.3 GHz. On the SandyBridge micro architecture, the performance for the benchmark went down with lowering frequency.

For the compute-bound kernel on both architectures, the performance went down when the clock frequency was reduced. This slightly increases the energy consumption on Haswell to 108 % the original one due to the increased runtime. On Sandy Bridge, the energy consumption stays roughly at 100 % because the longer runtime is fully compensated by the energy savings at the lower clock frequency.

Although the memory bandwidth is not affected by the changing clock frequency if all cores are used, the latency of a single memory access changes. We measured the memory latency with a pointer chasing benchmark. Figure 3 shows the memory latency for all available core frequencies. Obviously, the mem-

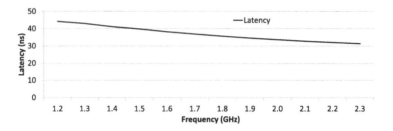

**Fig. 3.** Latency for a memory access at different clock frequencies on the Haswell system.

ory latency goes up when the clock frequency goes down, from 27 ns at 2.3 GHz to 44 ns at 1.2 GHz. The reason is a single memory access involves the core and the L1 and L2 caches and all those components are clocked down. For the bandwidth measurement, techniques like prefetching and out-of-order execution can hide the latency. For latency bound codes, i.e. codes where the prefetcher can not predict the memory access pattern, the core clock frequency influences the memory access time and thus the overall performance.

We did further tests on our system, similar to the tests done in [4]. The memory bandwidth with different numbers of active threads and different frequencies was measured and the results are shown in Fig. 4. It can be observed that when using a few threads, the core frequency has a serious influence on the memory bandwidth. However, that doesn't occur when many cores are employed.

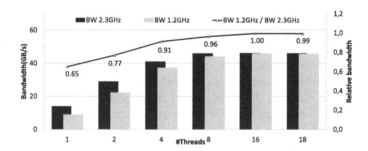

**Fig. 4.** Memory bandwidth using 2.3 GHz and 1.2 GHz with different number of cores

Although both Haswell and Sandy Bridge processors have the Turbo Boost feature, we decided to turn it off in our work due to its hard to predict behavior.

## 4    Optimization Steps

### 4.1    Wait Strategies

So far, we investigated the energy consumption and the performance of Haswell with kernel tests. For memory-bound applications energy saving could be achieved by scaling down the clock frequency without any performance loss, while for compute-bound applications doing so results in increased runtime. Several metrics have been developed already to determine if energy saving is worth the increased overhead, like the energy-delay metric in [6]. Those metrics are not subject of this work, since we want to save energy without any loss of performance. That benefits all metrics.

If we want to achieve means that no part of a serial program should be slowed down. However, for parallel programs it means that no part of the critical path should become slower. Non-critical path can get slowed down, as long as they do not become critical.

Many OpenMP programs synchronize at implicit or explicit barriers. The critical path is determined by the slowest thread arriving the barrier. All other threads have to wait inside the barrier before execution can continue. The OpenMP standard defines a runtime variable, OMP_WAIT_POLICY that controls waiting threads. OMP_WAIT_ POLICY=passive lets waiting threads be removed from the cores. These cores either become available to do other work or idle. With OMP_WAIT_POLICY=active cores stay occupied by the waiting threads. Only, no real work besides spinning is being done.

We implemented a simple compute-bound benchmark to investigate the energy consumption using passive and active waiting policies at different frequencies. In our measurements, we started 36 threads distributed over two sockets (T0-T17 on socket 0 and T18-T35 on socket 1) with a load imbalance as illustrated in Fig. 5. T0-T17 finish their work within 9.35 s while T18-T35 are busy for 24.51 s. Therefore, T0-T17 have to wait 15.16 s at the barrier.

The energy consumption and the runtime of T18-T35 are constant. The energy consumption of T0-T17 varies with the waiting policy; see the first two lines in Table 1. Using passive waiting, energy can be reduced by more than 35 %. At the same time, the runtime does not change.

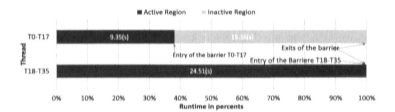

**Fig. 5.** Illustration of the load-unbalanced benchmark

So far, using the passive waiting is beneficial. However, this benefit vanishes as the time before running into a barrier become shorter, i.e. the time from the program start to a barrier or from a barrier to the next barrier become shorter. The passive waiting causes serious increase of runtime and energy consumption; see Fig. 6. That is because the thread context is flushed on entering the barrier

**Table 1.** Energy consumption using active and passive waiting at different frequencies

| Wait policy | Clock frequency | Energy (J) | Relative energy |
|---|---|---|---|
| Active | 2.3 GHz | 2079.68 | 100 % |
| Passive | 2.3 GHz | 1338.02 | 64.37 % |
| Active | 1.2 GHz | 1283.35 | 61.71 % |
| Passive | 1.2 GHz | 1167.29 | 56.13 % |

and has to be restored before execution can continue after the barrier. This overhead is high when the runtime is short.

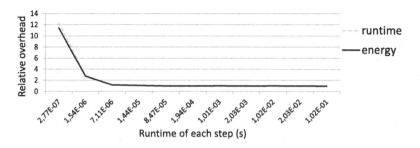

**Fig. 6.** Overhead caused by the passive waiting compared to the active waiting.

We would like to reduce the energy consumption further using DVFS. There are two ways to utilize DVFS:

1. We clock down T0-T17 while they are waiting in the barrier, while T18-T35 are running always with the same frequency, i.e. 2.3 GHz.
2. We clock down T0-T17 already at the beginning, while T18-T35 are running always with the maximum clock speed. T0-T17 can be clocked down to 1.2 GHz without becoming critical threads, because their runtime is only extended to 17.9 s and that is still shorter than 24.51 s.

The first idea is effective only if active waiting is employed. Furthermore, it can not be more energy efficient than the passive waiting.

The second idea can reduce the energy consumption effectively, independent of which waiting policy is used; see the last two lines in Table 1. Together with the passive waiting, our benchmark consumes the least energy. More than 45 % of the energy can be saved.

Using passive waiting, the energy consumption is reduced up to 8 % if the frequency is scaled from 2.3 GHz to 1.2 GHz; see the second and the fourth line in Table 1. That differs from the measurement whose result is presented in Fig. 2a. The runtime is increasing as the frequency is being scaling down. Here the runtime is constant determined by T18-T35.

## 4.2   Iterative Clock Adjustment

Based on the second idea described in Sect. 4.1, we have implemented a solution
for general OpenMP applications. The challenge here is of course to determine a
priori the clock frequency, which will lead to an evenly balanced load. This can
only be done if the compute time can be determined in advance by the input
data or if the load is repeated frequently during execution, e.g. if load balance
and work stay the same in every iteration of an iterative algorithm.

For such a case we implemented a framework that controls the clock frequency
of all cores. The framework is based on the OpenMP Pragma and Region Instru-
mentor (Opari)[11]. Opari inserts library calls before and after most OpenMP
directives, including barriers.

This allows us to:

– measure the runtime of all threads during one iteration;
– calculate the performance relative to the slowest thread and
– reduce the clock frequency by the fraction of time a thread was waiting in the
  barrier.

After several iterations, the energy-aware optimization library (called ENAW
for the rest of this work) reaches a steady state, where all clock frequencies are
adjusted and do not change in following iterations, as long as the load does not
change.

The implementation takes care of the following constrains:

– overheads of a DVFS operation in terms of runtime and energy consumption
  are taken into account when the new frequency is being calculated in order
  to avoid increasing runtime and energy consumption of the whole program.
  Especially, a DVFS operation is avoided if the same frequency is required by
  two consecutive barrier regions.
  The overheads are hardware-specific. The runtime overhead is measured using
  [10], while the energy consumption overhead is measured by repeated executing DVFS operations from the lowest to the highest frequency and vice versa.
– if the calculated frequency is between two available core frequencies, the higher
  one is always chosen so to avoid increasing the runtime.
– frequencies of sibling threads of a core are scheduled simultaneously to prevent
  disturbance.

An optimal frequency is calculated by each waiting thread in each iteration
step. However, the frequency is set only if it is beneficial. Overheads due to the
calculations are low compared to that of the DVFS operations.

How much energy can be saved using ENAW depends on the individual
workloads. It could save a lot of energy for OpenMP applications with serious
load imbalance where only one thread should run with the highest frequency
while all other threads can be slowed down.

### 4.3    Evaluation

We evaluate ENAW using two benchmarks: one is the already described compute intensive benchmark calculating sine and cosine of variables kept in CPU registers, called sin_cos for the rest of this paper; the other one is a sparse matrix-vector multiply (SMXV) kernel as it is used in many iterative solvers like GMRES or CG solvers. There, the matrix-vector multiplication is often the hotspot of every iteration.

We compare runtime, energy consumption and power of benchmarks using ENAW with the default OpenMP runtime configuration, i.e. using passive waiting.

**Sin_Cos.** Since practical applications have varying load balances, from perfectly balanced to extremely imbalanced, energy investigations with different loads of sin_cos should be interesting.

For an OpenMP application, a load imbalance occurs if threads reach a barrier after different duration. We use this duration variation to calculate the load imbalance, defined as:

$$lbl = \sum_{i=0}^{n-1} (\frac{t_i}{t_{critical}}) \tag{1}$$

$lbl$ is for load balance level. $i$ is a thread ID from 0 to $n-1$ where $n$ is the number of used threads. $t_i$ and $t_{critical}$ are duration of thread $i$ and of the critical thread to the barrier as both are running at the highest frequency.

$lbl$ depends on how many threads are used and how is the load imbalance. For tests with a constant number of threads, the lower is $lbl$, the more serious is the load imbalance. $lbl = 1$ only one thread is loaded, all other threads do not get any work to do. $lbl = n$ means that the load is distributed evenly through all threads.

We do tests with sin_cos. The total amount of work to be done is consistent and thread 0 is always the critical thread. The load can be manipulated to produce different $lbl$, where $1 \leq lbl \leq 36$ using 36 threads on our test platform. During the tests, we measure the runtime, the energy consumption and the power and compare these values using the ENAW with values measured without ENAW. The results of our tests presented in Fig. 7 are calculated using (Eq. 2):

$$\frac{ENAW\ runtime}{Default\ runtime}, \frac{ENAW\ energy\ consumption}{Default\ energy\ consumption}, \frac{ENAW\ power}{Default\ power} \tag{2}$$

As Fig. 7 illustrates, the most energy saving occurs at $lbl = 18, 19$, where the minimal frequency is set for threads $T1$ to $T35$. With a bigger $lbl$, the load is more balanced and a higher frequency must be set for T1 to T35 to ensure the runtime limit is not exceeded. With smaller $lbl$, the load is even more imbalanced. However, no lower frequency is available. DVFS cannot be more effective. Furthermore, the idle time of $T1...T35$ gets longer and DVFS has no effect at all.

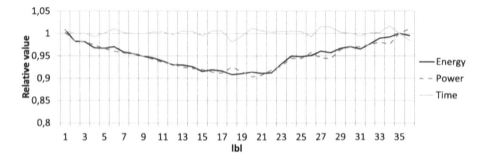

**Fig. 7.** Effectiveness of ENAW on sin_cos with different load balance levels

Figure 7 shows that by using ENAW energy can be saved; at the same time the runtime limit is rarely exceeded and the power is reduced.

**SMXV.** We use the SMXV implementation that is parallelized with OpenMP and distributes the rows of the matrix by the means of the static parallel loop scheduling (The scheduling strategy can be easily changed.). During a measurement the SMXV kernel will be called iteratively. Typically, the workload to the kernel does not change through the iterations. Therefore, the load balance does not change too. That leads to a repeating load imbalance if the matrix structure is unbalanced, since the number of non-zeros per thread, note the number of rows determines the computational load. We executed the kernel with and without our ENAW library attached with an imbalanced matrix structure extracted from a flow-solver. The *lbl* of the workload amounts to 21.85 with 36 threads. Thread T0 is the critical thread. Other threads are loaded individually. The lowest available frequency could be set on less than 6 threads, if ENAW would be used.

In contrast to sin_cos is the SMXV kernel memory-bound. For evaluation, measurements with SMXV were set with a different number of threads instead of different *lbl* as shown in Fig. 7.

During the tests, we used two different binding strategies in order to check whether ENAW has different effects. Figure 8 shows the results of our tests with the SMXV kernel. Values are computed using Formula 2. Using ENAW, energy consumption and power are lowered in all cases, up to nearly 20 %. The critical runtime is rarely exceeded, except when running with a few threads, in which case the memory bandwidth is throttled dramatically as the core clock is scaled down, see Fig. 4. This seriously impacts the performance of the critical thread.

With close binding, more than half of the measurements using ENAW takes less runtime than without ENAW. Lowering the core clock frequency of non-critical threads frees memory bandwidth for the critical thread. As a result the SMXV kernel is accelerated.

So far, we have evaluated ENAW against measurements with static scheduling, i.e. with load imbalance. If we switch the base measurement to using dynamic

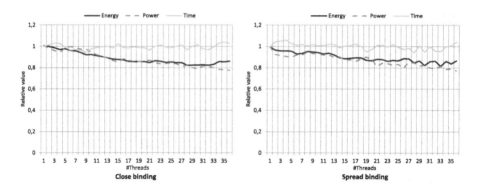

**Fig. 8.** Effectiveness of ENAW on SMXV with different numbers of threads

scheduling, the load balance is improved significantly. Could using ENAW still be beneficial? We do further tests where we measure the power, the energy consumption and the runtime as we have done before. However, we compare ENAW with the dynamic scheduling using Formula 3 The results from our measurements are shown in Fig. 9.

$$\frac{ENAW\ runtime}{Dynamic\ runtime}, \frac{ENAW\ energy\ consumption}{Dynamic\ energy\ consumption}, \frac{ENAW\ power}{Dynamic\ power} \quad (3)$$

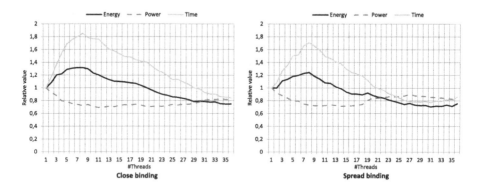

**Fig. 9.** Comparing ENAW to using dynamic scheduling.

With close binding, ENAW is not beneficial given less than 29 threads are used. Up to this point, the program runs faster with dynamic scheduling. After this point, the runtime get longer due to lots of remote memory accesses and data synchronizations.

With spread binding, although runs with few threads using dynamic scheduling are beneficial, the benefit is removed very quickly by the dramatic increasing of remote memory accesses, more dramatic than with the close binding. Therefore, ENAW outperforms the dynamic scheduling with 21 threads ore more.

## 5   Conclusion

The feature of Haswell that makes the uncore frequency independent of the core frequency allows better energy saving. For a memory-bound application, nearly 20 % of energy could be saved by scaling down core frequencys, without losing any performance. However, this energy-saving method does not work for compute-bound applications, if those applications are serial or parallel with balanced workloads, since both the runtime and the relative energy consumption are increased.

For imbalanced workloads, tests have shown that passive waiting threads are put into a sleep state, consuming nearly no energy. This significantly saves energy compared to active waiting. Clocking down cores that wait in a barrier turned out to not be profitable compared to the passive waiting mode.

Moreover, if the load imbalance occurs in several iterations with the same imbalance pattern, our ENAW library can be used to clock down non-critical threads. The new frequency is calculated and adjusted as low as possible to save more energy, but also as high as necessary to avoid an increase of the overall runtime. This library enables energy saving independent of whether applications are compute-bound or memory-bound. For our synthetic sin_cos benchmarks with varying *lbl*, it always saves energy, up to 9 %. For our sparse matrix-vector multiply kernel, it saves more aggressively, up to 20 %. The power consumption can also be reduced by 20 %.

**Acknowledgement.** Parts of this work were funded by the German Federal Ministry of Research and Education (BMBF) under grant number 01IH13001D (Score-E).

## References

1. Burton, E., Schrom, G., Paillet, F., Douglas, J., Lambert, W.J., Radhakrishnan, K., Hill, M.J.: FIVR—Fully integrated voltage regulators on 4th generation Intel® Core$^{TM}$ SoCs. In: Applied Power Electronics Conference and Exposition (APEC), 2014 Twenty-Ninth Annual IEEE, pp. 432–439. IEEE (2014)
2. Freeh, V.W., Pan, F., Kappiah, N., Lowenthal, D.K., Springer, R.: Exploring the energy-time tradeoff in MPI programs on a power-scalable cluster. In: Proceedings of the 19th IEEE International Parallel and Distributed Processing Symposium, pp. 4a–4a. IEEE (2005)
3. Gunther, S., Deval, A., Burton, T., Kumar, R.: Energy-efficient computing: power management system on the nehalem family of processors. Intel Technol. J. **14**(3), 50 (2010)
4. Hackenberg, D., Schöne, R., Ilsche, T., Molka, D., Schuchart, J., Geyer, R.: An energy efficiency feature survey of the intel haswell processor (2015)

5. Hager, G., Treibig, J., Habich, J., Wellein, G.: Exploring performance and power properties of modern multi-core chips via simple machine models. Practice and Experience, Concurrency and Computation (2014)

6. Horowitz, M., Indermaur, T., Gonzalez, R.: Low-power digital design. In: IEEE Symposium on Low Power Electronics, Digest of Technical Papers, pp. 8–11. IEEE (1994)

7. Li, D., De Supinski, B.R., Schulz, M., Cameron, K., Nikolopoulos, D.S.: Hybrid MPI/OpenMP power-aware computing. In: 2010 IEEE International Symposium on Parallel and Distributed Processing (IPDPS), pp. 1–12. IEEE (2010)

8. Li, J., Martinez, J.F., Huang, M.C.: The thrifty barrier: energy-aware synchronization in shared-memory multiprocessors. In: IEE Proceedings-Software, pp. 14–23. IEEE (2004)

9. Liu, C., Sivasubramaniam, A., Kandemir, M., Irwin, M.J.: Exploiting barriers to optimize power consumption of CMPs. In: Proceedings of the 19th IEEE International Parallel and Distributed Processing Symposium, pp. 5a–5a. IEEE (2005)

10. Mazouz, A., Laurent, A., Pradelle, B., Jalby, W.: Evaluation of CPU frequency transition latency. Comput. Sci. Res. Dev. **29**(3–4), 187–195 (2014)

11. Mohr, B., Malony, A.D., Shende, S., Wolf, F.: Design and prototype of a performance tool interface for OpenMP. J. Supercomput. **23**(1), 105–128 (2002)

12. Porterfield, A.K., Olivier, S.L., Bhalachandra, S., Prins, J.F.: Power measurement and concurrency throttling for energy reduction in OpenMP programs. In: IEEE 27th International Parallel and Distributed Processing Symposium Workshops and PhD Forum (IPDPSW), pp. 884–891. IEEE (2013)

13. Schöne, R., Hackenberg, D.: On-line analysis of hardware performance events for workload characterization and processor frequency scaling decisions. In: Proceedings of the 2nd ACM/SPEC International Conference on Performance Engineering, pp. 481–486. ACM (2011)

14. Schöne, R., Molka, D., Werner, M.: Wake-up latencies for processor idle states on current x86 processors. Comput. Sci. Res. Dev. **30**(2), 219–227 (2014)

15. Weissel, A., Bellosa, F.: Process cruise control: event-driven clock scaling for dynamic power management. In: Proceedings of the 2002 International Conference on Compilers, Architecture, and Synthesis for Embedded Systems, pp. 238–246. ACM (2002)

# Parallelization Methods for Hierarchical SMP Systems

Larry Meadows[✉], Jeongnim Kim, and Alex Wells

Intel Corporation, Hillsboro, OR, USA
{lawrence.f.meadows,jeongnim.kim,alex.m.wells}@intel.com

**Abstract.** We discuss several parallelization methods for multi-level hierarchical SMP systems using a stencil-based finite difference code. Performance comparisons and suggestions for OpenMP runtime improvements are provided.

**Keywords:** Stencil · Nested parallelism · Runtime support

## 1 Introduction

Modern symmetric multi-processors (SMPs) have multiple levels of memory hierarchy and multiple levels of parallelism. In this paper we explore various methods to exploit those multiple levels including OpenMP, nested OpenMP, OpenMP 4 teams/distribute, and a higher-level C++ template library called SIMD building blocks (SBB). Additionally we explore various methods of load balancing including manual load balancing and the OpenMP `collapse` clause. As a result of these experiments we offer suggestions for OpenMP implementors.

We use the diffusion test code from [1]. Our work shows alternatives to the plesiochronous barriers used in Chap. 5 of [2], some of which may be more understandable to and usable by most OpenMP programmers.

## 2 The Test Code

The diffusion test code (hereafter referred to as just *diffusion*) is a simple 7-point stencil code in three dimensions, shown in Fig. 1.

The diffusion kernel is memory bandwidth bound. To see this we can compute the ratio of floats (or doubles) accessed to floating point operations. Each iteration has 7 loads, 1 store, 7 multiplies, and 6 adds. There are thus 13 floating point operations and 8 memory accesses, resulting in a ratio of about 2.5 bytes/flop (single precision). As an example, the current generation Intel® Xeon Phi™ coprocessor[1] has a peak floating point performance on the order of 1000E9 flops/second and a memory bandwidth on the order of 170E9 bytes/second,

---

[1] Intel, Xeon, and Intel Xeon Phi are trademarks of Intel Corporation in the U.S. and/or other countries.

© Springer International Publishing Switzerland 2015
C. Terboven et al. (Eds.): IWOMP 2015, LNCS 9342, pp. 247–259, 2015.
DOI: 10.1007/978-3-319-24595-9_18

```
for (int z = 0; z < N; ++z)
  for (int y = 0; y < N; ++y)
    for (int x = 0; x < N; ++x)
      f2[z][y][x] = cc * f1[z][y][x] +
                    cw * f1[z][y][x-1] +
                    ce * f1[z][y][x+1] +
                    cn * f1[z][y-1][x] +
                    cs * f1[z][y+1][x] +
                    cu * f1[z-1][y][x] +
                    cd * f1[z+1][y][x];
```

**Fig. 1.** Diffusion psuedocode

which is only about 0.17 bytes/flops, far less than required. Thus, our optimization efforts are focused on memory optimizations.

There are two memory optimizations: achieving maximum memory bandwidth from the processor, and exploiting reuse by tiling for cache. The former is largely done by the compiler, though we do use non-temporal stores (which are particularly helpful on the Intel® Xeon Phi™ coprocessor. The latter is accomplished in different ways depending on the particular code version.

Reuse occurs because of the ±1 subscript arithmetic. For the contiguous (unit-stride) X dimension, the reuse occurs automatically (spatial reuse). For the Y and Z dimensions, the current iteration reuses two elements from the previous iteration (temporal reuse); Y becomes $Y - 1$, and $Y + 1$ becomes Y. The key is to tile the loops so that the previous elements from the Y and Z loops remain in cache.

## 3    SIMD Building Blocks

SIMD Building Blocks (SBB) is a C++11 template library providing concepts of Containers, Accessors, Kernels, and Engines to abstract out different aspects of creating an efficient data parallel (SIMD + threading) program. The Containers encapsulate the memory data layout of an Array of "Plain Old Data" objects. Kernels represent the work inside a loop body and use Accessors with an array subscript operator (just like C++ arrays) to read from or write to the objects in the Containers. Engines visit a Kernel over an iteration space. Since these concepts are abstracted out, multiple concrete versions can exist and can encapsulate best known methods, thus avoiding common pitfalls in generating efficient SIMD code.

For example, when speaking of efficient SIMD code, the terms "Array Of Structures" (AOS) and "Structure Of Arrays" (SOA) are often used. In order to utilize SIMD load/store instructions, the data must be in a SOA so that a vector register can be loaded with the same data members, instead of having to emit instructions to load each data lane separately or having to perform a gather over AOS data. However most object oriented code uses data in an AOS format.

Changing one's algorithms to work with SOA is cumbersome and difficult to maintain. With SBB, one can use an `SoaContainer < Object >` and the data will be stored in memory as SOA, but a kernel just sees an instance `Object`. This allows kernels to just work with the `Objects` and implement their algorithm and leave the complexities of SOA and data alignment to the container. SBB provides multi-dimensional 2d and 3d containers as well, with the added benefit of handling address calculation of multiple index variables through an accessor with multiple array subscript operators (just like a 2d or 3d c++ array). This often yields simpler kernel code.

Likewise the Engines abstract out iteration. Engines can be declared to generate scalar or SIMD code, to run single threaded, or with Intel® Threading Building Blocks (Intel® TBB), or with OpenMP threading. When an Engine runs a Kernel, it is given an iteration space and blocking size. The concrete engine can then divide the iteration space up into blocks and execute the Kernel over the blocks. 2d and 3d Engines are provide good cache blocking behavior out of the box. Switching threading models is as easy as changing a typedef and users can choose to make their own Engines that fit in SBB's framework (e.g., a team based threading Engine that uses threads on the same core to cooperatively work on the same block, as described in the next section).

## 4   Nested Threading

Intel® Xeon® processors and the Intel® Xeon Phi™ coprocessor consist of multiple cores. Each core has multiple hardware thread contexts, often called hyperthreads or simultaneous multi-threading (SMT) threads. The thread contexts each have their own register sets and other state but share all of the execution units and caches on the core.

In many cases it is helpful to have a two-level nested parallel structure that corresponds to the hardware threading structure. The outer level corresponds to the cores, and the inner level corresponds to the hardware threads within a core. The outer level determines the data decomposition (implicitly or explicitly), which in turn determines the data that resides in a particular core's caches. The inner level threads then cooperate on the data residing in the shared caches. This often reduces cache pressure since decomposition is per core, not per thread, and can lead to substantial speedups.

## 5   Code Variants

The following subsections describe the code variants used in the performance study. All of the codes use a common inner loop expressed in an inline function. The code for the inner loop is shown in Fig. 9 near the end of the paper.

The code in Fig. 9 incorporates some improvements from [2], namely alignment, streaming stores, and special treatment of the two boundary elements.

The latter improves vectorization efficiency and allows the alignment optimization by computing the 0th and nx-1th elements incorrectly as part of a vector operation, and then correcting the results with a scalar operation.

Note: the SBB implementation does not use the inline function. SBB templates take care of alignment and streaming stores, and handle the boundary elements with explicit halo regions.

## 5.1  Baseline

The baseline version is a modified version of the optimized code from [1]. An outline of the code is shown in Fig. 2. The outer loop is a timestep loop. Each iteration computes the stencil on the entire iteration space. There are two copies of the stencil array; one acting as an input array, and the other acting as an output array. The arrays are switched at the end of each timestep. A barrier is needed to ensure that all the threads have finished storing to the current output array before switching the two arrays.

```
#pragma omp parallel
for (int i = 0; i < count; ++i)
{
# define YBF 4
# define ZBF 4
# pragma omp for collapse(2) nowait
  for (int yy = 0; yy < ny; yy += YBF)
  for (int zz = 0; zz < nz; zz += ZBF) {
    int ymax = yy + YBF;
    int zmax = zz + YBF;
    for (int z = zz; z < zmax; z++) {
      for (int y = yy; y < ymax; y++) {
        diffusion_x_loop(f1_t, f2_t, nx, ny, nz, y, z,
          cc, cw, ce, cn, cs, ct, cb);
      }
    }
  }
#pragma omp barrier
REAL *t = f1_t;
f1_t = f2_t;
f2_t = t;
}
```

Fig. 2. Diffusion baseline

The Y and Z loops are tiled into 4×4 blocks. The 4×4 blocking factor was empirically determined using SBB and then back-ported to the various diffusion implementations. This loop nest is then collapsed and distributed amongst the threads. The inner loop is vectorized (see Fig. 9).

Note that in the baseline case, the load balance and data distribution are implicitly determined by the threads executing the collapsed for loop. We explore various other methods to improve load balance and data distribution in the implementations that follow.

```
#pragma omp parallel
{
    int z0, ze, y0, ye;
    // compute Y and Z begin and end points y0,ye,z0,ze
    ...
    for (int i = 0; i < count; ++i) {
        for (int yy = y0; yy < ye; yy += YBF)
        for (int zz = z0; zz < ze; zz += ZBF)
        {
            int z1 = zz + ZBF;
            int y1 = yy + YBF;
            for (int y = yy; y < y1; y++) {
                for (int z = zz; z < z1; z++) {
                    diffusion_x_loop(f1_t, f2_t, nx, ny, nz, y, z,
                        cc, cw, ce, cn, cs, ct, cb);
                }
            }
        }

        #pragma omp barrier
        REAL *t = f1_t;
        f1_t = f2_t;
        f2_t = t;
    }
}           // parallel
```

**Fig. 3.** Diffusion 2d decomposition

## 5.2  Hand Decomposed

The hand decomposed version of diffusion is very similar to the baseline version, except that the blocks are distributed by hand. An outline of the code is in Fig. 3. We begin by obtaining the thread number $mythread$, and then compute our position in the Z and Y dimensions. Our position in the Y dimension is $mod(mythread, nHT)$ and our position in the Z dimension is $mythread/nHT$ (using integer division) where $nHT$ is the number of threads per core: 2 for the Intel® Xeon® processor and 4 for the Intel® Xeon Phi™ coprocessor. Then we distribute the blocks in each dimension as evenly as possible. Finally, there are two nested outer loops (equivalent to the collapsed loops in the baseline code) that iterate over the Z and Y blocks, and two nested inner loops that iterate over the elements in each block.

One advantage of this hand decomposition is that a core always has all the Y blocks for each Z block. The collapsed loop might split some blocks between threads, since it distributes the full $Z * Y$ iteration space without regard to the original loop nesting.

One disadvantage of this decomposition is that the load balance is not always as good. For example, consider a problem size of 512 and a 60-core Intel® Xeon Phi® part. There are 512/4 or 128 blocks in each dimension. The number of threads in the Z dimension is 60, so the first 8 cores will each get 3 blocks of Z, and the last 52 will get 2 blocks of Z. Thus 52 of the cores will have 2/3 as much work to do as the other 8 cores.

In the collapsed case, there are 512*512/4 or 65536 iterations divided amongst 240 threads, resulting in 1092 or 1093 iterations per thread; the load imbalance is far less severe.

### 5.3    Nested Parallelism

As stated earlier, it is often useful to have the threads within a core cooperate on a single block of data residing in that core's caches. Nested OpenMP seems to be a good choice for this. Because current implementations of nested OpenMP have relatively high overhead, we placed the inner parallel region further out in the code than might have been desirable (this is explained more in the next section). This led to the code in Fig. 4.

```
#pragma omp parallel
{
  // compute decomposition in Z
  ...
  #pragma omp parallel for
  for (int yy = 0; yy < ny; yy += ybf)
  for (int zz = z0; zz < ze; zz += zbf)
  {
    int z1 = zz + zbf;
    if (z1 > nz) z1 = nz;
    int y1 = yy + ybf;
    if (y1 > ny) y1 = ny;
    for (int z = zz; z < z1; z++) {
      for (int y = yy; y < y1; y++) {
        diffusion_x_loop(f1_t, f2_t, nx, ny, nz, y, z,
          cc, cw, ce, cn, cs, ct, cb);
      }
    }
  }
}        // parallel
```

**Fig. 4.** Nested OpenMP

The parallel region enclosing the code in Fig. 4 computes its piece of the Z dimension just as described in the section on hand decomposition. Then the inner parallel for divides the blocks in the Y dimension so that each thread is working on 1/4 (or 1/2 for the processor) of the Y elements, but only on the Z elements for that core.

The cache footprint for each core for the Intel® Xeon Phi™ coprocessor is thus $NY * NZ/60 * NX * 4$ bytes, which is over 8 MB for the $512^3$ problem and thus far too large for L2. It would probably be better to tile the Y loop again, or to attempt the solution shown in the next section.

```
for (int z = zz+ymythread; z < z1; z+=nHTs) {
  for (int y = yy; y < y1; y++) {
    diffusion_x_loop(f1_t, f2_t, nx, ny, nz, y, z,
        cc, cw, ce, cn, cs, ct, cb);
  }
}
```

Fig. 5. Hand nested inner loops

### 5.4   Hand Nested

In the hand nested case, we divide the Z dimension as before, but we use a trick to ensure that the hardware threads on a core cooperate on the same block of data. The outer loops are the same as those in Fig. 4, but the inner loops are different as shown in Fig. 5. Here nHTs is the number of threads per core and ymythread is the thread number within the core. We divide the work amongst the threads by assigning the Z iterations round-robin to the threads (note that each thread gets only one iteration on the coprocessor).

So that threads that finish early don't race ahead to the next block, we follow the code above with a core barrier. This barrier is not required for correctness. The core barrier uses two 4-byte words. Each thread sets its byte in the first word, then waits until all the bytes are set. It then does the same for the second word. The value set by a thread toggles between 0 and 1 every time the barrier is encountered, thus removing any need for re-initialization. Two words are needed in case of back-to-back barriers (an alternate formulation using only one word is available but somewhat more complicated). The core barrier is quite fast (under 200 clocks) since all the threads on the core share a cache. The core barrier is also described in [3].

The hand nested code is really the code we want to use with nested OpenMP, but the overhead of nested OpenMP is too high. Again looking at the $512^3$ case, the computation performed by the tile loop in Fig. 4 is $4*4*512/16$ or 512 vector loop iterations (in other words, 16 calls to diffusion_x_loop). Using reference data we can compute the cost of a loop iteration as roughly between 5000 and 15000 clock cycles. Currently nested OpenMP overheads are greater than 500 clocks for fork-join of a nested parallel region, making nested OpenMP unusable at such fine granularity.

## 5.5    Crew and Teams

Finally we experimented with two different lower-overhead implementations. Crew is a very lightweight experimental nested threading model for OpenMP that exists in the Intel® C++ Composer XE compiler. Crew creates one OpenMP thread per core, and one extra thread for each additional hyperthread (3 extra threads for the coprocessor). The notation `#pragma intel_crew parallel for` then causes the main thread and the additional threads to divide the work for the following loop; however, no nested OpenMP regions are created and a dynamic scheduling policy is used. The lack of nested OpenMP overhead greatly reduces the overhead for nested parallelism.

Teams are designed for device code, but using `#pragma device if(0)` causes the code to be executed on the host. Creation of teams involves less overhead than nested OpenMP. Unfortunately, there is a need for a barrier of all of the threads in the team at each timestep, and the current definition of the teams construct does not allow a barrier. Thus the answers from the teams implementation are incorrect.

In both the crew case and the teams case, we parallelized the same loop as in the nested OpenMP case (rather than our preferred loop as was done in the hand nested case). Otherwise the code looks the same as the OpenMP nested code.

We ran the crew experiments only on the Intel® Xeon Phi™ coprocessor, and the teams experiments only on the Intel® Xeon® processor. The results are included for completeness.

## 5.6    SBB

The SBB version in Fig. 6 uses template programming to generate multiple versions of the same diffusion kernel (`diffusionOdd`) by varying Containers (AOS, SOA, Tiled), Accesors (YBF, ZBF), and Engines (OpenMP, TBB). Here, we present a set of data generated using `Soa3dContainer` and `OpenMP` engine and $YBF = ZBF = 4$. Essentially, this SBB version is the same as the baseline version. In fact, the optimal block sizes of the baseline code are "auto-tuned" based on the extensive SBB data. C++ 11 features (auto, lambda functions) and predfined `SBB_` macros faciliate compact and efficient codes that can be easily incorporate into the existing C++ applications.

## 6    Performance Experiments

We used two different systems for our experiments. The Intel® Xeon® system is a dual socket E5-2697 v3 (formerly code-named Haswell) @ 2.60 GHz. Each socket has 14 cores with two hardware cores per thread. The Intel® Xeon Phi™ system is a B1PRQ-7110 P/X @ 1.10 GHz. We used 60 of the 61 cores, each with four hardware threads.

Tables 1 and 2 contains the raw data (in GFlops/Second) for the two systems. Figures 7 and 8 show the performance in charts. The data in the charts is

```
//containers: SOA for 3D with +-1 Halo regions
const int StencilHaloSize = 1;
using Container=sbb::Soa3dContainer<float, StencilHaloSize, Allocator>;

Container inputContainer(nx,ny,nz);
Container outputContainer(nx,ny,nz);

//iterator space
sbb::Block3dBounds iterationSpace;
iterationSpace.d1.set(StencilHaloSize,nx-StencilHaloSize);// for d2 & d3

//block size
sbb::Block3dSize blockSize;
blockSize.d1=nx; blockSize.d2=YBF; blockSize.d3=ZBF;

auto in = inputContainer.access();
auto out = outputContainer.access();

//Define 2 kernels
//"Odd" that reads from "in" and writes to "out"
SBB_KERNEL_BEGIN(diffusionOdd)
  SBB_NON_TEMPORAL_BEGIN
  SBB_ITER_D321_BEGIN(z, y, x)
  {
    float result = cc* in[z][y][x] + cw* in[z][y][x-1] + ...;
    out[z][y][x] = result;
  }
  SBB_ITER_END
  SBB_NON_TEMPORAL_END
SBB_KERNEL_END
// "Even" that reads from "out" and writes to "in"
...

sbb::OpenMp3dEngine<sbb::VectorCode> the3dEngine;
for(int i=0; i<count; ++i)
{
  the3dEngine.run(diffusionOdd, iterationSpace, blockSize);
  the3dEngine.run(diffusionEven, iterationSpace, blockSize);
}
```

Fig. 6. SBB diffusion code

normalized to the memory bandwidth (Stream Triad) for the platform: 108 GB/s
and 158 GB/s, respectively.

On the Intel® Xeon® coprocessor, the hand-nested code is clearly the best
except in the $256^3$ case, where it is still competitive. One surprise is how well
the nested version performs.

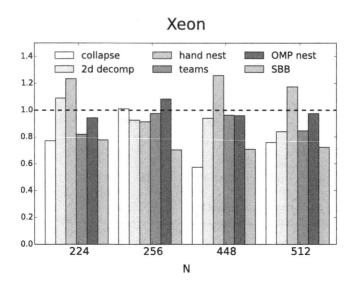

**Fig. 7.** Intel® Xeon® processor normalized performance

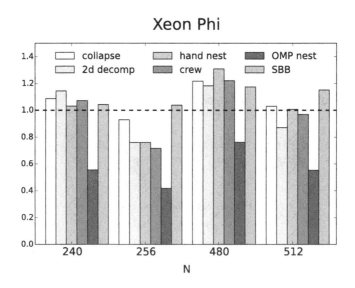

**Fig. 8.** Intel® Xeon Phi™ coprocessor normalized performance

```
static inline void
diffusion_x_loop(const REAL *f1_t, REAL *f2_t,
    int nx, int ny, int nz,
    int y, int z,
    REAL cc, REAL cw, REAL ce, REAL cn, REAL cs, REAL ct, REAL cb)
{
    int x;
    int c, w, e, n, s, b, t;
    const REAL *restrict pc; ...
    x = 0;
    c = x + y * (nx + NXP_DELTA) + z * (nx + NXP_DELTA) * ny;
    w = c - 1;
    e = c + 1;
    n = (y == 0) ? c : c - (nx + NXP_DELTA);
    s = (y == ny - 1) ? c : c + (nx + NXP_DELTA);
    b = (z == 0) ? c : c - (nx + NXP_DELTA) * ny;
    t = (z == nz - 1) ? c : c + (nx + NXP_DELTA) * ny;
    pc = &f1_t[c]; ...
    poc = &f2_t[c];
    __assume_aligned(pc, CACHE_LINE_SIZE);
    ...
    #pragma simd
    for (x = 0; x < N_REALS_PER_CACHE_LINE; ++x)
      poc[x] = cc * pc[x] +
        cw * pw[x] + ce * pe[x] +
        cs * ps[x] + cn * pn[x] + ct * pt[x] + cb * pb[x];
    // element 0
    poc[0] = cc * pc[0] +
      cw * pc[0] + ce * pe[0] +
      cs * ps[0] + cn * pn[0] + ct * pt[0] + cb * pb[0];
# pragma vector nontemporal
# pragma simd
    for (x = N_REALS_PER_CACHE_LINE; x < nx; x++)
    {
      poc[x] = cc * pc[x] +
        cw * pw[x] + ce * pe[x] +
        cs * ps[x] + cn * pn[x] + ct * pt[x] + cb * pb[x];
    }
    // element nx-1
    poc[nx-1] = cc * pc[nx-1] +
      cw * pw[nx-1] + ce * pc[nx-1] +
      cs * ps[nx-1] + cn * pn[nx-1] +
      ct * pt[nx-1] + cb * pb[nx-1];
}
```

Fig. 9. Diffusion inner loop

**Table 1.** Intel® Xeon® processor (GF/Sec)

|  | 224 | 256 | 448 | 512 |
|---|---|---|---|---|
| Collapse | 83.2 | 109.1 | 62.1 | 81.9 |
| 2d decomp | 117.7 | 99.8 | 101.4 | 90.6 |
| Hand nest | 133.3 | 98.6 | 135.8 | 126.7 |
| Teams | 88.4 | 105.2 | 103.8 | 91.2 |
| OMP nest | 101.7 | 117.0 | 103.5 | 105.2 |
| Sbb | 83.9 | 75.9 | 76.4 | 78.0 |

**Table 2.** Intel® Xeon Phi™ coprocessor (GF/Sec)

|  | 240 | 256 | 480 | 512 |
|---|---|---|---|---|
| Collapse | 171.8 | 147.0 | 192.4 | 162.7 |
| 2d decomp | 180.9 | 120.2 | 187.1 | 137.8 |
| Hand nest | 162.9 | 120.3 | 207.0 | 159.2 |
| Crew | 169.3 | 113.3 | 193.0 | 153.1 |
| OMP nest | 87.7 | 66.0 | 120.4 | 87.3 |
| Sbb | 165.0 | 163.5 | 185.0 | 180.0 |

On the Intel® Xeon Phi™ coprocessor, the hand nested version is still most competitive. One pleasant surprise is how well the original blocked and collapsed version performs; this is nice because it is relatively easy to write compared to the others. This data also demonstrates the strength of SBB. For users that are comfortable with C++ template libraries, SBB is an excellent choice that also enables easy experimentation with different containers and blocking factors.

## 7    Conclusions and Future Work

Nested OpenMP is a natural way to exploit hardware with two-level thread-ing, but the overhead is currently prohibitive for very fine grained threading, especially on the current generation of the Intel® Xeon Phi™ coprocessor. Alternatives such as hand nesting are possible, but can be tricky to write and to maintain, and may not be portable (especially with respect to performance).

Some of the performance issues with nested OpenMP are inherent in the OpenMP specification (thread teams, various query functions, ICVs, etc.) and it would be beneficial to consider changes or additions to the specification to make nested parallelism more lightweight. Other performance issues are related to quality of implementation. Hopefully this paper gives more impetus to the developers to improve their implementations.

Some of the OpenMP requirements can be relaxed when using OpenMP 4.0 teams, but currently those have restrictions (most importantly, that they need to be used in a device region) that make them unsuitable for general use. Making teams more general is a possible alternative to loosening the requirements for nested OpenMP.

One problem with picking diffusion for this paper is that there isn't enough work in the stencil. Real codes (e.g., various oil and gas codes) have far more complex stencils. Our experience has shown that in these cases, nested threading and blocking have much greater impact.

With the exception of SBB, none of these codes address load balancing, which is significant when the problem size doesn't match the number of cores and threads available. This is clearly evident in the $256^3$ and $512^3$ problems run on the Intel® Xeon Phi™ coprocessor, where SBB is the best performer. More work is needed to create a pure OpenMP dynamically scheduled code that still has good cache locality. Attempts using OpenMP tasking did not achieve good performance. We attribute this to high overhead when creating OpenMP tasks.

There are a few anomalies in the data: core threading on the Intel® Xeon® processor is poor for the $256^3$ problem; nested parallelism on the Intel® Xeon Phi™ coprocessor is far worse than on the processor; SBB performance is worse on the processor than on the coprocessor; tiled/collapsed code performs reasonably well on the coprocessor but not as well on the processor. We are investigating these issues.

SBB is a useful alternative for C++ programmers and is reasonably easy to use compared to some of the more complicated techniques.

# References

1. Jeffers, J., Reinders, J.: Intel Xeon Phi Coprocessor High-Performance Programming. Morgan Kauffman, Boston (2013)
2. Dempsey, J.: High performance parallelism perls. In: Jeffers, J., Reinders, J. (eds.) Pesiochronous Phasing Barriers, pp. 87–115. Morgan Kauffman, Boston (2015)
3. Briggs, J., et al.: Separable projection integrals for higher-order correlators of the cosmic microwave sky: acceleration by factors exceeding 100. Cornell University Library. http://arxiv.org/abs/1503.08809

# Supporting Indirect Data Mapping in OpenMP

Thomas R.W. Scogland[1]([✉]), Jeff Keasler[1], John Gyllenhaal[1], Rich Hornung[1], Bronis R. de Supinski[1], and Hal Finkel[2]

[1] Lawrence Livermore National Laboratory, Livermore, USA
tscogland@llnl.gov
[2] Argonne National Laboratory, Lemont, USA

**Abstract.** Code-passing abstractions based on lambdas and blocks are becoming increasingly popular to capture repetitive patterns that are amenable to parallelization. These abstractions improve code mantainability and simplify choosing from a range of mechanisms to implement parallelism. Several frameworks that use this model, including RAJA and Kokkos, employ OpenMP as one of their target parallel models. However, OpenMP inadequately supports the abstraction since it frequently requires information that is not available within the abstraction. Thus, OpenMP requires access to variables and parameters not directly supplied by the base language. This paper explores the issues with supporting these abstractions in OpenMP, with a particular focus on device constructs and the aggregation and passing of OpenMP state through base language abstractions. We propose mechanisms to improve support for these abstractions and also to reduce the burden of duplication in existing OpenMP applications.

## 1  Introduction

Abstraction is a critical part of computer programming. The languages and libraries that we use, even basic constructs such as functions, are all examples of abstraction. Abstraction allows us to hide the complexity of actions behind simple facades, and to concentrate effort on higher level concepts. While lambda expressions, closures and other forms of general "code passing" mechanisms have been integral parts of functional languages such as LISP and Haskell for many years, they have not been available in mainstream systems programming languages until recently. The C++11 standard [4] introduced support for lambda expressions that was expanded in C++14 [5]. Further, the growing support for C blocks in Objective-C suggests a path for their support in C as well. Frameworks such as RAJA [3], Kokkos [1] and Grand Central Dispatch [7] employ these mechanisms to abstract the implementation and management of parallelism away from the use of that parallelism in user code.

This material is based upon work supported by the U.S. Department of Energy (LLNL-CONF-671602).

OpenMP [6] provides a programming model that abstracts the specifics of threaded programming on a variety of platforms across the C, C++ and Fortran languages. It provides high-level constructs to represent parallel regions, work-sharing, synchronization, ordering, and atomicity as well as data sharing and dependencies. Using lambda expressions to wrap around these constructs seems natural.

Take an example like the C blocks parallel loop function in Fig. 1. It effectively abstracts the specific annotation on the loop out of the user code, which allows a library or header to switch between OpenMP or Cilk+ to parallelize the loop. However, interfaces such as these create a challenge for specifying data sharing attributes and data mapping. Clauses to support reductions, variable privatization, and perhaps most notably data mapping for device constructs rely on the user listing variables explicitly as part of the construct *at compile time* and they do not offer mechanisms for static polymorphism. Because OpenMP constructs are composed of pre-processor directives, some of which are actually evaluated after pre-processing and template expansion, they cannot exploit base language mechanisms for passing information like reduction variables or map-types through a language abstraction like a lambda. Further, C++ lambdas and C blocks are intentionally opaque objects, so the code that they are passed cannot inspect their details in order to glean the information.

```c
void parallel_for_all(size_t start,
                      size_t end,
                      void (^fun)(size_t i)){
#if defined(USE_OPENMP)
#pragma omp parallel for
  for(size_t i=start; i < end; ++i)
#elif defined(USE_CILK)
  cilk_for(size_t i=start; i < end; ++i)
#endif
  { fun(i);
} }
void add_arrays(double *a, double *b, size_t N){
  parallel_for_all(0, N,
    ^(size_t i) {
      a[i] += b[i];
    });
}
```

Fig. 1. An example parallel loop function using C blocks

Traditional OpenMP parallelization works well for simple examples such as that in Fig. 1. Implicit data sharing rules easily combine with the base language code passing mechanism to handle most use cases correctly. Variable privatization for example is provided by declaring a local variable inside the scope of the block, and sharing provided by simply using the captured value. Issues can arise with reductions or more complicated decisions for features such as loop schedules but the required information is usually needed for the base language abstraction. OpenMP 4.0 device constructs and their support for mapping array sections create new challenges. The code in Fig. 2 shows a desirable abstraction using a C++11 lambda with templates to abstract over a target region in OpenMP or OpenACC [2]. However, neither of these parallelization mechanisms have mechanisms to make the arrays available on the device within the abstraction. As noted in the comment, the arrays must be explicitly listed in map clauses, which is impossible since the variables effectively do not exist where they must be listed. While data mapping clauses are our primary focus, there is a general lack of support for passing state through the base language to OpenMP constructs, and lack of support for aggregation of constructs that should be addressed as well. It is equally impossible to externally select the reduction operator or variable to use in a template lambda function for example.

```
template<typename FunT, typename It>
void target_forall(It begin, It end, FunT fun){
#if defined(USE_OMP)
#pragma omp target teams distribute parallel for
// need to list map(tofrom: a[begin:end-begin]) map(to: b[begin:end-begin])
// unfortunately, they do not exist here
#elif defined(USE_OPENACC)
#pragma acc kernels loop
// need to list copy(a[begin:end-begin]) copyin(b[begin:end-begin])
#endif
  for(It i = begin; i < end; ++i){
    fun(i);
} }
void add_arrays(double *a, double *b, size_t N){
  target_forall(0, N,
    [&](size_t i) {
      a[i] += b[i];
    });
}
```

**Fig. 2.** An example target loop function using C++ lambdas

With the growing popularity of these abstraction models, OpenMP needs mechanisms to pass information through base language constructs. Otherwise, each instance that uses one of the abstractions must anticipate the parallelization mechanism within the abstraction, thus breaking the advantages that it offers. This paper explores the challenges of supporting abstractions like lambdas, proposes adjustments and extensions to OpenMP to support abstraction of target regions, and discusses extensions that generally support abstraction models.

The remainder of the paper is structured as follows. Section 2 provides background on the behavior of the **map** clause and the device data environment in OpenMP 4.0. Section 3 proposes adjustments to the handling of **map** clauses to support abstraction better. Section 4 presents a preliminary design for a general mechanism to pass OpenMP information through base language mechanisms.

## 2    The OpenMP 4.0 Data Environment

OpenMP 4.0 introduces the concept of target devices and their associated data environments into the programming model. While those data environments may share storage with host memory, they can also be completely disjoint. Thus, OpenMP now supports a limited form of potentially distributed memory programming that expands the requirements and functionality of its data sharing and data motion constructs substantially. The original data sharing attributes, such as **private**, **shared**, are still available within device environments but programs must map data into the device data environment. While default mapping rules support many implicit mappings, dynamic arrays or other pointer-based structures require explicit mappings. This section details the OpenMP 4.0 memory mapping interface, its use, defaults, and interactions.

### 2.1    Mapping Syntax

The **map** clause of the target and target data constructs *maps* data from the host data environment, which is the system memory space as viewed from the encountering thread, into the device data environment, which is the memory space that is visible on the target device. In other environments, copy-based constructs are common for this task, but OpenMP has carefully specified that the operation does not require copying, which allows systems in which the host and device share memory to avoid unnecessary allocations and copies. Nonetheless, mapping requires a concept of directionality to ensure that data can be copied for environments that do not support a shared memory between the host and the target device. Figure 3 shows the syntax of the **map** clause.

```
map([map-type:] list-item[, list-item...])
    map-type: alloc | to | from | tofrom
    list-item: <variable-name>[array-section]
    array-section: [<start>:]<length>
```

**Fig. 3.** The options and syntax of the map clause

Despite its few options, the map syntax can specify a wide variety of cases. The **map-type** specifies which direction a value should be copied in if copies are necessary. Specifically **alloc** specifies that no copies are ever necessary, to copies to the device at the beginning of the region, from copies back from the device at the end of the region and tofrom copies in both directions. Each list item specifies the variable to be mapped and, if it is an array section, the offset and number of elements to map. For C and C++, OpenMP 4.0 includes array section syntax that lists the element from which to begin the mapping and how many elements to make available starting from that point. For Fortran, OpenMP uses the base language syntax. Any variable listed without an array section is treated as a scalar, and the default behavior for any variable accessed in a device region that is not specified in a map clause is to treat it as though it had been listed as a scalar with a map type of tofrom. For C and C++, the mapping of dynamic arrays or their sections is composed of two parts. A pointer is mapped into the device data environment with map-type alloc and an array of the specified size is mapped in with the map-type specified. The new pointer in the device data environment is then set to point to the mapped array. These steps allow manipulation of the pointer on the device and multiple disjoint mappings of an array.

```
void omp4_foo(double *arr, int len, double arg){
  #pragma omp target map(from: arr[0:len]) \
                     map(to:len)
  //                 map(alloc: arr)
  //                 map(tofrom: arg)
  {
    // arr = arr_data_array;
    arr[len - 1] = arg * arg;
    len = 5;
  }
}
```

**Fig. 4.** A simple example of data mapping

Figure 4 shows a simple mapping example, which explicitly specifies two mappings. The map clause maps the array arr as an array section and len as a scalar. The construct results in four separate mappings occuring, with two *implicit* mappings shown in comments. The array arr has an implicitly mapped pointer at global scope to hold a pointer to the device data that the first map clause explicitly maps. The mapping will copy the elements between 0 and $len - 1$ of arr in the device data environment back to the host, if necessary. Both len and arg are mapped as scalars. The value of len is explicitly mapped to the device data environment so it will be the same value as in the host data environment at the start of the region. The assignment to len in the target region makes its value in the host data environment unspecified after the target region executes since it may share storage with the version with the device environment version. The scalar value of arg is implicitly mapped tofrom the device data environment since it is not listed in a map clause.

## 2.2   Presence

If the host and device environments share storage then mapping has no cost. However, if they do not share storage then it can entail a significant allocation and copying costs. Thus, applications require a method to reduce the frequency of mapping. The `target data` construct adds variables to the device data environment across a region of *host* code. That region can include `target` regions, which use the already mapped data rather than transferring it repeatedly. Effectively, mapped variables are added to a *presence table* that is consulted whenever a variable is mapped, re-using the existing version if one is found. Thus, a variable can be logically mapped at each code location that requires it while allowing it to be transferred only once in an outer scope.

The presence table semantically lists mappings between host variables and their device-side counterparts. It is not as simple as a hash table or direct-mapped array because applications can map multiple sub-arrays of larger arrays through different pointers. Thus, implementations must perform a range-based search over the table to support all features of OpenMP 4.0. Nonetheless, a user model of a table that maps the address of a variable to its device-side counterpart if one exists generally suffices. For scalars, a presence check is that simple. However, array sections are handled in two phases. First, the address of the host pointer, `&arr` in the example above, is checked for presence and then the address of the array, `arr`, is searched then assigned into the device side pointer found or allocated in the first part.

## 3   Map Refinements

OpenMP needs to provide mechanisms that allow the user to map the data elements used inside abstractions such as the lambda expression in Fig. 2. The mechanism must support type abstraction but must not require the variable name within the lambda expression in order to be consistent with the base language construct. At first thought, the `target data` construct seems to provide a solution. However, annotating the lexical scope that contains the use of the abstraction may be difficult or impossible. Thus, these abstraction mechanisms require the TR3 unstructured data mapping constructs, `target enter data` and `target exit data`, that map data without requiring an enclosing lexical scope. Since they can map data for dynamically encountered target regions and reduce the number of times items are mapped, they may seem like an ideal solution. Unfortunately, the mechanism does not solve the problem due to the mapping defaults and how the presence table mechanism is specified.

Figure 5 shows unstructured data mapping of the data that the abstraction layer in Fig. 2 requires, after inlining of the template code and the lambda function. The example may appear correct since both a and b are appropriately mapped by the `target enter data` region and i is automatically privatized by the `target` construct. Unfortunately, as discussed in Sect. 2, the default mapping for variables not listed in a map clause is equivalent to listing them in `map(tofrom: <var>)`. Thus, the variables will be mapped to and from the device

```
void init_arrays(double *a, double *b, size_t N){
  #pragma omp target enter data map(to: a[0:N])\
                                map(to: b[0:N])
}
void release_arrays(double *a, double *b, size_t N){
  #pragma omp target exit data map(from: a[0:N])\
                               map(release: b[0:N])
}
void add_arrays_inlined(double *a, double *b, size_t N){
  init_arrays(a,b,N);
  double * inner_a = a, *inner_b = b;
  #pragma omp target teams distribute parallel for
  for(size_t i = 0; i < N; ++i){
    inner_a[i] += inner_b[i];
  }
  release_arrays(a,b,N);
}
```

**Fig. 5.** Unstructured data mapping example

data environment as desired. However, *all* unlisted variables are treated as scalars rather than array sections or references. Since array sections are mapped in two parts, and the presence check works on each of them independently, the desired behavior would result if the addresses of the pointers, in this case &inner_a and &inner_b, matched those of the originally mapped pointers, &a and &b. Since inlining typically uses temporaries, the host pointers would be mapped instead of finding the already mapped array sections. If the host and device data environments do not share memory, then memory errors or segmentation faults are likely when the array accesses are performed. Thus, we propose two changes for OpenMP variable mapping. The first adjusts the presence check used for array sections. In the second, the default mapping depends on the type of the variable. We detail both changes in the following subsections.

### 3.1    Data only Array Sections

Since array sections are mapped in two parts, a presence check can fail for an array section *even if it is present* when it is accessed through a copy of the pointer other than the one used to map it. This issue may seem minor, except that C and C++ pass function parameters by value. Thus, a target data construct used in a function does not map the variable of the calling function. Thus, init_arrays does not map the variables of add_arrays_inlined. Thus, unstructured data constructs can map function parameters and stack-based local variables to the device. The device copies can then become unreachable when the host variables cease to exist. Further, passing another function a pointer to mapped data as an argument creates a new copy of that pointer, and the presence check inside the sub-function fails. The second phase of the presence check can rectify the situation if the array section is explicitly mapped. However, that solution again requires the variable name within the abstraction.

We propose one step mapping semantics for array sections. These semantics do not implicitly map the pointer variable or add it to the presence table. Instead, they only add the base address of the array section and its associated offset and length to the presence table. An application must explicitly map the pointer in order to modify it on the device. Thus, the presence check for a function called with an array argument will find the array. These semantics have the potentially beneficial side-effect of allowing pointers to array sections to be passed as parameters to kernel function implementations of target regions in programming models such as CUDA and OpenCL. Alternatively, we could retain the double presence check for pointer and reference types, but reverse the order such that the value of the pointer is first checked for presence, and its address is checked only if that fails. While this option is heavier-weight, it is closer to the current semantics. Neither of these solutions addresses the implicit behavior, which we require since the abstraction mechanism prevents naming the variable explicitly.

### 3.2   Type-Based Implicit Mappings

The default `tofrom` mapping has the closest semantics to the `shared` data sharing attribute, which is the default for most variables for other OpenMP constructs. The `tofrom` map-type ensures that the device data environment has the host value initially and that changes in the `target` region are propagated back. However, the additional implicit behavior that treats pointers, as well as other scalars, as value types causes problems for nested mappings of array sections. We propose that the default be split between two different groups of variable types, the *value types* and the *reference types*. The reference type class includes pointers and C++ references. The value type class includes scalars and structures.

We then can specify that the default for any reference type is a minimal array section including the address pointed to by the variable. The explicit equivalent would be `map(alloc:<var>[:0])`. These semantics essentially assume that implicit mappings of reference types follow a previous explicit mapping of an array section that the variable references. Thus, these semantics are closest to those for Fortran array types, given that C and C++ lack the dope vectors that support implicit array mapping. These semantics ensure that pointers and references are always checked for presence by the address that they hold rather than their own address, unless they are explicitly mapped as value types. Combining this change with the adjustment to the mapping of array sections allows the code in Fig. 5 to work as expected without explicitly annotating the target region.

We can also consider whether the existing default is appropriate for value types. As previously mentioned, `tofrom` is the closest to the `shared` data sharing attribute. However, OpenMP includes a range of implicit and predetermined data sharing attributes that reflect the expected use of variables. For example, loop iteration variables of loop constructs are `private`. The `tofrom` mapping can imply significant overhead for value types. For example, allocating and initiating a small variable in the global memory space of some devices, such as GPUs, entails significant overhead, which the current default requires since the variables must have globally modifiable state between all threads on the target. Semantics similar to firstprivate could entail lower overhead and provide similar benefits to our proposed array section changes. Overall, we suggest the specification of default mapping attributes based on the expected use of the variable similarly to the predetermined and implicitly determined data sharing attributes. A default clause for device constructs could also be useful.

# 4    Clause Grouping and Binding

Our proposed solutions in the previous section address finding mapped values in the device data environment without listing the variables on a construct. That can be sufficient to address mapping in target regions, but does not solve the more general problem of defining or passing OpenMP state through abstractions. In this section, we propose a general solution that can declare re-usable groups of clauses and methods for binding those groups to constructs. This extension to the OpenMP name space that currently supports user-defined reductions would better support abstraction within OpenMP, thus reducing its verbosity and the need for replicated code.

```
#pragma omp declare group <binding clause> [<binding clause>...]\
                          [<general clause>...]
   clause: name(<group name>)
           bind_all(<construct name>)
           bind_type(<variable type>)
   general clause: any valid OpenMP clause

New general clauses: bind_groups([<action>:]<group name>[,<group name>...])
                     bind_types(<type or var>[,<type or var>])
   action: merge (default) | inherit | exclude | override
```

**Fig. 6.** The options and syntax of the declare group construct

The basic construct provides an OpenMP-visible name to a group of related clauses. This standalone construct, which we call declare group and present in Fig. 6, can specify any number of clauses and accepts any clause that can be specified on any construct in OpenMP. The only clauses that *apply* to it, however, are the name, bind_all and bind_type clauses. The bind_all clause of the declare group construct takes a list of construct types, such as target, parallel or target teams distribute. The declared clauses are then applied to every instance of the listed construct types that are in the same lexical scope as the declare group construct, or a sub-scope thereof. The name clause creates a name for that group of clauses that can be referenced later to control the inclusion, or exclusion, of the clause group with a bind_group clause. The <type> argument to bind_group specifies how clauses are incorporated from the group:

**merge** pulls in all clauses from the group, and merges them with those specified on the construct, two conflicting clauses will result in an error; **inherit** pulls in all clauses from the group, but allows them to be *overridden* by clauses specified directly on the construct; **exclude** causes a group to be excluded from the construct even if it would have been bound to the construct by a **bind_all** on the group's definition; finally **override** includes all clauses, but allows the clauses in the group to override clauses specified directly on the construct. For cases where override precedence is required, it is defined be in simple left-to-right order of the specification in the clause list of the construct. If any of the clauses do not apply that construct, then the behavior is unspecified. For order-dependent clauses, the order is preserved from the original **declare group** construct.

```
#pragma omp declare group name(privs)\
   firstprivate(a,b,c,d,e,f,g,a1,b1,c1...)

void foo(){
  #pragma omp declare group bind_all(parallel) name(par) \
                            default(none) if(use_threads)
  #pragma omp parallel bind_group(privs)
  ...

  #pragma omp parallel bind_group(privs)
  ...

  #pragma omp parallel
  ...

  #pragma omp parallel bind_group(privs)
  ...

  #pragma omp parallel bind_group(exclude: par)
  ...
}
```

**Fig. 7.** Group binding

Figure 7 provides an example of applying clause groups to simplify a complex set of constructs. The first **declare group** construct has only one clause, but it is a voluminous list of variables that should be **firstprivate** on several constructs, but not on all. While ideally this usage would never be necessary, it is not uncommon to see many constructs with such long lists repeatedly specified in a code. Our proposal provides a convenient shorthand. While one could argue that C99 macros, if fully supported, implement the same functionality, the second **declare group** offers more. Since it is inside the function, and is specified to bind to all **parallel** regions, it applies to all of the regions in that function, except the last from which it is specifically excluded, factoring out the specification of the conditional clause and default data sharing.

This relatively simple extension addresses many issues of clause duplication. However, it does not obviously address the more general issue of being able to write polymorphic OpenMP, where a library writer can provide users an abstraction that allows their arguments to supply information to construct an OpenMP construct dynamically at compile time. In order to discuss how it can be used to help address header-based libraries and other such abstractions, we will discuss an example. The code depicted in Fig. 8 is a straightforward OpenMP function, summing all elements of two arrays into a single sum variable.

```
double sum_two_arrays(double *a, double *b, size_t N){
    double sum;
    #pragma omp parallel for reduction(+:sum)
    for(int i=0; i<N; i++) {
        sum += a[i] + b[i];
    }
    return sum;
}
```

Fig. 8. A simple reduction function

Now, lets say that a library writer wants to write an abstract for_all_reduce function that uses OpenMP underneath. This may sound like a toy, many libraries implement reduction operations, but reductions are exceptionally difficult to implement in a performance-portable manner, so allowing higher-level abstractions to rely on OpenMP optimized reductions could be a significant benefit for library writers. It will need to take a range of values, and somehow populate both the operator and the variable parameters of the reduction clause at compile time. Using C99 macros, it can be done as depicted in Fig. 9.

```
#define FOR_ALL_REDUCE(iter, start, end, operator, variable) \
    _Pragma(omp parallel for reduction(operator:variable)) \
    for(int iter=(start); iter<(end); iter++)

double sum_two_arrays(double *a, double *b, size_t N){
    double sum;
    FOR_ALL_REDUCE(i, 0, N, +, sum){
        sum += a[i] + b[i];
    }
    return sum;
}
```

Fig. 9. A macro reduction wrapper

Now we have a general wrapper that will do a reduction on a single variable. The real challenge begins when multiple reductions, or other variable listing effects are required but invisible in the abstraction. Take the example back in Fig. 2, while the previous section described a means of supporting the mapping behavior, there remains no way to reasonably support a reduction in the context of a variable captured into a C++11 lambda.

We provide an additional clause for a wide range of OpenMP constructs, similar to the bind_group clause. This bind_types clause allows the declare group construct to bind clause groups to *variable type names*, either by being placed in their type definition or as an extra clause that modifies an existing type. Thus, we can use the type system of the base language to pass information to OpenMP. Note that binding to a type name, rather than the type itself, allows us to bind behavior to a typedef or using declaration that doesn't actually create a new base-language type per-se. Figure 10 shows an example of our preliminary proposal for this functionality.

```
// Library header
typedef double ReducSum;
#pragma omp declare group bind_type(ReducSum) reduction(+:omp_self)

template<typename FunT, typename It, class ... Types>
void target_forall(It begin, It end, FunT fun, Types ... args){
#pragma omp parallel for bind_types(args...)
  for(It i = begin; i < end; ++i){
    fun(i, args...);
} }

// User code
void add_arrays(double *a, double *b, size_t N){
  ReducSum sum;
  target_forall(0, N,
    [&](size_t i, ReducSum& c_inner) {
      c_inner += a[i] + b[i];
    }, sum);
}

// Post-expansion and variadic template inlining result
void add_arrays(double *a, double *b, size_t N){
    double sum;
    #pragma omp parallel for reduction(+:sum)
    for(size_t i = 0; i < N; ++i){
        size_t _i = i, &c_inner = sum;
        c_inner += a[_i] + b[_i];
    }
}
```

Fig. 10. Binding a clause group to a type

Conceptually, the `declare group` construct annotates the `ReducSum` type with the necessary information for OpenMP to generate the proper reduction for the wrapped code, expanding `omp_self` to the variable from which the clause was extracted on the construct. Thus, nearly any OpenMP information could be passed as part of aggregate types, and have that information passed by existing base language mechanisms. The bigger challenge is to declare a cross-language mechanism to handle this process. In the example we use C++ because it supports definition of an abstract function that not only takes arbitrary types, but can identify the types independently of out-of-bound information, something C variadic functions cannot do. We are continuing to explore this direction for a broader solution in future work.

## 5   Conclusion

This paper has explored the challenges inherent in supporting lambda or block based abstractions in OpenMP. We find that as currently specified, many of the important features of the newest standard, notably device constructs, do not support interfaces that such abstraction layers can use. The map interface in particular poses a significant challenge. We propose adjustments to mapping semantics and defaults that will both address this issue and simplify existing code. Beyond the mapping support, we also explore the issue of reducing clause duplication in OpenMP code and passing of clauses through native mechanisms. The ability to define *clause groups* along with binding specifications could eliminate significant duplication required in OpenMP applications currently. Attaching the same information to the type system of the base language would allow OpenMP information to be passed through abstraction layers for a more general solution to the abstraction support problem.

## References

1. Kokkos. http://trilinos.org/packages/kokkos/
2. OpenACC 2.0 application programming interface specification, June 2013. http:// www.openacc.org/sites/default/files/OpenACC%202%200.pdf
3. Hornung, R., Keasler, J.: The RAJA portability layer: overview and status. Technical report, Lawrence Livermore National Laboratory (LLNL), Livermore, CA (2014)
4. ISO/IEC: Iso international standard iso/iec 14882:2011 - information technology - programming langugages - c++ (2011). http://www.iso.org/iso/iso_catalogue/ catalogue_tc/catalogue_detail.htm?csnumber=50372
5. ISO/IEC: Iso international standard iso/iec 14882:2014 - information technology - programming langugages - c++ (2011). http://www.iso.org/iso/home/store/ catalogue_ics/catalogue_detail_ics.htm?csnumber=64029
6. OpenMP ARB: OpenMP 4.0 specification, June 2013. http://www.openmp.org/ mp-documents/OpenMP4.0.0.pdf
7. Sakamoto, K., Furumoto, T.: Grand central dispatch. In: Proceedings of Multithreading and Memory Management for iOS and OS X, pp. 139–145. Springer (2012)

# Author Index

Printed in the United States
By Bookmasters